# Trials of the Whistle King

by

## Dr. Howard W. Wright

Invention: Surviving ADHD, Dyslexia, Treachery and Deceit
Armed with Faith and Family

# Trials of the
# Whistle King

Invention: Surviving ADHD, Dyslexia, Treachery and Deceit
Armed with Faith and Family

by

# Dr. Howard W. Wright

First paperback edition May 6, 2020

ISBN: 978-0-9600547-6-3 (paperback)
ISBN: 978-0-9600547-7-0 (eBook)

Printed in the United States of America
Published by Puhala Publishing


For information:
Email: info@puhalabook.com

## Other books by Dr. Howard Wright

Puhala and the Temple of Refuge

Puhala and the Revenge of the Matu

Puhala and the Secret of the Menehune

# Contents

Preface..........................................................................................1

Chapter 1: Dealing with the Pros....................................3

Chapter 2: The Invention..................................................19

Chapter 3: School, Hell on Earth...................................29

Chapter 4: Acceptance to Whittier College.................35

Chapter 5: UCLA – Redemption....................................39

Chapter 6: Rebooting.........................................................48

Chapter 7: More Than Just Science...............................53

Chapter 8: Rejection Times Two.....................................62

Chapter 9: Guadalajara......................................................67

Chapter 10: Dental School...............................................74

Chapter 11: The Proof is in the Pudding......................82

Chapter 12: The Other Howard Wright........................93

Chapter 13: The Homeless..............................................103

Chapter 14: Taking it to the Streets..............................116

Chapter 15: Dr. Allen.......................................................133

Chapter 16: Understanding the Market.......................149

Chapter 17: The U. S. Patent..........................................157

Chapter 18: The New Product Pitch.............................167

Chapter 19: The Injection Tool......................................177

Chapter 20: Marketing......................................................186

Chapter 21: Manufacturing.............................................195

Chapter 22: Keeping the Ogres at Bay.........................203

Chapter 23: Brand Diversification.................................210

Chapter 24: Getting Knocked Off..................................215

Chapter 25: Toothpaste, the Idea..................................222

Chapter 26: SmithKline Beecham........................................229

Chapter 27: The Hammer Falls...........................................237

Chapter 28: Starting Anew.................................................249

Chapter 29: Teaching.........................................................253

Chapter 30: Extracurricular Activities...............................266

Chapter 31: Toothpaste, The Do-Over...............................279

Chapter 32: Handing Off Operations................................284

Chapter 33: Making the Toothpaste..................................286

Chapter 34: Back in the Saddle Again...............................305

Chapter 35: Writing...........................................................314

Chapter 36: A Framework for Success...............................319

Chapter 37: Moving Forward.............................................329

# Dedication

In all that I have lived and all that I have longed for, you,
Vicki, are my greatest, most enduring love.

# Preface

This is my story. It is not intended to instruct anyone on how to run a company or give advice on patents, trademarks, or any laws or regulations. I am a retired dentist, educator, writer and inventor. I am not an attorney, business consultant or have a degree in finance. I never attended a business school nor studied international marketing.

This is simply a retelling of what I endured at the hands of some of the most self-serving and dishonest ignoramuses in the world while at the same time being lifted up by some of the most wonderful, caring and generous people in existence.

I have tried to recreate events, locales and conversations from my memories of them. In order to maintain their anonymity and not hurt anyone's feelings, in most instances I have changed the names of individuals and places, I may have changed some identifying characteristics and details such as physical characteristics, occupations and places of residence.

# Chapter 1:
# Dealing with the Pros

*"High expectations are the key to everything."*

Sam Walton – Owner, Walmart Stores

It was 1995 and the noise on the floor of the convention hall was deafening. It reminded me of the first time I walked into a Las Vegas casino, the lights, the noise, the excitement. Surrounding me were executives from nearly every country on the planet. They were young and old, male and female, all dressed for success looking to market their products to the world. But this was different than the cards, dice and slots of Vegas. This was no game. This convention was just about as serious as any commercial enterprise could get and I could taste the tension.

I had arrived early with the other exhibitors. Under one arm I held a box of 250 whistle samples and a slew of brochures while in the other I carried a three-by-four-foot color poster of the Storm whistle, the loudest whistle in the world. I had just arrived at the International Home and Housewares Show in downtown Chicago, the annual event that put on display anything and everything you had ever imagined. I, for my part, was as nervous as a prize turkey in November.

All across the convention hall, representatives from hundreds of different companies were putting the finishing touches on their exhibit spaces. Booths that ranged from tiny ten-foot by ten-foot cubicles to mega displays that stood larger than a two story house. All around me computers were being powered up, lights plugged in and samples arranged.

The International Home and Housewares Show extends some 785,000 square feet and houses over 2200 exhibitors, the convention so large it took me nearly a half an hour to find our booth.

The space I was to occupy for the next three days was a twenty by ten foot stall located in the center-rear of the hall. I finally found it and quickly set up my assigned area. I was allocated a three foot section of back wall and a single foot of the "rail section" at the corner of the Mueller Manufacturing booth. My space was small, but I was delighted to have it.

Like everyone around me I rearranged my area, hung my poster and laid out my whistles in anticipation of the start of the convention. It was then, as I chatted with a neighboring exhibitor, that a horn was blown and everything changed. Mid-sentence he stopped, turned and without saying another word, hurried back to his booth. I did the same.

It was 8:30 a.m., the doors had swung open wide and the buyers had just entered the building. Throughout the hall, exhibitors, who a moment ago were relaxed, casually milling around their displays, suddenly trashed their half-drank coffees only to take their positions inside their booths.

The crowd of buyers moved thick down the carpeted aisles. Some quickly, looking as if they were late to a scheduled appointment or meeting, while others wove their way slowly, their eyes taking in each and every item as they looked to acquire that all important "next big thing."

In an odd way, it reminded me of a shipwreck I once explored SCUBA diving off the coast of Florida. The sand at a depth of a hundred feet was smooth, white and empty, until up ahead I spotted a large dark blurry shape in the distance. I approached the structure slowly. It was huge, over seventy feet long and twenty feet high. As I got closer, I started making out the details: wires and masts, railing and crossmembers, all encrusted with decades of growth and decay. Then I noticed the fish.

Hugging close to the dilapidated wreck were millions of small bait-fish that moved through the water in tight protective schools, their masses glistened as they shifted and spun always staying close to the safety of the sunken ship. The small fish were beautiful as they swam weightless and relaxed around the wreck.

Suddenly, far off on either side of the shipwreck, I saw the predators circling like shadows at dusk. There were large barracuda, silvery amberjacks, and sharks hanging back in the distance until, one by one, the hunters would move in to attack. As the predator approached searching for food, seeking out that something special to eat, the once calm schools of baitfish disappeared running for their lives into the body of the wreckage.

As I stood at attention behind my array of multicolored whistles and watched the buyers filter into the great convention hall at Mc-Cormick Place, I realized I was much like one of the millions of bait-fish that surrounded that wreck. However, unlike the terrified anchovy or little pin fish that wanted to disappear, I wanted to be that something special. I needed to be noticed.

No matter where I looked there were deals being made, samples being displayed and widgets being demonstrated. Across the hall I saw the booth for Proctor and Gamble, 3M, Rubbermaid and a thousand other companies large and small. Many I recognized; most I had never heard of.

In the midst of it all, I stood there humbled and awestruck as I watched the interactions like some freshman high school student on the first day of classes. Around my neck I wore a string of seven whistles, each a different color. In my hand I held a short stack of brightly colored brochures. My mission was simple: I desperately needed to promote and ultimately sell the loudest whistle in the world, my invention, my baby, to anyone and everyone that would listen.

"Don't talk to those two," Karl slurred, "they're nobodies."

Karl was the lead salesman for Mueller Manufacturing and despite his gruff command, I walked up to an older couple and introduced myself as the inventor of the Storm whistle. I explained how they can double their money on each sale, how the whistle was made in the USA and that it was the loudest in the world. They took a price sheet and sample of the whistle. They asked questions about postage, our return policy, minimum orders and suggested retail price.

"FOB St. Louis (buyer pay the postage from St. Louis), 100% return policy, minimum order thirty-six pieces with a wholesale price of $2.98 each, an SRP of $5.95." I answered.

They filled out an order sheet for the minimum of thirty-six Storm orange. I'm ecstatic.

From a cheap folding chair in the back of the booth, Karl shook his head in disgust and looked at me with disdain. "That was a colossal waste of time."

I looked at him like he's crazy. "I just sold thirty-six whistles. They have three stores in Buffalo!"

Karl was unimpressed. Short, squatty, balding and weary of it all, he wore a dark suit, a dark tie and an even darker expression. He had been slogging away selling mop buckets, creepers (those low flat carts auto mechanics lay on to go under cars) and fish fillet boards for Mueller Manufacturing in St. Louis for over thirty years and had seen it all. As he stared at me, he just shook his head at the idea of being forced to add whistles to his fine line of household products.

"Walmart will be here any minute," Karl snarled as he gritted his teeth. "You're wasting time selling to those mom and pop stores."

"That is like my sixth order today." I smiled holding a short stack of crinkled order forms. "Do you have any idea how many cavities I need to fill in order to make this kind of money? How many mouths I need to look into?"

Karl glared at me irritated. "And by the way, when Walmart gets here, keep your mouth shut."

"I know," I replied. "That's like the fiftieth time you've told me."

Karl never wanted me in the booth. Thinking back, I guess my whistles were just one more thing for him to worry about. One more product he had to schlep around and peddle. One more set of forms to fill out. One more pain in the butt.

"I'll be good," I promised, "as quiet as a mouse."

But Karl's wasn't buying it. He could see that I am enjoying this way too much.

The booth was owned by Mueller Manufacturing, a large corporation located in Fenton, Missouri that dealt with dozens of companies making hundreds of products, one of which was my whistle. As part of the promotional aspect of our manufacturing agreement, I was to be allowed to attend the Home and Housewares Show and help sell the whistle. While being at the convention was great, what I really wanted was to go to Bentonville, Arkansas and visit the world headquarters of Walmart to meet the buyers. I wanted to see how the "sausage was made," what it was like going toe-to-toe with some of the savviest deal makers in the world.

I had heard stories of glass booths and interrogation type interviews. I had read stories about long lines of companies begging to be a vendor for one of the largest retail outlets in the world and I wanted to see it for myself, but it never happened. Truth be told, I had nothing to do with getting into Walmart. I wasn't even there when the deal to sell whistles to Walmart went through. Amazingly, it was a senior vice president at Walmart who discovered my whistle and that, like so many things in my life, happened by accident.

The whistle was first signed with Walmart in late 1994 while I was away with my wife Vicki on a cruise to Mazatlán, Mexico. We were mid-way through the vacation, wearing floppy sun hats and Bermuda shorts, when we were interrupted by one of the stewards from the cruise ship. We had been walking laps around the upper deck, holding hands and relaxing when we were stopped.

"Are you Dr. Howard Wright?" he asked. "You have a phone call from the mainland. It's not an emergency, but it is important."

Now, this was before internet and cell phones, so to receive a shipboard call was both rare and expensive. My sister Joanne was back in Missouri watching over our three kids while we were away, so Vicki and I, fearing the worst, hurried to our stateroom where we took the call.

"Are you having fun?" my sister asked.

With Vicki and I huddled tight around the handset, I answered with a hesitant and nervous, "Yes. What's up?"

"Well," she said over the crackling phone, "The kids are fine. It's, well, I just got a call from Mueller Manufacturing, your whistle maker. They say Walmart is having a big employee gathering and want their vendors to supply noisemakers. They want whistles sent to Bentonville for the corporate meeting. Mueller Manufacturing wants to know if you are willing to donate a thousand whistles to Walmart for their party. That's a lot of whistles and I wanted to ask you first."

Walmart it seemed, was so cheap that when they organized these huge corporate mega-conventions, rather than buy gifts and gadgets for the employees, they would solicit freebees from vendors. Mueller Manufacturing, being a vendor, had received the request for a noise-maker and had come up with the idea of sending my Storm whistle as a gift to Walmart for the gathering. The only hiccup was that they didn't own the whistles, only made them. It wouldn't be Mueller Manufacturing giving the product away, it would be me.

Mueller Manufacturing, with their thirty plastic injection presses and hundreds of employees sold proprietary products, products they controlled and owned the rights to. They were also a contract manufacturer who, for a price, would take my tool, put it in one of their presses and make my whistle. They didn't own my tool, didn't own the whistles it made and had absolutely no right to sell any whistles unless I said they could.

Vicki and I looked at each other for half a second and with mutual nod, answer, "Sure, send them the whistles. No charge."

We immediately forgot about the call and went back to our slow walks on the upper deck.

A couple of days after the event in Arkansas, unbeknownst to me, Mueller Manufacturing received another call from Walmart, but this time it wasn't asking for free swag, it was from a buyer. It seems that a corporate executive from Walmart, was at the convention, saw the whistle and liked it so much that he wanted it in their stores!

Without my knowledge and without my approval, Mueller Manu-facturing jumped at the opportunity to have my whistle as part of the Walmart family of products and further agreed to fill an initial order of thirty thousand whistles along with reorders of fifteen thousand whistles a month.

Unaware of the dealings between Mueller and Walmart, Vicki and I finished up our cruise, drinking margaritas and relaxing poolside. Back in Missouri, Mueller Manufacturing had just made a deal with one of the largest, most contentious and controversial retailers in the world.

In all likelihood, we probably would have agreed to sell the whistle to Walmart. At that time, I was working as a dentist five and a half days a week, spent an average of four hours a day on whistles and was helping with our three children, twin ten year old girls and a son twelve. While I was drilling, filling, and billing, Vicki worked at the dental office two days a week, helped me box whistles till midnight no less than four nights a week, and ran the household 24/7.

Our whistle company, the All Weather Safety Whistle Company, was limping along happily selling between two and three thousand whistles a month. While we were not as big as IBM, we made nearly a dollar a whistle, so we were delighted.

A day after we returned from the cruise, I got a call from Mueller Manufacturing telling me they wanted to talk about possibly licensing the whistle to Walmart. They seem really excited about me signing some papers and offered to take me to lunch at the most expensive restaurant in St. Louis to discuss this "life changing opportunity."

My dad always told me there is no such thing as a free lunch, and he was right. I smelled a rat, but none the less, I agreed to go.

I had read stories about Walmart: how they had this bad habit of gobbling up their competition and then spitting them out destroyed, how they would undercut pricing on your product only to drop you cold, tales abound of how Walmart was the worst of all that is free enterprise, a perversion of capitalism.

I was wary of the entire deal, but knew that I had to keep my eyes open and consider the opportunities when they presented themselves. While I didn't like Walmart, I understood that markets change. First, you had the transformation of the single store to the strip mall, and then from the strip mall to the superstore. Walmart, the king of superstores, hadn't become one of the largest retailers by doing anything particularly innovative. They didn't offer great service, a trendy store environment, or the coolest products. The draw Walmart had was low price along with the fact that most anything anyone would want was in one central location.

Vicki and I discussed the upside and downside of working with Walmart and realized quickly that the only thing we really knew about licensing a product to a big-box retailer was that you get paid a royalty for letting someone else sell your product. What could be so bad about that?

Leonardo da Vinci is quoted as saying, "The greatest deception men suffer is from their own opinions."

I realized quickly I had to learn more and decided to find out for myself, just what, indeed, could be so bad?

I visited my neighborhood Walmart and searched the shelves, writing down at least twenty product names and manufacturers. Ol' Roy Dog Food, Great Value Soda, GV Coffee, to name a few.

I then called each of the companies found in Walmart and asked to speak to the manufacturer, the owner of the company that actually made the product. I asked them: what it was like working with Walmart? What was the downside? Was it worth the added sales?

I got nowhere, until I finally received a call back from one of the store's auto parts manufacturers. The guy on the line sounded both bitter and cold. He spoke in short sentences like a callous and nasty cop, wanted to know who I was, what company I was with and most importantly, what the hell was I doing calling him.

"My name is Howard Wright, I make whistles and I..."

"Who are you really, what do you want? Are you from Walmart?" The parts manufacturer didn't only sound nervous, he sounded angry.

"I'm just a small business owner. Look up my company; I make the Storm whistle. Call me back whenever you like, but I am considering getting into bed with Walmart and I am concerned."

He hung up on me.

The next day I got a call from the same parts guy, "So, you're for real." He said, "So? You asked about Walmart. What do you want to know?"

I told him we made whistles, were a tiny family business and had made whistles for about five years. I continued and explained that we didn't make the whistles, but had it manufactured and that I was just told that there's a possibility Walmart may want to license it and I don't know what to do.

There was a long pause on the line. It was more than a pregnant pause, it was deep thinking kind of silence. After about ten seconds this older, ruddy sounding guy that reeked of stress to the point of breaking, told me a story. "Imagine," he said as he thought long and hard considering what he was going to say, "Imagine if instead of

making auto parts or whistles you made swing sets. You had employees and suppliers and you made twenty a month, maybe two hundred
fifty a year and you're happy as a pig in cool mud. Then, out of the
blue, Walmart comes to you and gives you an order for five thousand
of these hypothetical swing sets, but at half your wholesale price. You
sharpen your pencil, do the math and figure you can make it work,
barely. You hire more people, take out a loan and expand. The retail
outlets you've had a relationship with, people you have sold to for
years, see your low-priced swing sets popping up in Walmart and
they hate you for it, but you don't care. You have Walmart."

I listened, took notes and didn't say a word.

The voice on the phone goes silent then starts up again, dread and
anguish dripping from each word. "After two years, Walmart, without any notice, stops buying your swing sets and instead comes out
with a swing set of their own. It's just like the one you make but
cheaper, made in Cambodia or India or somewhere. Now you're
screwed like a one-legged monkey. You have outstanding loans, un-
used inventory and you're laying off employees; but worst of all, your
phone doesn't ring. All your old customers won't talk to you."

After a moment I ask, my voice heartfelt and concerned, "So what
are you going to do?"

There is quiet. I hold the receiver close to my ear until he sadly
confides, "I don't know."

He hangs up.

I agreed to meet the representative from Mueller Manufacturing
for lunch two days later at a swanky French restaurant in downtown
St. Louis, a place I would never have chosen and could definitely not
have afforded.

I'd been with Mueller for over five years and knew a lot of the people who worked there, but this "representative" is somebody I'd never
seen before. He looks slick with a thousand dollar suit, gold wrist-
watch and one of those metallic briefcases. He told me I should try the

"*Poulet aigu ⸱e Tarragon*" or some odd dish. I agreed but leave the meal untouched.

"So," he said, using his napkin like a six year old child, "Walmart has shown some interest in your whistle, and given the right price, we can sell quite a few."

He looked at me expecting a "Wahoo, I'm rich!" but I sat still, stone-faced. All I could think about was the trembling voice of the auto parts guy and the swing set story. I knew the only way this is going to work out in my favor was if I forced Walmart's price on the whistle to be somewhat close to my own retail price of $5.95.

"What are you thinking?" I asked.

"We do everything: packaging, shipping, inventory, everything," he said with a slick smile. "You are paid twenty-five cents a whistle."

I looked at him and shook my head sadly. "I want $1.50 per whistle."

He is clearly shocked at my quick decline and is taken aback. "We could possibly go to $.40 per whistle, but that is our final offer."

I got up, thanked him for lunch, and told him how much I regret not coming to an agreement. "I am a successful dentist and am just doing the whistle thing for fun. I would be willing to accept $1.25 and not a penny less." I walked out.

The next morning, I got a call from Mueller Manufacturing saying they accepted the $1.25.

Selling the Storm whistle to Walmart was truly exciting. The money was great, the price was high enough so it didn't alienate too many of our distributors and it was fun seeing my whistle in all the stores. Now, what I had my eye on was to attend the mega conventions.

It took me over two years of hounding Bob Mueller, the owner of Mueller Manufacturing, before he finally let me have the seller's badge and sit in the booth with Karl. In order to get permission to attend, I promised I wouldn't cause any problems or upset any proverbial apple carts. I paid my own way, bought my own food and swore that I'd be "good."

Allowing a newbie like me into the corporate booth was a gamble, but I was persistent and I'm sure Bob thought that tough, old, nasty Karl could keep me under control and out of trouble for the three days of the convention in Chicago.

"I am not babysitting him!" I remember hearing Karl argue from down the hall. I was sitting in the lobby listening to the heated discussion boiling two doors down. It was almost sad as I heard Karl lament the idea of having me in the booth. Bob Mueller listened patiently but held firm insisting that I was to go along.

From the moment I walked into the conventional hall, I was struck "convention drunk." Buyers from all over the world would step up to our display table and examine the mop bucket, the filet board and the whistles while Karl, always unimpressed and unmoving, sat in the back of the booth. I, on the other hand, worked the crowd like P. T. Barnum, and waved people in to see the "greatest whistle on earth." I would introduce myself to as many people as I could while detailing the features and benefits of the whistle, always ending with the comment, "The loudest whistle in the world." Most were uninterested.

Napoleon Bonaparte is quoted as saying, "An army marches on its stomach." On the battlefield that may be true, but on the convention floor, things were different. Buyers and sellers, rather than propelled by food, were driven by the name tag: the badge. Like a soldier's uniform, the badge conveyed four key bits of information. First, whether the person was a buyer, seller or visitor, second the person's name, third the persons position in company and lastly, the company name. All Karl was concerned with was the blue buyer's stripe that covered the top third of the badge and the company name. If the person wasn't a buyer and Karl didn't recognize the company, he ignored them.

I stepped up to yet another potential customer, a couple of men from a company I had never heard of. Their blue buyer name tags made my introduction simple, "You must be Joe and Stan from Sarasota. Let me give you a sample of the loudest whistle in the world, and explain how…"

They take the samples, ignore the brochures and drop the bright orange whistles into their overstuffed bags and walk off.

"Told you," Karl scoffed with a shake of the head as he sat finishing off the dregs from a lukewarm cup coffee, "I've done this for forty years. These people you're trying to sell to are nobodies."

I ignore him and continue introducing myself to each and every person that walks by. I have been to a number of conventions. As a dentist I would go to the American Dental Association meetings, attend the seminars, learn new x-ray techniques and look over the new equipment. Now I was on the other side of the desk and it was as different as night and day. It was like going to a restaurant, but this time you're not going out to dinner, you're the cook. You're in the back wearing a soiled apron and funny hat, flipping burgers and cutting salad.

As a whistle manufacturer I was now the seller. The huckster behind the counter trying to get some person's attention as they walked by glassy-eyed, using every trick in the book to encourage them to stop and look.

Karl is not a bad guy. It takes a great deal of energy to stand on your feet all day and put up with the rejection that 19 out of 20 people who walk by give you. Maybe when Karl was thirty years younger, he was pounding the pavement just like I was now, but this was my time and my invention, and I wanted everyone to know about it.

There is that old adage that goes, "If a tree falls in a forest and no one is around to hear it, does it make a sound?" The answer, as far as I was concerned, was an emphatic "No. Not a peep." If nobody knows what you've created, then it only exists in your mind. For some people that's ok, but for me, the Storm whistle was a safety device that had and would continue to save lives and I wanted people to know about it. Unless I got out there and made as many people aware of my whistle and what it could do, it is as if it never existed.

Suddenly everything went quiet. Certainly, there were noises banging across the hall, but in our aisle, in our narrow corner of the world, everything seemed to collapse into a muted hush. I looked over my shoulder and saw Karl as he quickly lifted himself from his chair, centered his tie and smoothed his jacket. The guys next to us selling automatic jar openers, biodegradable dishwasher soap and those small square organic pot scrubbers abruptly became silent mid-pitch.

I looked down the aisle and watched as a small cluster of buyers walked straight toward us in a tight unwavering formation. They approached us like a squadron of F16's you see in those combat movies, loaded for bear, hunting for rabbits.

In front walked a solid man, fiftyish in age, his stark white hair cut short and neat, his tie and expensive jacket conservative. Beside him, on either side, walked two women who looked like executive secretaries, each with an open notebook, a pen at the ready. A step behind trailed two men, lieutenants of some kind, at their sides each held what looked like an extra wide carrying case.

All up and down the aisle it went quiet, vendors were silent as they watched the human wedge make its way to our booth. As they entered, Karl gently pushed me to the side, forcing me out of the way. The lead buyer's blue badge had written in block print the name "Mr. Chris Chiburis," but what takes my breath away is what is written beneath. The single word, "Walmart."

"Hello Mr. Chiburis," Karl blurts out. "It's good to see you. I have the sales numbers…"

Mr. Chiburis raised his hand and quieted Karl with a look, "I have bad news. We have decided to cancel the mop buckets."

Karl was clearly shaken; all the blood seemed to have left his face and I thought he is going to faint. "You can't, the sales have been good and, well we've been in Walmart..."

"I'm doing you a favor," Mr. Chiburis interrupted as cold as ice, his tone reminiscent of a condescending schoolmaster. "We were going to have YOU remove the buckets that are still on the shelves. I've convinced the heads in corporate to let them sell out."

Karl looked down petulantly, "What about the creepers?"

"We'll leave them where they are," Mr. Chiburis answered, "for now." Behind him the secretaries scribbled on their notepads.

I waited and watched shocked at Karl, his face contorted as if he had just heard his mother died.

"You must be the whistle guy," Mr. Chiburis remarked as he turned and pointed to the whistles that hung round my neck.

"Yes," I answer quickly. I don't offer to shake his hand or mention my name. I am blindsided by the air that has just been sucked from the room. "I'm the whistle guy."

"You need to lower the price of the whistle by ten cents." he demanded as the scribes scrawled dutifully into their yellow pads.

I held up my index finger to hold a pause and concentrated as I looked him in the eye and countered, "The whistles are in half the Walmarts... I'd be willing to drop the price by seven cents if you put us in the rest of the stores."

Chiburis looked at me like I was a bug he could squish if only just one more nerve cell in his brain told him to do so. "Fine," he stated as he turned. "Seven cents, all the stores." And without a smile or a goodbye, he walked out of our booth as hard and as fast as he entered it, the secretaries scribbling away in his wake.

I turned back to Karl with a smile that vaporized the moment I saw the shock and anger on his face.

"I told you to keep quiet," he hissed. "You never negotiate with Walmart."

I learned a month later that Walmart didn't want to cancel the mop buckets after all. Threatening to destroy a person's livelihood was just their silly way of asking for a little lower price.

Negotiating pricing and distribution at the International Home and Housewares Show with one of the largest retailers in the world seemed natural for me, effortless. It wasn't always that way though, not by a long shoot. As a young person, I was slow, timid, stuttering and introverted; hardly able to complete even the simplest of tasks. It wasn't until later, after a series of life altering events, that everything changed and I became a new person.

# Chapter 2:
# The Invention

*"Invention, it must be humbly a•mitte•, •oes not consist in creating out of voi•, but out of chaos."*

Mary Shelley - Author or Frankenstein

I first invented the underwater whistle when I was a kid in eighth grade, a few months after my fourteenth birthday. The idea came to me while at a friend's place for a pool party. We were playing a raucous game of Marco Polo and his mom, after hearing the famous Italian's name thrown back and forth for twenty minutes, claimed it was driving her insane. My friend lived in a two-story circular apartment complex that had the pool in the center and I guess the noise of us yelling "Marco" followed by the resounding "Polo" was giving her, and everybody else in the building, a migraine.

Forced to stop, my buddy, Ray McEwan, swam up to me and complained, "If only we had something that would make noise underwater, then we could keep playing."

Without a second's hesitation I told him that I could build it. He, of course, said it was impossible.

I don't know what gave me the confidence to even dream that I could make a whistle work underwater. I had always been a terrible student, a worse athlete and as blind as a bat without my glasses. Truth be told, up until that point, hadn't achieved anything.

Nonetheless, as soon as I got home, I started building the underwater whistle. My father, Harvey Weston Wright, Jr., was a NASA rocket scientist, literally a mechanical engineer that built the valves for the rockets that went to the moon, and, for as long as I could re-member, lived by two basic credos. The first declared that, "There is no better memory than a two-inch pencil." The second involved the Latin phrase, *"Re•uctio A• Absur•um,"* reduce it to the absurd.

*Re•uctio A• Absur•um* meant that when confronted by a seemingly impossible question, the answer often becomes clear when specific as-pects of the problem are taken to the extreme, basically taken to the absurd. The classic example is the story of a child on a garden path who asks its mother, "Can I pick a flower? It's just one flower." The mother responds, "But if every single person who came by picked 'just one flower,' there would be none left." Exaggeration can bring clarity to the question, (or confusion) depending on the case.

With this in mind, I hid myself in my bedroom and finding an old clear plastic shoe box, cut a hole in its upper side using a paper clip heated over an old Christmas candle. I then carefully fitted a cheap blue and white plastic whistle inside the cut opening, holding it in place with tape. I figured, if a whistle worked in the open air then it would probably also work in a box the size of a refrigerator (*Re•uctio A• Absur•um).* Moreover, if the whistle worked in an absurdly large box the size of a large household appliance, then it might just work in a shoe box.

It looked strange, the clear plastic box with the whistle stuck half in and half out, held there by a wad of black electrical tape. The way the mouthpiece stuck through the side of the box made the whole contraption look more like a small blue and white parakeet peaking its beak through the side of a rather small cage than the first rendition of an underwater whistle.

I tried to blow the whistle, but it didn't work. The box was sealed and there was nowhere for the air to go. How moronic of me, of course it wouldn't work. It was like trying to blow air through a straw while blocking the opposite end with your finger.

Taking hold of my trusty paper clip, I heated it up again and carefully cut open a small air vent on the bottom of the plastic box. After a dozen small holes were opened, I blew the whistle hard and it worked, emitting a smooth even trill.

I wasn't surprised it worked. The whistle didn't know if it was in the open air in my back yard or sitting stuck on the inside of one of my mom's old shoe boxes. The sound was muted and hollow, but it performed like a champ.

My next task was to see if the whistle–in-a-box noisemaker would work underwater. After rummaging in the garage, I took an old piece of garden hose, attached it to the mouthpiece of the whistle and then submerged the whole gizmo in a large bucket of water. As expected, I watched as water poured in every hole and loose joint in the box until everything, including the whistle and hose, were completely flooded.

I waited as the whistle box lay flooding on the bottom of a five-gallon pickle bucket. Once the bubbling stopped and I was certain that the entire mechanism was completely swamped, I then placed the free end of the garden hose in my mouth and blew hard. The forced air first purged the water from the hose, then the plastic whistle and finally created a shallow air pocket at the top of the shoebox.

It didn't work. All it did was gurgle.

The whistle was a standard toy type referee's whistle that had a ball that rolled around a small circular bowl until the air was eventually forced out through a slot in the top. As I looked closely at the whistle with the cork ball floating in a pool of water, I had an idea.

What if I rebuilt the "whistle–in-a-box noisemaker" but this time turned the whistle upside-down so the little slot where air escaped pointed down? That way any water that had flooded the bowl would empty out on its own. Breaking the whistle loose of the plastic shoe box, I turned it upside down and re-inserted it into the clear shoe box's sidewall, taping it in place.

Dunking the entire device back into the water, I again placed the hose in my mouth and blew. Same as before, the forced air ran through the hose, into the whistle and, bubbling, pushed the water from inside the box leaving the whistle suspended in a pocket of air. This time however, because the whistle's air slot was pointed down, the water didn't get caught up inside of the whistle bowl. Instead everything was blown out, purging it clean.

The whistle screamed from beneath the water. As bubbles poured from the bottom of the box, I could hear the trill of the whistle as it reverberated through the walls of the bucket. It worked! Granted it was as clumsy as clown shoes on a duck, but it worked.

Now it was time to start making the box that held the air pocket smaller, less "absurd," more compact and easier to hold. Nobody in their right mind wanted an underwater whistle the size of a shoe box.

Using a small pen knife blade heated over the candle, I trimmed the box in the same way you might heat a steak knife to slice through a block of cold butter. Over and over I heated the small knife to red-hot, cutting through the plastic panels of the box until it was a third of its original size. Now came the hard part, welding the individual parts back together again.

Back in the early 1970s, we didn't have super glue, glue guns or fast set epoxies, so it was a true challenge for me to rejoin the trimmed parts of the smaller plastic whistle box. Elmer's white glue dissolved in water, carpenter's glue took too long to harden, and rubber cement wasn't strong enough. What I needed was some kind of quick drying cement that was easy to use, hardened in seconds, worked on plastic and was totally waterproof.

Looking closely at my cluttered desk, I suddenly saw that the answer was literally, right in front of me. Splattered on nearly everything around and pockmarked across my desk were dark blebs of once molten plastic. Some were glossy smooth while others were charred and coarse, the black plastic was stuck hard and fast to pretty much everything it contacted.

I realized in a split second, that while I was pressing the searing hot knife blade through the plastic shoe box, little specks of liquefied plastic had dripped down and were now stuck like some kind of magic adhesive to every surface imaginable.

Feeling the now cool blobs of plastic, I realized that if I could find the right kind of plastic and learn to heat it to just the right temperature, it would melt smooth, drip down like honey and once cooled, be the perfect glue to fuse my whistle box together.

Discovering the right plastic became a real challenge because not all plastics melted the same way. Some of the materials I tried burned when I put them in the flame. Others just sat there and smoldered. It wasn't until I searched the garage, the back yard and, as a last ditch effort, my little sister's room that I discovered exactly what I was looking for. Troll dolls.

What I learned was that when you put one of those unpleasant little troll dolls in a flame, it would slowly melt into a thick black goo. The sludge was sticky and thick, but wait five seconds and it hardened like stone to anything it touched. Lucky for me my sister had a mess of the ugly little spuds, more than enough to complete my work. It was not until much later that she noticed that they had disappeared. To this day my sister Claire still glares at me for destroying half of her troll collection.

Over and over I remade the underwater whistle, each time making the plastic box that held the air pocket smaller. What I soon came to realize was that the sound produced by the whistle didn't come from inside the whistle bowl like I assumed, but instead was actually produced outside the whistle.

What I discovered, after working with the whistle for hours on end, was that all the sound created came from an area located just outside the whistle's air slot in a space no bigger than an M&M candy. I learned that if I could in some way protect that small area and keep water from interfering with the way the air spun and vibrated just outside the whistle's small square opening, I could make the whistle both small and functional.

Using small pieces of thin flat plastic that I broke off used photographic flash cubes, I built a protective box around the vibration-producing area of the whistle and added a small vent to allow the blown air to escape. The underwater whistle, with its black crusty welds and charred plastic walls looked more like a half-melted ball of wax than an innovative safety device.

I took it to the beach the next day and while diving under a wave, tried blowing it while underwater. It was ugly, rough and the mouthpiece was too small, but it worked! It blew underwater.

I showed my father what I was working on, and while I think he was truly surprised I had actually done something constructive, he didn't spend much time patting me on the back. At the same time that I was building the underwater whistle, he was working on Apollo 11 trying to land Neil Armstrong and Buzz Aldrin on the moon.

My father was a great engineer who invented the valves that controlled the rockets on the Lunar Excursion Module that allowed the space craft to land on the moon. It was, by the way, that same valve assembly that later allowed the Apollo 13 crew to return home after becoming disabled half-way to the moon.

I can distinctly call to mind when my father got the call from NASA after the command module of Apollo 13 exploded. It was April 14th, 1970, just hours after the initial blast. NASA telephoned my father and asked if his valve, having been built to fire a half dozen times, would function the twenty to thirty times necessary to save the men.

"When you build something," my father always told me, "design it to last ten times longer than required."

I recall my father watching the wonderful movie *Apollo 13*. He was sobbing as he watched the scene where the NASA's flight director, Gene Kranz, asked an unnamed engineer by phone if the valves on the descent rockets on the LEM would work enough times for the men to return home. In the movie that unnamed engineer, my father, supposedly said, "Yes."

Through tears my father told me, "I didn't tell them, 'Yes.' I told them it would work a thousand times."

So, my father, at the very pinnacle of his career, didn't have a lot of time for my toy underwater whistle. He did give me two pieces of advice however. The first, absolutely correct, the second, completely wrong.

My first instruction was to go to the library and search through the existing patents and see if my underwater whistle was already out there as part of the "public domain." He told me the search process was a great way to learn about patents and would also teach me how inventors thought, built and designed new things.

My father's second instruction was totally wrong; a veritable menu for disaster. He told me to write down my idea, include a drawing and then seal it in an envelope. I was to then go to the post office and have a postal worker stamp all over the envelope's glued flap the date stamp. The last step was for me to mail the letter to myself, keeping the unopened envelope as proof that I had the idea as of the date printed by the United States Postal Office.

I remember getting the envelope back in the mail and then hiding it in the back of my desk where no one but the most devious thief would find it. Every few days I would pull it out and look at it and dream of seeing my underwater whistle used by divers all over the world.

It was Walt Disney who said, "If you can dream it, you can do it." and at age fourteen I would dream of seeing my underwater whistle on diver's gear everywhere.

My father was correct that the sealed envelope might, in a small way, document who came up with the idea first, but it was NOT in any way a legal document and totally useless as any form of patent protection. Putting your idea in a sealed envelope and mailing it to yourself as a "poor man's patent" was useless.

My mother, Mary Jo Wright, however, loved the idea of the underwater whistle. I remember my father saying that it was just a silly toy, while my mom argued that it was "wonderful" and thought it was worth pursuing. Despite working part-time at her own real estate office and raising my brother and four sisters, she drove me to downtown Los Angeles at least three times over a two week period and waited hours upon hours as I searched the existing patents for any prior mention of an underwater whistle.

Back In 1970s, in order to complete a patent search, you had to visit one of the over dozen Patent and Trademark Depository Libraries spread across the United States and physically look at each patent. Indexes found at these depositories allowed research individuals to cross-reference patents by numbers, topics and inventors, all in an attempt to make the laborious search as streamlined as possible.

The downtown Los Angeles Public Library was one such depository that had volume after volume of patents dating back to the 1700s. The arduous task of doing a patent search was explained to me by the reference librarians and involved writing down hundreds of patent numbers from a catalog and then pulling four-inch-thick volumes, one by one from enormous shelves, reading the descriptions and finally determining if the idea of an underwater whistle was ever thought of before.

There are many sections that make up a patent. There is the title, the abstract, the description and the drawings, but one key section, particularly when doing a search, was the references. The references consisted of a list of patent numbers put together by the patent examiner that itemized any relevant prior art, any patents that had anything to do with the patent you were looking at getting.

For every whistle patent I read, I would write down ten more patent numbers from the references and then look up those. One patent for a whistle from the 1950s might mention six other whistle patents from the 1940s. The patents from the 40s often referenced ten more comparable patents from the 20s and 30s. On and on I went, writing down patent numbers, pulling books, reading descriptions and inspecting drawings.

I spent hours at the Los Angeles library surrounded by stacks of books, my head down as I scribbled nearly illegible notes while all around me attorneys and legal assistants worked silently, all doing the same thing. It was amazing reviewing the patents, seeing the progression of an idea over decades. I would often stop while flipping through one of the thick volumes and read the description for a new sewing machine from the 1860's or a drawing of a "new and improved" 1912 rope fabricator.

My mother loved the idea of my doing the patent search. She loved the idea that somehow, I could muster the focus to power through pages and pages of patents until, at the end of the day, I was forced to leave.

For me, the search for any sign of an underwater whistle in those hundreds of patents with their beautiful line drawings and wild descriptions was a blast. Every patent that I was able to cross off my list as unrelated moved my underwater whistle one step closer to being unique. Every whistle patent that failed to deal with anything water related was a small step closer to me becoming an actual inventor.

The good news was that after it was all said and done, there was nothing ever documented, drawn or suggested that was similar to my underwater whistle. It was new and truly distinctive.

In school I was a failure. I found it impossible to follow directions, was unable to memorize anything, hated math and couldn't spell. I clearly remember at the end of seventh grade when my teacher pulled me aside to tell me she had recommended to the school board that I repeat the school year. That the principal wouldn't listen and instead decided to let me move on to eighth. At the time, I foolishly thought her comment was some kind of compliment rather than the threat laced warning that she truly intended.

My successful patent search did one thing for me besides attest to the originality of the underwater whistle. It proved to me that the teachers were wrong. I could do something special and I wasn't the total failure they all said I was.

I had always judged myself by my performance in school; saw myself through the eyes of my instructors who, with every test, quiz and homework I struggled through, convinced me of the depth of my stupidity. Now, it seemed, I had done something special. I had thought of something nobody had ever dreamed before and in doing so, realized that there was hope for me after all.

Albert Einstein is quoted as saying, "Everybody is a genius. But if you judge a fish by its ability to climb a tree, it will live its whole life believing that it is stupid." School for me as a teenager was tantamount to trying to teach a fish to climb a tree. It wasn't my fit.

# Chapter 3:
# School, Hell on Earth

*"When you come to the en• of your rope, tie a knot an•*
*hang on."*

Franklin D. Roosevelt -
32nd president of the United States

I was a terrible student. It wasn't that I was disruptive or a trouble-maker, it was just that nothing made sense. My penmanship was nearly impossible to decipher, I couldn't grasp math or read very well and on top of all that, I had a very difficult time memorizing anything. What made school all that more difficult was that I had a stutter (my mom insisted that it was a stammer) and was unable to say the letter 'r' until fourth grade. Needless to say, having speech problems along with being the dumbest kid in class made things much more enjoyable for the bullies.

I hated everything about school. The teachers, the books, especially the homework. However, as I started my freshman year of high school, I did hook up with a handful of good friends. Friends that watched out for my back and stayed with me through the day-to-day grind. When I wasn't grounded for having flunked another test or forgetting to turn in homework, my buddies and I would meet up, es-cape to the beach and either surf or go snorkeling till dusk.

The beach was my greatest refuge. There was nothing to memo-rize and no lines to stay within; it was a place where you were tested every day, but never judged. I loved the ocean. My parent's house was atop a sandy cliff overlooking the Pacific Ocean in Redondo Beach, California. It was a wonderful place to grow up with the beach just a short jog away.

I was fifteen years old in 1971, a time when there was no internet, no online sales and the era of mega sporting goods outlets was a decade away. In my world, when it came to acquiring gear for water-sports and more specifically SCUBA diving, everything centered around what I considered the Disneyland of dive shops, Dive N' Surf. From my house, it was only a short twenty minute bike ride away.

Dive N' Surf was located two blocks from the beach, reeked of surf wax and old wetsuits and carried the most amazing aquatic devices imaginable. They sold high tech pressure air gauges, SCUBA tanks, surfboards and spear guns and it was there that I decided I would un-veil my underwater safety whistle to see once and for all if they were at all interested in buying the idea.

Dive N' Surf was owned by twin brothers Bill and Bob Meistrell who were innovators in their own right having designed the first practical wetsuit. I called and spoke to the Meistrells over the phone and convinced them that the underwater whistle was a great safety device for divers and that it would save lives. I am not certain if they knew I was only a kid at the time, but they agreed to meet me at the nearby harbor the next day at noon to check it out.

My mom drove and as we pulled into the parking lot at the ma-rina, I was overwhelmed to see a group of Dive N' Surf divers huddled together overlooking the water waiting for me. They were clearly SCUBA professionals. It was a combination of their swagger, the way they were decked out in the most modern wetsuits and high-tech equipment, but more than anything it was the way they looked at the water. They watched the water with respect and confidence, joy and fear, all rolled into one. I don't recall if it was Bill or Bob Meistrell who showed up, but whoever it was, he had brought along four expe-rienced divers to go into the water and try out the whistle.

I was beyond excited.

I had always been that dorky stammering loser. The lonely guy who the teachers would stick in the very back of class in the "group table." People never cared what I had to say, and with my stutter, I didn't want anybody to hear me anyway. My Uncle Bob told me that as a young man he used to call me "The Professor," because of the way I would just sit in the corner with my big oversized glasses and just watch, rarely saying a word. But here I was with professional divers, my heroes, and they were waiting for me, and they wanted to see what I had invented.

I was worried the guys from Dive N' Surf would want me to explain the whistle, how I invented it and how I made it. I cringed at the idea that they would laugh at the way I talked. Over the last few months I had come up with an idea that I thought might help smooth out my speech. I figured if I listened really hard to the way the radio broadcasters talked, the way they spaced out their words and paced themselves, maybe I could stop the stammering. I practiced every night as I lay in bed, a small transistor radio pressed to my ear as I listened to talk radio while trying desperately to mimic the smooth cadence of the professional announcers.

To my surprise, the guys from Dive N' Surf didn't want to talk. They took my whistle looked at it for about a half a second and without saying a word jumped straight into the water. After about two minutes underwater they'd surface, toss the whistle to another diver, and down they would drop.

Mr. Meistrell, my mom and I watched from the edge of the boat dock as the divers went up and down talking about what they heard and how far away they could hear it. The underwater tests didn't last more than ten minutes. The divers surfaced, took off their masks and while treading water not more than a few feet away, called out. "It works."

I got a call three days later from Dive N' Surf. They said the corporate guys wanted to perform one more set of tests. That they were going to be at Catalina Island over the weekend and wanted to know if I could go there and meet up with them. They went on to say that the Dive N' Surf's yacht could take me there and back.

Catalina is located about thirty miles southwest of Los Angeles. It has crystal-clear water, great fishing and even better diving. The idea of going there to pitch my underwater whistle was straight out of dreamland. For perhaps the first time in my life I felt I was right where I knew I should be.

"That sounds great," I told the guys at Dive N' Surf, "but I normally work on weekends painting, I'll lose like thirty bucks."

"We'll pay you the thirty dollars."

I then thought back to the divers and all their wicked good high-tech gear that I could never afford. Asking the person on the phone to hang on, I ran to my room, rifled through my stack of old magazines and snagged a SCUBAPRO dive catalog. Sprinting back to the phone, I snatched the receiver and calming my voice asked, "I could skip work and go if Dive N' Surf could throw in the SCUBA regulator like the one in the latest catalog, top of page 12."

There was a pause. He agreed.

"And there is a dive knife on page 47. One of those."

"Fine," the Dive N' Surf guy agreed impatiently, "but that's it."

"Well," I added, "I'm only fifteen, I'm a freshman in high school. My brother has to go with me and he also works. How about two sets?"

"Ok," the executive agreed with a huff. "You and your brother, sixty dollars, two regulators and two knives. Meet at Dive N' Surf at seven Saturday morning."

"Cool!" I shouted into the handset.

The guy on the phone hung up abruptly. He didn't seem happy being hustled by a kid, but I didn't care. I was on top of the world.

The day finally arrived.

My brother Ken and I showed up early at Dive N' Surf. We were quickly shuttled over to the marina where we boarded the large, 62 foot Body Glove yacht and headed off to Catalina. Ken was six years older than I, and from the start was skeptical of the whole affair. As we motored the nearly thirty miles toward the island, the weather turned choppy, windy and dark, quickly turning my long awaited day trip to Catalina, into anything but tranquil. My brother and I were fine, but the corporate guys looked like they were seasick. By the time we got to the island they were grumpy, annoyed and nauseous.

To make matters worse, these guys were executives and lacked the kind of diving experience the other divers displayed. These two, with their tailored clothes, immaculate haircuts and brand-new gear, looked like they had never "dropped down" in rough seas before. My brother and I had offered to dive with them during the tests, but the executives said they wanted to try the whistle solo and demanded that we stay on the surface to answer questions.

I knew things were going from bad to worse when they struggled to get their gear set up and their tanks strapped on. Then, when the first guy jumped in the water without his mask, I knew without a doubt the tests were in trouble.

They dropped down and within 60 seconds were back on the boat. "It didn't work," they said pulling themselves quickly aboard.

"Of course it works." I tried to explain, "Let me get in the water and I'll show you."

"Nope," they said unequivocally, "we're going back."

And that was it. After all my work and energy, I had left the fate of my underwater whistle to a couple of guys who either didn't care or who were so uncomfortable in the water that they abandoned the whistle in order to make it through the dive.

Dive N' Surf never did call back and despite my repeated attempts to reestablish contact with them, the opportunity to work with one of the largest dive centers in the world was lost.

I never forgot my disappointment that day. I threw the whistle with my drawings and "poor man's patent" into a large box of old abandoned junk and closed the lid. Looking back now I can't believe I had allowed someone else to demonstrate my whistle, let someone else showcase what I had spent so much time on. I was devastated. Except for that silly underwater whistle, I had always been a complete failure, and now that the whistle was proved inadequate, my failure was complete.

# Chapter 4:
# Acceptance to Whittier College

*"If you can't fly then run, if you can't run then walk, if you can't walk then crawl, but whatever you ·o you have to keep moving forwar·."*

Martin Luther King, Jr. - Civil Rights Leader

I fumbled my way through high school with the underwater whistle abandoned at the bottom of a junk box and the memory of the failed underwater whistle tests buried deep in the back of my mind. Ninth grade was no different than tenth, eleventh no different than twelfth. By the time I finished my senior year of high school my grade point average was 1.9 with me receiving nearly as many D's and F's as C's and B's.

In June 1974, despite having to repeat several classes in summer school and in the face of all the teachers that threatened to hold me back, I graduated from high school.

My mom was one of those old school Italian mothers who insisted that you owned your own business, became a doctor or became a lawyer. Anything else was a failure. I think that was why she was so intent on getting the whistle to work. She saw the whistle as my only hope at success, my only hope of running my own business. But now that it was relegated to the trash bin, that left only two alternatives, each of which demanded good grades.

It was the constant drone of my parents insisting I go to college that propelled me to move ahead with college applications. I hated school, but once I learned that after graduating high school all my grades were wiped clean, the idea that I could start anew was compelling.

I applied to college with the hope of starting again, of putting the pain of both grade and high school behind me. But with such a horrible grade point average, no college or university would consider me. Sure enough, I was rejected from every school I applied to.

That was until my older sister, Karen, stepped in. She had just graduated top of her class at Whittier College, a small liberal arts college located southeast of Los Angeles. My sister was a great student who won academic awards and had been active in clubs and organizations, so when she heard I hadn't been accepted to college, she approached the Dean at Whittier.

Karen told the Dean that I was special and despite my low GPA, had never caused trouble and was an honest and caring person. The Dean was unfazed until my sister told him how imaginative I was and how I had a patent on the world's first underwater safety whistle (an exaggeration at the least), how I was an inventor and was creative and that I just needed the right school to focus that ingenuity.

I remember when I received the final decision letter from Whittier. I opened the envelope and unfolded the letter with the embossed "Whittier College" printed across the top.

I think back to the dread I felt as I read the first paragraph. It was the same anxiety I lived with every time I took home a report card. The same sickness that churned in my stomach as I read the rejection letters from so many colleges. But this time it was different.

When I read the words that said I had been accepted, it felt like a great weight had been removed from my shoulders. I truly felt like I suddenly had been absolved and set free to start again. The fact that the letter said I was on "special probation" and that I needed to meet all my freshman professors and show them my high school transcript before starting class was immaterial. It was like I had a new lease on life.

I chose to meet with the department heads as soon as possible after receiving my acceptance letter to make certain that there were no problems later on. I telephoned Whittier and made the necessary appointments having no idea what to expect once I got there.

The math department's chairman was younger than I had expected. His name was Dr. Mike Massa and as I entered his office, I was shocked to see him sitting smoking a pipe, his feet propped on his desk, a tattered paperback book held loose in his hands. He looked like a young Indiana Jones, the stacks of journals piled on the floor and the shelves of tattered texts giving the room a sooty, library kind of smell. Behind him a row of windows sat half open and on a far wall a blackboard spread wide taking up half the wall.

"My name is Howard Wright," I told him as I handed over a beige folder. "I'm a freshman and was told I needed you to agree to accept me in your class before I can attend. My high school transcripts are in the folder."

Dr. Massa took the file and with a muted laugh he read, turning pages slowly and keeping his feet on the desk.

"OK," he said with a smile. "Go to the blackboard and let's do a few problems."

I visibly cringed.

"Don't worry," he added as he pointed to the board.

I stood at the ready, the chalk tight in my hand.

"Let's start with this," then after a pause, "five plus twelve."

I looked at him saddened. "Seriously?"

"Please."

I wrote "5 + 12 = 17".

The math professor picked up his paperback and from behind the pages said, "Six times six."

After a slight pause I wrote the answer.

"Seven divided by twelve."

I stumbled through the problem, dividing them best I could, writing the answer alongside the long division.

"One half multiplied by one quarter."

I started making things up, flipping fractions and adding numerators and denominators.

He was totally indifferent by my odd calculations, never once giving me the smallest hint if the answers were right or wrong. He would look up occasionally, smile and ask a slightly harder question. I trudged on, trying my best as I filled the whole board with numbers. I would stop uncertain and then, with a wave of his hand, he would tell me to just keep going and "work the puzzle."

The final question was something like "$(2x +5) \times (5y - 4) =$."

I made up the answer guessing my way through as I tried desperately to remember back to the math classes I had flunked, my confidence evaporated and feeling totally humiliated.

He closed his paperback book and studied the board for the longest time, the only sound being the drowning whirr of some distant lawnmower. With a thoughtful kind of curious grin, he shook his head sadly, "It's all wrong, well, not everything, but nearly everything. You've broken virtually every rule there is."

Then raising his hand to his chin, he continued, "But what's interesting is, as you were working the problems, I could actually see you learning, seeing relationships, making adjustments. I think you can do this if you work hard." He reached down and signed his name to the cover sheet attached to the front of the folder.

As I walked slowly past the wide green lawns of Whittier College I was elated. This was not the mathematics I stumbled through year after year filled with formulas and concepts that never made any sense. This could be different. I could feel it. I could do this.

I attended the next two meetings, one for biology and one for English, and in both cases I was greeted by professors who saw me as a challenge, an opportunity for them to knock the rough edges off a valuable, albeit dull, stone. Whittier College was a Godsend.

# Chapter 5:
# UCLA – Redemption

*"Most of the important things in the worl⬧ have been accomplishe⬧ by people who have kept on trying when there seeme⬧ to be no hope at all."*

Dale Carnegie - American Writer and Lecture

The day after I was officially accepted into college, my mom told me I was going to spend the summer working as a volunteer at UCLA's teaching hospital. Every year since I was ten years old, I had been was stuck in summer school. Now it seemed, having graduated and accepted into college, I foolishly hoped that a part time job and surfing would fill the next few months. My mom, however, saw things just a little bit differently.

"How do you expect to be ready for your premed classes if you've never worked in a hospital?" my mother asked not expecting an answer.

Groaning out loud I looked at her, "How am I expected to make any money?"

"We're paying for your school. You don't need any money. You're spending the summer working at UCLA as a volunteer." She answered smartly, "Your first day is Monday."

The commute to UCLA from Redondo Beach took a good hour with most of that time spent creeping along bumper-to-bumper on the notoriously congested 405 Freeway. On arriving at the volunteer office, I was greeted by a pleasant white-haired matron who took down my information and once satisfied, asked me where I wanted to work.

"We have an opening in the patient transport or you could help in the information booth in the east wing," After rifling through a stack of papers, she smiled and said, "and there is an opening for a lab assistant in nuclear medicine."

Nuclear medicine? I didn't have a clue what nuclear medicine was, but compared to spending my summer propped in an information booth directing people to who knows where or wheeling people from x-ray to orthopedics, I took the mystery gift behind door number 3. "Nuclear medicine; Let's try that."

I don't know why I picked nuclear medicine. I guess because it sounded "cool." While in high school, I hated everything to do with chemistry. I tried valiantly to pass the general chemistry class in my senior year with a C but was confused with all the talk of moles and electrons. Now, I had just been forced to volunteer in a lab surrounded by the stench of formaldehyde and the buzz of dingy fluorescent lights. My only escape from the monotony being the opportunity to clean dirty glassware.

The woman in charge of the volunteer center grinned cheerfully as she handed me a clip-on badge with the declaration, "VOLUNTEER" written boldly across its surface.

"If you have any questions or you want to change to another department, just come back here," she said with a smile. "We'll set you straight."

I thanked her, clipped the badge to my shirt pocket and headed down the polished white corridor in search of the Department of Nuclear Medicine. As I walked, lost in more ways than one, I was totally unaware that what would happen in the next ninety minutes would change my life completely.

UCLA's hospital was immense, the hallways running for over twelve miles, many of which were painted with color coded lines to help people navigate the myriad of corridors that ran in every direction. After asking several people for instructions, I finally found the offices of Dr. Milo Webber located deep in the hospital's sub-basement.

I am not certain what I expected to see when I walked into the lab. Perhaps a tired guy with thick glasses and a pocket protector hunched over a microscope just staring apathetically at microbes as they swam around? Maybe there would be some open books laid out on the desks and one of those dreaded periodic tables hanging crooked from a nearby wall?

I found the lab, entered through a pair of wide-open double doors and was immediately awestruck. The lab was gigantic. It extended at least fifty feet straight back with lab desks, sinks and work areas that filled every corner of the space. On the jet-black epoxy desks, there was every form of glassware, microscopes and analytical devices one could imagine. Against the left wall were chalkboards strung end to end; on their dark green surfaces were written cell counts, calculations and formulas as foreign as Egyptian hieroglyphics.

On the right wall of the lab there were row upon row of metal cages stacked from floor to ceiling, each one the size of a small microwave. Taking a step further into the room I looked closer and peered through the perforated metal door of the closest hutch and found that each held a single white rat, it's pink eyes and white fur stark against the wood chipped cage floor. There must have been well over a hundred rats cooped up in the lab, water bottles and food trays hanging from each door.

The lab smelled of alcohol and rodents, but what dominated the space more than anything was the tension that seemed to ooze from the dozen or so doctors and lab techs that scurried in every direction. I couldn't tell who was in charge, but as I stood and watched, it was like nothing I had ever seen before.

"Ya," the powerful Swedish accent startled me, "Vell, and who'd , may I ask, are you'd?"

She was middle aged, standing no taller the five feet with short cropped hair and a rumpled white coat that hung down to her feet.

I'm Howard. Howard Wright," I stammered, showing her my nifty badge and handing her my papers. "I'm a volunteer."

"Ja," she said as we stood side by side and watched the lab hum with activity, "My name is Olga."

"Hello, Olga."

We both stood silently as we looked over the laboratory until I noticed something on the far wall. It was odd, like when you see an object move out of the corner of your eye, but you can't quite figure it out.

For me it was the writing on the chalkboard. Even from across the room it looked strange; as if something was out of place. It was like seeing a document and knowing there is a typo somewhere in the lines, but not knowing where the problem was or how to fix it. It was like entering your room an knowing somebody moved something, but you just can't figure out what.

I remember staring at the chalkboard with all its figures and equations and having no idea what I was looking at or what it meant; but understanding to my very soul that something was wrong and to leave it unannounced was impossible.

Bending down so no one else would hear, I pointed to the chalkboard where the rows of numbers were written and whispered to Olga, five simple words that changed my entire life: "I think the math's wrong."

It never entered my mind that what I said was important. I don't even know why I mentioned it. For me, making a mistake on a math paper was standard. As a matter of fact, the idea that I would complete a worksheet that wasn't covered in red marks was a day to be celebrated.

Olga looked at me with an odd kind of head tilt and without saying a word, stepped three strides further toward the middle of the room and then stopped.

She looked around as if she hadn't a care in the world, straightened her rumpled lab coat and taking a deep breath screamed out to everybody in the lab, "STOP, STOP! HOWARD SAYS DE MATH IS WRONG."

Oh my god I could have killed myself. If I had one of those Japanese knives, I would have committed *seppuku* right then and there. I felt like I was just kicked in the groin and could barely speak as I moved toward Olga and begged her to keep quiet.

"No, no, no."

My first day, my first five minutes on the job and I was right back in sixth grade being humiliated in front of the whole class. I seriously thought I was going to barf my entire breakfast right on top of Olga's head.

"Who said the math's wrong?" He was at least six feet four, bald, well over forty and looked like he was from somewhere north of Russia. I suddenly realized I may not have to worry about killing myself because this guy standing right in front of me with his starched white coat, white shirt and narrow black tie was about to murder me.

Olga pointed with a nervous nod my way.

"And who the hell are you?" He spat.

He was right in my face and all I could think of was to run. Seriously, that whole fight or flight thing never made any sense to me until that day. I wanted to run and find a hole and dive into it.

"What's wrong with the math?" It was a softer voice, but no less intimidating. The Russian stepped back and so did Olga as the entire lab watched an elderly man with graying temples and a hard, serious expression approach. He was wearing a short white lab coat, and as he moved forward the entire lab fell silent.

"I'm sorry, I should just leave. I shouldn't be here." I cringed and stood there holding my hands together to keep them from shaking.

"No," The doctor said looking me straight in the eye. "Tell me. What is wrong with the math?"

The entire lab stood petrified as if all time and space had suddenly stopped.

I pointed to the chalkboard furthest from where I stood. "I don't know, but it doesn't look right. Something seems wrong."

The doctor in the short coat kept staring at me as he gave the order to redo the math.

"I double checked it." the Russian objected as he glared at me with the seething look of bitter resentment.

"I said, redo the math," the elderly doctor commanded, clipped and forceful.

A moment later I could clearly hear the crack of the chalk from across the room as the figures were reworked. Anger fumed each time the chalk slammed into the board as the Russian was forced to recalculate the numbers. Suddenly it became quiet, the chalk stopping mid calculation.

The Russian turned, the math involving fractions and percentages laid out before him suddenly halted. "I... It seems that I wrote down the conversion from liters to milliliters wrong, I had it reversed, inverted. Instead of dividing by a thousand I multiplied by 1000. The numbers are all wrong. I don't know how I could have..."

The doctor in his short white coat took a short step closer to me and leaned in, his face mere inches from mine. In a voice that was both surprised and curious, he asked me, "Who ARE you? What are you doing here?"

I remember looking first to Olga and then to the doctor, "I am Howard Wright," I stuttered. "I'm a volunteer. I'm supposed to help clean stuff up, wash glassware. That kind of thing."

In a loud voice, the doctor, his eyes unmoving as he looked deep into my very soul, called out, "Olga, get me a coat."

Olga disappeared in a blur of motion. A moment later she returned and in her hand she carried a white doctor's coat. She helped me put it on, clipping my UCLA Volunteer badge to the breast pocket.

"My name is Dr. Milo Webber. This is my lab and from now on you will be my personal assistant."

And with that everything changed.

It was amazing how Dr. Webber's acknowledgement of my worth transformed how I saw myself. How, up until that moment, I always had the impression that I had nothing to offer and, with the loss of the whistle, I was simply stupid and useless.

But now, Dr. Milo Webber wanted me at his side. A man who was, I would come to learn, one of the foremost authorities on nuclear medicine in the world, and he had seen value in me.

It seems that by having spoken up, I saved the project from certain disaster. The lab was at the very start of a three-year multimillion-dollar program to study ascites cancer, a disease that affects millions of people around the world. It seems that if I had not intervened, they would have injected the rats with one thousand times too much cancer, destroying the project.

I ended up working with Olga and Dr. Webber, and yes, the Russian PhD, for the rest of the summer and carried on working with them for the next three summers. My mother was right. I never understood what it meant to be a doctor, and if it wasn't for her insistence that I work with great physicians like Dr. Webber, I would have never seen my true potential or have demanded so much of myself.

To this day I don't know what it was about the calculations on the chalkboard that got my attention. What subtle hint screamed out to allow me to see the error stuck deep inside the complex factor labeling scrawled on the board? I only know that something caught my attention and compelled me to speak up.

I cannot accept any credit for finding the mistake and saving the project. I had no idea what I was looking at. The voice with which I called out was not mine. Albert Einstein said, "There are only two ways to live your life. One is as though nothing is a miracle. The other is as though everything is a miracle." Personally, I believe in God's miracles in my life.

Like all of God's miracles, it was a free gift. Totally undeserved.

In my senior year in high school I was in a tough wrestling match winning 4 to 0 with a minute left in the third and last period. I dominated the match, working hard and moving constantly to control my opponent. My adversary was sluggish and dog-tired as we wrestled, until I made a fatal mistake, lost my balance and was flipped onto my back.

"Two points reversal, three points near fall," the referee screamed.

I built back to my base and tried to even the points by wrestling myself free, but the other kid just held on, keeping me from getting the escape that would offer me the one point I needed to even the match.

There was only fifteen seconds left on the clock and I moved as fast as I could, but the other wrestler just stuck to me like a wet T shirt. I tried standing again with five seconds to go but couldn't work myself free. In my last attempt to escape, I took hold of my opponent's wrists and tried to wriggle my way clear, but it was too late. The buzzer screamed.

"One point escape," the referee called out.

I was shocked. I didn't think I got out in time. The other coach was as mad as a hornet as he ran onto the mat and yelled at the referee for missing the call. I stood at the center of the mat confused.

"Overtime," the ref shouted. "The score is tied five to five."

I wiped the sweat from my face and dropped down immediately onto my hands and knees at the center of the mat. While I kneeled stock still and waited for the two-minute overtime period to begin, the other wrestler visited his corner and plotted strategy with his coach.

Trying to relax as I waited for the other wrestler, I thought about how lucky I was to get a second chance to win the match. Lucky to get the proverbial second bite at the apple. It was then, as I lifted my head that I saw the referee lean forward and whisper in a voice only I could hear, "Now, let's see what you can do."

In a split second, I realized that there was no luck involved. It wasn't anything I did that got me the second chance and it wasn't some silly mistake by the referee. The official, the person in charge of everything, had permitted me a redo. Right or wrong, good or bad, legal or not, the official in charge has just given me a second chance. The words of the referee reverberated in my head. "Now, let's see what you can do."

My adversary came back to the center of the mat and covered me, one hand on my elbow, the other tight around my waist. His chin dug deep into my back.

"Ready, wrestle!" The referee called out and in the split second it took for those words to be said, I jumped to my feet.

I burst up and out with all the energy I had, ripping with a ferociousness I never knew I possessed. I broke loose, turned and without a moment's hesitation attacked.

"Now, let's see what you can do," reverberated in my mind. I pinned my opponent thirty seconds later. "Now, let's see what you can do."

On the wrestling mat, it was a referee who gave me the opportunity to be the champion I kept hidden inside. Then it was a professor at Whittier College who told me that he believed that I could indeed learn and finally it was a doctor at UCLA that reminded me that I had the ability to see what others couldn't. Through the grace of God, I was given the second chance to be the person God wanted me to be.

# Chapter 6:
# Rebooting

*"Success is not final, failure is not fatal, it is the courage to continue that counts."*

Winston Churchill - Prime Minister
of the United Kingdom

College gave me the opportunity to start over again, to mold my-self into a new person and while I didn't know what I wanted to become, I knew what kind of person I was not willing to remain. I wouldn't accept the mentally unprepared dolt that I had gotten used to in high school and I refused to remain the slow, half assed block-head that I had become.

I decided, after my time in Dr. Weber's nuclear medicine labora-tory at UCLA, that I liked being responsible, wanted to be respected and was willing to fight to win that relevance. During that first sum-mer before college I shadowed doctors, nurses and assistants and watched them; really watched them.

What I came to realize was, that when it came to being successful, these professionals weren't any smarter than I was and didn't work any harder than I did. What they were was organized. Organized in understanding what they wanted to achieve and organized in know-ing what they had to do in order to achieve it. Observing these UCLA professionals as they completed complex tasks, I came to realize that the framework for their organization was, to a large degree, built around a very simple tool: lists.

Ever since I was ten, my mom and dad told me that the answer to my bad grades lay in the "making of lists and sticking to them." Unfortunately, as far as I was concerned, all lists did was highlight up-coming stumbling blocks and itemize my failures.

Having worked at UCLA and taking the time to watch as the re-searchers outlined daily schedules, create detailed agendas and itemize lab protocols; I came to see that I had viewed lists in completely the wrong way. Lists shouldn't be approached as some kind of sadistic collection of Herculean tasks to stumble upon, but rather as a mecha-nism to break difficult tasks down into achievable steps. Each individ-ual line-item representing a doable kind of mini finish line which, when completed and strung together, represented a stairway to vic-tory.

By creating lists with specific achievable microtasks, I was able to force my brain to narrow its focus, concentrate and finally get things done. With this in mind, I started creating lists for everything: how I would spend my day, what exactly I would study, what pages I would cover and what paragraphs I would outline. Each mini-detail allowing me to effectively divide and conquer the largest of tasks.

What creating detailed lists did for me was to break down daily re-sponsibilities to such a degree that each task became not only attain-able but easy. If I found that when a particular task became too tough, I would go back and break that individual job down further until the parts were achievable. Rather than having a list of failures staring me in the face at the end of the day, I had a long list of victories, each item crossed off representing dozens of individual mini-successes.

Lists not only helped me to formulate a path to success, they also helped me to focus. Jerry Seinfeld, the great comedian, said "The lack of focus is why we have a lack of greatness." For me that was abun-dantly true. Having individual tasks on a list that were narrow, con-fined and defined to the degree that I couldn't help but stay on task was key to my becoming a good student.

Researchers have determined that, in order to focus, the brain spends 75% of its energy powering special cells that silence the constant barrage of sensations that hammer us every second of every day. Most people don't feel the weight of their body when they sit on a chair, they don't feel the shirt on their back or hear the thousands of noises that surround them. Most people are able to focus because our brains have these extraordinary dampening neurons that act as gate-keepers to selectively quiet the torrent of sensory impulses that con-stantly surround us.

But, not everyone.

It seems that for many attention deficit individuals, those dampen-ing cells aren't fully engaged forcing them to fight defenseless and un-protected against a ceaseless stream of sensations, ideas and feelings. As a remedy, stimulants such as Ritalin and Adderall are prescribed with the goal of activating those gatekeeper neurons to basically "quiet the room."

I wasn't aware of all the psychological studies and was never diag-nosed by anyone, except those shortsighted teachers who called me stupid. What I did know, however, was that by making numbered lists that contained distinct micro-goals, I soon found that I could fi-nally focus and complete tasks, exhilarated as I wrote "DONE" across each item on the list. Amazing as it sounds, I actually started enjoying school.

What changed? How was it that by turning to using lists, a tech-nique I always detested, all of a sudden became a major force for me allowing me to be able to get things done?

I changed. I stopped doing things for my parents or teachers and started to accomplish goals for myself.

I once had a conversation with an individual who worked at a drug rehabilitation center. I was amazed when he told me how those indi-viduals who showed up surrounded by family and friends rarely suc-ceeded in staying "clean." He explained that is was the solitary individ-ual that entered the rehab facility alone that typically turned their lives around. He said it was because that lone addict had truly seen his problem and wasn't detoxing for anyone but himself.

It appeared that I had made the decision to change not because of my mom's threats or my dad's screams. I decided to change because I decided to be a different person, a more responsible person, and I knew the sooner I made that change the better.

Another aspect of learning to focus centered around my tendency toward distraction. It was amazing how the smallest, most inconsequential snippet of conversation or insignificant bit of background noise could pull me off task. To combat this tendency to become side-tracked, I started waking up early to study. I would set my alarm for five in the morning and study till eight. Then I would go to breakfast, go to class and then study again. At five in the morning there was nobody knocking on the dorm room door, no noises from outside, nothing.

The last major obstacle I had in school involved my difficulties with memorization. It seemed that no matter how many times I tried to force myself to store obscure facts into my brain, they just wouldn't stick. What are the four parts of the scientific method? Outline the steps in the Calvin cycle? Name the organelles on a cell diagram. It was like torture trying to recall these kinds of random facts.

What I learned from the tutors at Whittier College was that if I could create each bit of information into a continuous story instead of trying to remember unrelated facts, I could both understand the concepts on a deeper level and also be more effective at memorizing the details. This meant first understanding the concept completely and then, after securing the image of the story in my mind, adding the related facts. This was critical because, neurologically, individual facts are typically held on a single spot or engram in the brain. Pictures and stories, on the other hand, are held in groups of thousands of engrams. Attempting to retrieve information efficiently off a single engram is difficult while finding and gaining access to strings of thousands of engrams is much simpler. By first creating a solid story in my mind as an underlying framework for the facts to attach, my brain was able to access the information quicker allowing everything to make more sense.

Math, however, was another issue. My success in math was solely due to my roommate Tim. Tim was a math guru, having taking the most difficult classes the college had to offer and passing each and every one of them with an A. For Tim, math was nothing but a game; because for him, that is just what it was. A game.

The first thing Tim taught me about math was that it was no different than Monopoly, or Hi Ho Cherry-O. It was just a game with rules, a start and an end. Math, Tim explained, was like a board game where you move step by step in order to get to a particular spot with each stage guided by a set of rules that must be obeyed. The more rules you know, the more efficiently you can move around the board.

Tim taught me to write down four or five math rules (equations) on my paper before ever attempting a problem. Then, after reading the problem and determining what numbers you had, go back to the rules, pick out the ones that were relevant and then plug-in the available data. It took me just days to go from hating math to enjoying it immensely.

Michael Jordan, the famed basketball star, has been quoted as saying "If you run into a wall, don't turn around and give up. Figure out how to climb it, go through it, or work around it." Tim taught me how to make math fun by making it a game.

# Chapter 7:
# More Than Just Science

*"Everyone thinks of changing the worl•, but no one thinks of changing himself."*

Leo Tolstoy - Russian Writer

Every day I got better at school. I became more efficient at organizing my studies, making lists, developing my memory and learning to negotiate my way around the game of math.

It wasn't just making lists or learning to memorize obscure factoids that allowed me to excel in my classes. It was also by building close friendships with a small handful of likeminded classmates that allowed me to succeed. By surrounding myself with good people who had the same yearning for greatness, the same drive and work ethic to excel, that I was able to persist undeterred in achieving my goals.

Whittier College provided me with a great college experience where I was able to get better grades, learned to expect more from myself and focused my goals. Most importantly, and clearly unexpectedly, I also had the opportunity to learn about God.

My parents never spoke about the Holy Spirt, Christ or the Lord. The only time I recall my father ever speaking with me about God was one evening when I was young, probably no more than twelve years old. He and I were watching a TV show together when the program must have mentioned something about "the afterlife." I remember my father turning the volume on the television down and then, looking at me square in the face with his no-nonsense stare that screamed 'you better listen boy,' went on to explain his thoughts on the subject.

"Howard, don't listen to those jerks. There is no afterlife and there is no God." Then, using his hands to emphasize his words, went on to give examples. "If you step on a worm, it's dead. There is no afterlife for the worm. There is no worm heaven. It's gone."

Leaning closer my father expounded, "Kill a squirrel and it's the same thing. No afterlife, no squirrel paradise. It's dead. And if you kill a man, it's the same. There are no mystical spirits, no angels, only death."

Then, pointing right in my face, he slowed his words and moving within an inch of me uttered these words. "People made up all this afterlife crap. It's so they feel better when they die. It's all lies. There is no God."

While at Whittier College I came to understand that my father was wrong about God. Completely and unequivocally wrong. I learned there is one God and He loves me. That there are evil spirits intent on forcing our attention away from God's grace and there are godly spirits directing us toward His glory.

It was not just God's miracles in nature and science that convinced me of His existence; it was also the prophecies in the Bible and my own personal experiences that convinced me of the truth of God's presence in my life and His yearning for a relationship with me.

One personal experience that forced me to question these strictly analytical beliefs concerning science and the nonexistence of God, involved an old glass table I had borrowed from my mom and dad when I went off to college.

The table was rickety to say the least, had an extremely heavy square glass top and was supported from the center by an odd kind of wooden pedestal. I used it to hold my clock radio and a cheap lamp and really never thought much of it until one Friday night during my freshman year.

I remember distinctly how I was studying in my dorm room when a group of students knocked on my door pulling me from my books.

I opened the door and found three guys and one girl crowding my door, hoping to borrow a table in order to have a seance. They didn't seem drunk or high, just stupid.

"Come on," they whined, "yours is like the fifth room we've tried. We won't break it."

I reminded them, "You know, seances are stupid and a waste of time. Right? There are no ghosts and no spirits. When you die, you die like a worm. There is no 'afterlife.'"

"Just for a little while," they all begged. "Yours is the only one around."

"Fine," I gave in. "Just get it back to me before eleven. No later."

I tossed the lamp and clock radio on the bed as two of the boys moved to either side of the table. They struggled to lift it from the ground, half dragging it, half carrying it toward the hallway while the girl held the door. Shuffling their way outside they were doing fine until *whack* they slammed the glass against the door jamb, not once, but twice.

"Stop," I yelled, "you'll crack the glass. Just stop. Put it down."

"We got this," one of the guys grunted as he smashed the table into the wall again.

"NO!" I yelled. "Put it down. Find somebody else's table to use for your stupid game."

"What if we did it here, in your room?" one of the guys suggested. "It will be fun."

Being an amateur magician, I loved sleight of hand, card manipulation and the art of misdirection. The guy was right, I thought to myself. It just might be fun catching these dorks in their ridiculousness.

"Ok," I agreed, "but I promise, you'll just end up feeling stupid."

One of the boys snatched my chair while the others ran down the hall to the dorm commons where they grabbed another three.

Hurrying to their spots across from one another, they settled themselves, leaving me to sit atop my desk and watch.

Between spurts of laughter, they calmed themselves, placed their hands atop the table and in less than three seconds fell silent.

It was unnerving watching them with their heads held high and their eyes closed. I expected constant jokes, stupid mantras and silly calls for the "undead," but they sat perfectly still with their eyes softly shut, completely and absolutely asleep.

The only movement was the table as it rose from the ground.

As slow as slow can be, the table, my mother's old glass table, left the ground as soon as they closed their eyes.

I remember the book I was studying. It was orange and had *Biology* written across the front. I shifted it off my lap and onto my desk.

I walked around the four students. Each had their eyes closed, the tips of their fingers barely touching the surface of the glass; each in a deep trance.

As the table rose, I swept my arm over their heads and in front of their chests in search of a wire but found nothing as the table lifted to six inches above the floor. I looked at their hands and was stunned when I noticed that only the smallest portions of their fingertips touched the clear glass tabletop's surface.

I grabbed one of the boys, the one I felt was the largest of the four, and hooked his shoulders and pulled him hard and fast from his chair. He immediately woke, screamed and ran, bolting for the door.

The table rose higher. I grabbed the second boy pulling him from the table with the same results.

The table was now no less than two feet above the ground and rising.

I grabbed the wrists of the third boy and ripped them from the table. They came free easily like the others. Once loose from the table he awoke, screamed and threw the door wide. He ran away without looking back.

The girl was the last of the four. She sat alone with her eyes closed and her fingertips barely adhering to the top of the glass. The table now floated three feet from the floor. Her hands were unmoving just above her head, palms down like she was about to pull herself over a six foot cinderblock wall, but there was no wall, only a girl I had never seen before and a glass table I had known my entire life.

Unmoved by the fact that she had been abandoned by her friends, she sat stone still, her eyes closed, shoulders relaxed, her head forward.

I checked her feet for lifts, swept under the pedestal for any kind of jack and found nothing. It was my room and it was my table and everything I knew about physics, math and science had just been blown away.

Louis Pasteur, arguably one of the greatest scientists of all time, said, "Little science takes you away from God, but more of it takes you to him."

I realized at that moment that I knew nothing of science and nothing of the world.

I gently grasped her wrists and lifted her hands from the table. Her fingers came free from the glass with absolutely no resistance. The table slowly returned to the ground as she turned to me and slowly opened her eyes, a terrifying pain contorting her face. It was then, as she sat and, her eyes wide and aflame, glared at me that she hissed in a voice that can only be described as demonic. "How dare you toy with what you know nothing about, you pathetic bastard."

I stood in shock and watched as whatever it was inside this woman continued to spew strings of condemnation and hatred until I finally answered back in the only way I knew how.

As a middle child I had always been a pleaser. When my siblings screamed at each other or my parents went on a rampage, I always tried to quiet the maelstrom by making jokes and acting the clown. It is what I did to endure the heart wrenching pain of a dysfunctional family; humor was my medicine. Comedy, my cure-all during difficult times.

Looking at the contorted face of the girl as she spat every form of hatred at me, I leaned close and asked with a quirky smile, "Bastard? Are you saying my parents weren't married? Because I'm pretty sure they were. I've seen the pictures."

More rants and vile threats until, all of a sudden, she went quiet.

Unmoved from the same wooden chair she had occupied for the last five minutes, the girl suddenly settled down. She brought her hands to her face and cried, unable to fathom what she was happening to her until once again she fell into a trance.

It was after a short time that she raised her head, opened her eyes and spoke; this time the tone was totally different, now peaceful and compassionate. The new calming voice was instructive telling me to pray to God for His mercy, His grace and repeatedly reminded me to cling tight to the Holy Scriptures. The voice told me to not give up on the girl and stay the course away from evil. To embrace what is blessed and Godly.

I scrambled to my desk, grabbed a slip of paper and a pen and started scribbling notes.

The schizophrenic flip flopping occurred again and again; one minute the girl speaking of the peace found only in the one true God and then moments later vile retribution of any and all that was good.

Half of me wanted to throw the girl out the door, to just forget the entire event ever occurred and go back to my life where everything made sense. Back to the world where the laws of physics were all that existed.

But I didn't throw her out. There was a side of me that wanted to help her, to do what I could to break her free of the torment. And also, deep down inside, I was also curious.

I had hoped the upheaval inside the girl would simply stop but after about an hour of back and forth, good and evil, I decided to look for help. It was during a moment when the girl fell into a quiet trance that I ran next-door to ask my neighbor for support but neither he nor his roommate were home. I went to another room and another until finally someone answered.

It was Ryan who opened the door. He lived down the hall, was from England, was freshman like me and, although I didn't actually know him, he always seemed a good guy.

I figured once I told him about the table, the girl and the "seizures," that he would just slam the door in my face, but he didn't and immediately offered to help.

Part of me expected that by the time I came back with another person, the girl would have left, disappeared somehow. Run away or in the very least stopped the ranting. But no, she was still there, now directing her vile ramblings toward both of us.

Ryan was a Christian and quietly prayed with none of the "Be Gone Satan," hogwash I had seen on TV, but instead confronted the situation with simple prayer. I, on the other hand, deflected the vile spewing comments with my own defensive offbeat humor.

It was two hours later that the girl finally returned to her right mind, free of the bizarre rantings. She sat exhausted and clear headed with the exception of one horrible side effect: she had become blind. Not blind in as much as she saw only darkness, but now, eyes wide open, she reported only seeing white, a blinding stark white and nothing else.

We did the only thing we could think of and guided her to the student health center where there was an emergency nurse/doctor on duty.

After a short cursory exam, the practitioner looked at Ryan, the girl and me and asked, in no uncertain terms, "Ok, so speak up. Which one of you imbeciles has been toying with witchcraft?"

I pointed at the girl and she just hung her head down low.

Furious, the physician looked at us like we were the most foolish creatures on the planet. "You should know better than this; she could have been killed." Then, after a long moment he shook his head in disgust. "Her vision will return, but never, ever toy with the black arts."

As we left the infirmary, the girl's eyesight began to return and, listening to her request, returned her to her dormitory.

The next day I walked to a park not far from school and, moving to a secluded area, tried to wrap my head around what I had seen, what it all meant and how the existence of the "supernatural" fit into my understanding of who I was and what I believed.

It was quiet as I sat and tried to put everything I had experienced into perspective. I sat looking over the notes I took the night before until an older gentleman walked up.

"Excuse me," the man said. "I don't mean to disturb you, but I have got to tell you something."

He was wearing a tan suit and bland tie and looked incredibly uncomfortable.

"Yeah," I replied not knowing who he was or where he had come from.

"I know this sounds stupid," he went on, "but I was driving down Whittier Boulevard to check on one of my accounts when suddenly I had this powerful urge to pull over and look for somebody. I think it's you."

"Really?" I smiled nervously.

After a moment's hesitation, he pulled his eyes off his fumbling hands and looked down at me sitting on the bench and explained, "I'm supposed to tell you that everything is OK, and that God loves you and you are not alone."

I grinned.

"Does that make any sense to you?" The man said as he stood painfully confused, "because I have no idea why I came over here."

"Yeah, it's all good," I insisted.

He turned and walked away.

I didn't know why I was permitted to see, up close and personal, the spiritual exchanges that I witnessed. All I can conclude is that I must truly be the dumbest of the dumb requiring spiritual intervention in order for me to believe in the existence of God. It is sad when you think about the fact that without some crazy table floating a good three feet off the ground, I would have never considered the existence of our Lord or the wonderful gift of the Bible.

Despite my fear and apprehension, I didn't reject what I saw. It crossed my mind to ignore everything I had experienced. I considered disregarding what I witnessed with my eyes and felt in my heart, but I decided at that moment to see the world for what it was. I decided to remove the blinders of disbelief and instead open my eyes to everything; both natural and spiritual.

Albert Einstein was quoted as saying that "Once you stop learning, you start dying."

Years later when I coached varsity wrestling, one of my better athletes asked me why I always pushed him so hard. I told him that it was because I saw greatness in him; a wonderful untapped potential and I wanted to show him the power he held inside.

Maybe, just maybe, the Lord forced me that night to open my eyes to the reality of God, and yes, the existence of evil. Pushed me to broaden my outlook on life in order to unleash in me some great untapped potential that, without a great deal of prodding, would have never been exposed.

# Chapter 8:
# Rejection Times Two

*"A failure is not always a mistake; it may simply be the best one can ∘o un∘er the circumstances. The real mistake is to stop trying."*

B. F. Skinner - American Psychologist

After having completed my first two years of college at Whittier, I was disappointed to be told by my parents that I had to transfer to the University of California San Diego. At this point, with my brother in medical school and two of my four sisters attending the university, my parents felt they could save money by sending me to a state school. I understood how expensive everything was and reluctantly agreed.

UCSD was as different as night and day from Whittier. At Whittier, my classes had twenty to thirty students per class with professors who would speak to you one-on-one explaining each concept and principle in detail. At UCSD, my classes were attended by upwards of 300 students packed in auditorium-style lecture halls. Labs, that were taught by the professor at Whittier, were now being taught by teacher's assistants and the idea of asking a question in class was crazy.

What UCSD did provide, however, was a tougher caliber of student. Like at Whittier, I would wake up early and study from five till eight in the morning. I would then go to breakfast, arriving for my first class at nine. At around three in the afternoon I would visit the teacher's assistants and review everything covered in my classes till five and then rewrite my notes till dinner. In the evening I would hook up with a study group or finish a paper and start it all again the next day.

The realization that I wasn't a good student and would have to work twice as hard as anyone else in the school was clear. Derek Jeter, the great baseball shortstop is quoted as saying, "There may be people that have more talent than you, but there's no excuse for anyone to work harder than you do." At UCSD, as I competed against some of the brightest students in the country, I knew to my very core that I had to work harder than everyone else.

Nearly every day I would meet classmates that could read a paragraph twice and memorize every term with understanding, but that wasn't me. My hopes and goals were only going to be grasped if I focused and worked smarter, harder and longer than the other guy and maybe, by the grace of God, be able to fulfill my dream of becoming a … dentist.

My mother wanted me to be a physician like my brother. She said that dentists were losers, people who wanted to be a "real" doctor but couldn't hack it. I considered being a medical doctor but being a physician didn't seem like a good fit. The idea of giving a patient a drug and then having to wait a month to see if it worked sounded boring to me. In the same way, training for ten years to be a surgeon to do the same procedure day in and day out seemed incredibly dull. Dentistry sounded more exciting.

I saw dentistry as a melding of art and engineering applied to people. It was owning your own business, treating a problem and fixing it in less than an hour. Being a dentist meant creating objects made from porcelain, gold and metal that were both beautiful and functional.

I told my father of my dream of being a dentist and he suggested that if I was serious, I should work with a family friend named Dr. Francisco Ramirez. He had a small dental office in a primarily Hispanic area of east Los Angeles, had been there for years and, according to my father, was very successful.

What I found during my weeklong visit to Dr. Ramirez's office was exactly what I was looking for. He, along with his assistant Maria, treated patients for every kind of problem: adjusting loose dentures, placing new crowns, filling cavities and performing difficult extractions. Every patient paid with cash and thanked him profusely at the end of each procedure. Each day, as we walked down the crowded street to lunch at his favorite restaurant (they reserved a window table just for him), nearly every passerby knew his name and greeted him with respect.

He was a legend in his community.

But my mother would have none of it. Whenever I would talk about going to dental school or take the dental admission test, she would turn her back on me and brush me away.

"Dentists are failures. They are wannabe doctors who couldn't make it in medicine. Being a dentist is foolish, you will be a real doctor."

Finally, she laid down an ultimatum. "If you want to go to dental school, fine. Go to the bank and get a loan ON YOUR OWN. You will get no help from me. I will cosign nothing. Apply to medical school and we will pay for everything."

I weighed my options. It would take me 10 years to save enough money to become a dentist by working as a mechanic or in some warehouse, or I could become a medical doctor like my brother.

I gave in. I took the medical admission tests, obtained recommendations from all the doctors I had worked with at UCLA and applied to every medical school in the country.

By the end of my senior year at UCSD I had a 3.56 GPA and was in the 50th percentile on the MCAT (Medical College Admissions Test.) The average person being admitted to medical school in 1978 had a 3.8 GPA and an MCAT percentile above 88.

I was rejected from every medical school in the nation.

"Now can I apply to dental school?" I asked my mother, as the last of the rejection letters arrived at the house.

My mother was clearly humiliated and depressed. "Fine. Apply to dental school."

To get into a U.S. dental school you needed a 3.3 GPA and earn above a 70 percentile on the dental admission test. I had a 3.56 GPA from UCSD, received a 96 % on the dental admission test and had recommendations from Dr. Ramirez, Dr. Webber and others.

But there was an issue. One of the questions on the application asked, "Have you ever applied to Medical School?"

My mother said I should lie. "You should mark 'No' on that question. You don't want them to think dentistry was your second choice."

"I won't lie," I responded.

My mother looked at me and shook her head disgusted, "Then you'll never get in."

I remember looking at my mother and telling her, "If God wants me to go to dental school I will be accepted, but I won't get there with a lie."

My mom never liked my Christian leanings. She had a terrible relationship with the Catholic Church and told me repeatedly what a fool I was for attending.

"Fine," she said, "You mark that box 'YES'. Tell them you applied to medical school. You will see what happens."

My mother was right. Over the next four months I received letters from dental schools all across the nation, over sixty schools, each one a rejection.

But there was another way I could become a dentist. I had heard of a school in central Mexico, the Universidad Autónoma de Guadalajara. It was a large university that had a dental school that accepted students from all over the world, including the United States. By attending UAG and completing the four-year dental program, I could receive a degree to practice dentistry. Then, after passing a battery of exams and participating in a "fifth pathway clerkship," I could then become a licensed dentist in the United States.

It was an incredibly difficult approach to becoming a dentist. Going to school in Mexico involved taking all the classes in Spanish, performing all clinicals in remote venues in the mountains around Guadalajara and submitting yourself to a government and legal system that was steeped in corruption and dishonesty.

I asked my mother if I could apply and if she would support me.

I was amazed when she said, "Yes."

It was a month later that I was accepted to the Mexican dental school. I remember looking at the University's brochure, reading the description of the classes I would be taking and in particular, the orientation for American students that was to take place three months before classes were to begin. The orientation was critical because it was during that twelve-week period that I would need to learn to speak Spanish, a necessity for getting through the difficult curriculum.

My mother, curious as to where I was going and what I would be doing down in the middle of Mexico, read over my shoulder about the philosophy of the school and its history when suddenly she stopped.

"Wait, this says that you've been accepted to the university and that you have been admitted to all their schools. You can go to their school of Antiquities, Gemology, Dentistry or Medicine." Slapping the brochure hard with her fist, she stared at me with a satisfied smile, "You don't understand, do you?"

I shook my head confused, "No, what are you saying?"

Grinning wide like the Grinch on Christmas Eve, she laughed, "You've just been accepted to medical school."

# Chapter 9:
# Guadalajara

*"It's hare to beat a person who never gives up."*

Babe Ruth - American Professional
Baseball Player

I had been on the crowded bus for a little over 20 minutes, just long enough for me to stop noticing the blaring mariachi music, the dust or the way the pictures of the Virgin Mary swayed over the driver's windscreen. I stood, one hand clutched tight to the bus's overhead handrail, the other gripped snug to my bookbag that lay tight over my shoulder. I had been going to classes in Mexico for three months having just recently started feeling like things were going my way.

All around me my fellow bus riders rocked and swayed with the movement of the bus while either reading their novelettes, looking out the window or tending to their children. I had just left the Banco de Mexico having withdrawn twenty dollars in *pesos* for another week's groceries and was heading back to my tiny apartment when suddenly I felt a person's hand on my groin.

*"Oye, no toca hombre!"* Hey, don't touch, I yelled at the guy as I stepped between two older women in an effort to distant myself from the sexual deviant. But the man just offered an odd kind of sexy smile and wormed his way toward me and groped again.

Shifting with the sway of the bus, I then crawled over the back of a crowded bench seat and wedged myself behind an older gentleman as I shouted back, *"Estas loco? No toca!* Are you crazy? Don't touch. But the molester kept moving toward me while I backed away.

The bus took a hard turn to the right and ground noisily to a halt at the curb as the door opened and the depraved individual, along with all the other riders and their associated bags and bundles, were emptied onto the sidewalk.

After a moment's pause the bus continued down the road with me and a lone woman, a nurse I assumed by her white cupped hat and nurse's smock, standing alone in the center aisle.

*"Viste eso?"* I declared to the nurse, *"una pervertido!"* Did you see? A pervert!

The nurse looked at me like I was an idiot child and sadly shook her head. *"No era un pervertido, es un ladrón."* It wasn't a pervert, it was a robber.

I looked at her, both shocked and irritated as I asked in broken Spanish, "Why didn't you tell me?" Then, raising my fist, I added, "If I would have known, I would have hit him."

"I know, fool," she said in Spanish, "that's why I didn't tell you. If you would have hit him, his partner, who you didn't see standing behind you with the knife, would have killed you." Then, shaking her head in frustration said, "Why do you think everyone got off the bus?"

I finally stopped and looked around at a rare oddity on the streets of Mexico. A bus with rows upon rows of empty seats. It was only then that I realized the truth of her statement. Knew to my very core that my foolish arrogance had nearly gotten me killed, knifed to death on a crowded bus in Mexico.

Guadalajara could be a very dangerous place. On two separate occasions I had a gun placed at my head by thieves. The school itself was surrounded by a ten-foot chain link fence topped with razor wire, but despite all the violence and crime, I learned to love Mexico and the Mexican people.

I had visited Mexico many times on surfing trips and family vacations, but I never really understood what Mexico was truly about until I lived there.

It took three and a half days for me and my childhood friend Bill to drive down to Guadalajara. Three and a half days of traveling straight south on Mexico's Highway 15 over immense deserts, incredible beaches and thick jungles.

The roads south of the border were a mess, so much so that we only drove during the day; each evening forced to stop at small roadside motels for the night. Mile after mile we motored in the blistering heat taking turns navigating the torn up highway, the unmarked detours and the narrow mountain roads on our way south. Worst of all were the potholes.

The potholes or *baches* are often huge. These large craters in the streets were so common and so large that they made driving even at the best of times a challenge. Many of these highway *baches* were simple annoyances, while others were so deep that when the car's tire fell inside, the bumper would simultaneously careen off the surrounding asphalt. It took nearly two days of constant pounding for my old red Pinto station wagon to eventually succumb to the potholes, its front left shock absorber pressed straight through the driver's side fender plate.

It happened on a Sunday evening when we were an hour outside of our next scheduled hotel stop. After sustaining the damage, we were forced to limp the car at near walking speed to a small town in the middle of nowhere. Every shop was closed and as we sat in the car, the sun dipping below the horizon, we knew we would be spending the night in a parking lot in who knows where.

As we sat nervous in the dark, the car doors locked, the windows open two inches for air, we suddenly noticed a person slowly walking toward us from beyond the dirt parking lot. He was an older man: short and stocky with thick gray-hair and deeply wrinkled features. Bill and I, realizing our predicament, stepped from the car and met the gentleman with a kind smile and a handshake.

It took a few minutes, but after a lot of weird hand gestures, we finally understood what the man was trying to say and motored the short distance to a service station at the edge of town. The garage was closed, but digging in his pocket, the old gentleman pulled out a key, opened the service bay and after inspecting the damage, started to work. He jacked up the car and using a torch, welded the parts back in place. We tried to pay him for his time, but he refused any money.

It wasn't just the road conditions that made driving dangerous. It was gun wielding border guards that delighted in playing "let's make a deal" in order for travelers to secure passage across state lines. It was cows that walked aimlessly on highways and it was unmarked one lane bridges that made travel a veritable life and death game of chicken.

And then there were the trucks.

It almost seemed that the truckers in Mexico had a death wish the way they swerved headlong around and through traffic with total abandon. They would fly down mountain roads, pass stopped cars on either the right or the left and blow through towns as if their vehicles were Ferraris and not ten-ton trucks.

Upon arriving at the southern outskirts of Guadalajara, I drove directly to the international airport to drop Bill off for his return home to Los Angeles. Thanking him deeply for making the long and dangerous trek, I remember the deep level of loneliness that poured over me as I watched him disappear into the terminal.

I motored my small red station wagon north through the city center of Guadalajara and headed straight for the Universidad de Autónoma. As I drove, I focused on what I had to do to succeed: generate daily lists, utilize the study techniques that had gotten me through college, focus on the details rather than the enormity of the full mission and, most importantly, pray.

My first order of business was to find a place to live. I was told by the school that the local paper had a few apartments for rent that offered students two meals a day and laundry service for as little as two hundred dollars a month. I found one, and after struggling with my broken Spanish, got settled.

Just as the advertisement stated, the room was a studio apt with private bath, two meals a day and laundry service once a week. That being said, the room I rented was a disaster on every level. It was built atop the flat roof of a family home with access gained by climbing a steep set of makeshift wooden stairs that dumped, whoever was fool-hardy enough to climb them, at the door of the simplest of 12 by 12 foot cubicles.

The cell that I called home, was modest, to say the least. Con-structed of cinderblocks and a loosely fit corrugated tin roof, the room came with no furniture save a worn out bed and the powered end of an extremely old extension cord. The single small window that lay centered on the furthest wall from the door was nothing more than a simple opening without glass, screens or shutters. After the first night trying to sleep in a mountain jungle and getting bit by ev-ery bug imaginable, I purchased mosquito netting that I hung loose over the bed like a tent. I lit the room with an old lamp I purchased from a second-hand store and built my desk out of an old beat-up door and stacked bricks.

The meals were advertised as breakfast and dinner while the bath-room was promoted as private. What I found waiting for me each morning was a raw egg mixed in milk and a bread roll. For dinner I was fed a pair of boiled chicken feet and a handful of rice in clear liq-uid. It wasn't until much later that I learned chicken feet were only eaten by the poorest of the poor and consuming raw egg in Mexico was tantamount to playing Russian roulette with salmonella.

The bathroom was indeed private, but only because no one in their right mind would want to use it. The toilet was built as clearly an af-terthought wedged just beyond view beneath the same set of dilapi-dated stairs that I used to climb to my roof room. Having a single cold-water supply line that fed both the commode and a low-lying shower head, my morning shower consisted of me freezing as I hunkered beneath the stairs like a troll, one foot atop the toilet seat, no walls to provide even the slightest bit of privacy.

I held fast to the schedule that I developed at UCSD and studied early in the morning, after school and after dinner. As a first-year student, our classes included embryology, anatomy, histology and biochemistry. Each class was taught entirely in Spanish, so I studied both in English and Spanish in an attempt to learn the information and be able to pass the tests.

All in all, the Universidad Autónoma was not all that bad. One of the highlights was the community "*Guar♦ias*" where we would go into the small towns surrounding Guadalajara and perform health assessments, do exams and offer vaccinations. It was after my sixth month in the medical school, just as I was starting to get things wired, that there came a totally unexpected late-night knock on my door.

"Don't worry, everybody is ok."

I hardly recognized him standing in the dark on my stoop, his rumpled shirt and disheveled hair screaming the impromptu nature of the visit.

"Can I help you?" I asked, astonished that someone had found their way to my rooftop abode.

"I'm the phone guy. Remember? You paid me to come here in case there was an emergency."

And then I did remember. I had hoped never to see him, but here he was, standing at my door at eleven at night on a Wednesday evening. He was not unlike one of those military officers who was sent out to the notify a family that their loved one was missing or killed in battle. I just stood there and stared at him and waited.

One aspect of living so far from home, isolated, in the early 1980's was the difficulty for a family back in the states, to contact their loved ones in case of an emergency. What we did at the University in

Guadalajara was to have a person who owned a phone keep all the addresses of the other students who didn't. We made sure our family back home had the phone guy's number so if there ever was an emergency, that person, for a fee, would drive to your house and tell you to call home immediately.

"Do you have a car, Howard?" he asked as he wiped the sleep from his face.

"Yes," I acknowledged.

"Great," he said with a nod. "Follow me. You can use my phone."

I tailed the phone guy back to his house and called home as soon as I got there.

My mother answered on the first ring, her voice excited and animated.

"Mom, what's going on? Is everybody ok?"

"Yes, everybody is fine. We just got back from our road trip and have been going through the mail. I have great news. You've been accepted to dental school in St. Louis. You must arrive no later than five days from today. Call me tomorrow."

"Are you sure? I was rejected from all those schools."

"I have the acceptance letter right here!" she exclaimed. "It's late. Call me tomorrow."

My entire world changed in a flash. I was leaving a school where cadavers were floated in baths of formaldehyde like dead carp at a third world fish market. A school where the campus security guards carried machine guns and you were happy that they did.

But with one phone call and one simple letter, everything changed. It was unbelievable, because deep in my heart I knew it was impossible and that somebody must have made a mistake.

# Chapter 10:
# Dental School

*"The only goo♦ luck many great men ever ha♦ was being born with the ability an♦ ♦etermination to overcome ba♦ luck."*

Channing Pollock - American Magician

My older sister, Joanne, flew into Guadalajara just two days after I received the phone call from my parents. In that time, I notified the university of my leaving, sold my Spanish textbooks and said goodbye to some of the most amazing friends I had ever met.

The famed American dancer and choreographer, Martha Graham, once said, "Fire is the test of gold; adversity, of strong men." That axiom never rang truer as I watched myself and others tested daily to our very wits end in Guadalajara. Day after day I was pummeled emotionally by arrogant professors, selfish fellow students and ruthless thieves, all the while clutching to my goal, or more precisely my mother's goal, of becoming a medical doctor.

From that furnace of adversity where I studied high in the mountains of central Mexico, I saw great people become even stronger despite the constant berating of unscrupulous teachers and administrators. On the same token, I also saw others who, under the same pressure, quickly surrendered into a hateful cocoon until all that remained was contempt and selfishness.

I had heard stories of the Auschwitz and Dachau concentration camps, where the good became better and the bad became worse, but it wasn't until I lived six months in central Mexico that I had the opportunity to see it firsthand. I watched as people who would have never thought of lying or stealing turned vile under the stress and

74

frustration of oppression. I also observed others, under the same un-relenting pressure, rise to near sainthood.

But now I was going to the Midwest. I had never been to Missouri, never traveled any further east than the Grand Canyon. I recall speaking to a guy from Texas who told me that Washington University was one of the top schools in the country. Honestly, I didn't even re-member applying there. The idea that I had been accepted to dental school felt surreal, dreamlike.

In addition to having studied chemistry, biology, anatomy and a fair amount of Spanish while in Guadalajara, what I truly came to learn while in Mexico was the amazing spirt and strength of the Mex-ican people. Clearly, learning a new language can be frustrating and there is no question that dealing with a foreign government is often maddening, but I came to love Mexico and the incredible Mexican people. It rapidly became clear to me that despite the poverty that en-veloped nearly half of the families in Mexico, they were an amazingly generous people, extremely family centered and incredibly happy. Mexico and the Mexican people were incredible.

I could have probably gone to a bookstore and tried to find out specifics about St. Louis and Washington University School of Dental Medicine but, as odd as it sounds, I didn't care. I just wanted to get out of Mexico and return to a place where teachers spoke English, you could drink the water and where you were innocent until proven guilty.

I didn't speak very much on the long drive back to the States. While in Guadalajara I had learned to control my emotion and not let the daily ups and downs break my spirit.

"Never too high, never too low," it was an adage I lived by in the Universidad Autónoma. If you let your unbridled emotions run unchecked, momentarily feeling of happiness could easily overwhelm your rational thought leading you to subsequent bouts of deep depression. Never let yourself get too excited because the depression that follows, and it most surely did follow, could be devastating. It was that mindset that caused me to remain quiet and sullen on my trip out of Mexico. It was a good thing that I did.

We arrived in St. Louis three days later and after consulting our AAA travel guide book, we decided to stay at the Chase Park Plaza Hotel.

We picked that hotel because it was only four blocks from the school and was described as both historic and iconic. Driving down Kingshighway Blvd., it was easy to pick out the Chase with its art deco archways and tall twenty-five story tower. Staying at the Chase was Joanne's idea. She figured after driving nearly three thousand miles over mountains, deserts and rivers, we'd earned it.

Registration for classes began at eight, but I decided to arrive at seven-thirty in hopes of finding a dorm room, posting fees and buying books. Washington University School of Dental Medicine was housed in a relatively new, four-story building attached to the renowned Barnes Hospital complex. The entrance was modest; a simple placard hung alongside large glass double doors announcing the school's name and the year of its founding.

"Please sign in," the guard instructed as he handed me the clipboard and attached pen.

It was odd hearing him speak English. Refreshing to say the least.

It was then that I noticed that there was nowhere to sign. The horizontal box that lay wide next to where my name was typed had already been written in. The scrawled cursive of Howard Wright looking both familiar and totally foreign.

"It looks as if I have already arrived?" I responded staring at the odd-looking signature that was indeed my name, but not by my hand.

The guard smiled, "Well, then I guess you're done here."

Never too high. Never too low.

"Can you point me the way to the Admissions Office?"

"Third floor, you can't miss it."

Like every other admissions office throughout America, the reception desk at Wash U was busy. Students laden with stacks of papers zoomed here and there as they asked their standard questions of "Where is this?" and "When will that begin?"

Seeing the line to speak to the receptionist, I cued up behind what looked like a fourth-year female student and waited.

It didn't take long until it was my turn. Placing my briefcase on the tall counter that separated us, I began my introduction.

"Hi," I said to the middle-aged female receptionist, "I'm Howard Wright and somebody already signed in for me downstairs and they USED MY NAME."

I said it with a serious smile with the hope of conveying both the gravity of the situation and my willingness to forgive. At this point I hoped that it was a mistake, a minor slip up. But deep in my mind, the warning bells were ringing loud and clear. Having lived in Mexico for the last six months, I had learned to listen for the brain's alarms and believe them when they rang.

Right now, the alarms were wailing bigtime.

The receptionist was clearly experienced, time tried and not to be trifled with. She looked as if she had dealt with annoyances of my kind her entire life and that I was just another "i" to be dotted, another "t" to be crossed. She looked at me and I could see her considering the various options available: was this a practical joker or could the attendance sheet have misspelled his name? Then the unmistakable look of fear splashed across her face.

"One moment please."

She turned and stepped away from the desk, moved halfway across the room and stopped before a large filing cabinet on top of which rested a long metallic filing box. Taking hold of the container, she centered it in front of herself and grasping the lid, opened it slowly. It contained three by five cards which she flipped through like a seasoned Los Vegas dealer. Halting mid-riffle, she pulled two cards from the deck and held them side by side, her eyes shifting back and forth as she examined them.

It was as if a switch had suddenly been flipped. Her face, a moment ago the picture of self-assurance and control, was now overshadowed by the look of doubt and fear. I could see it in her eyes as clear as day. I recognized it because I had seen that very same expression most of my life whenever I looked in the mirror. It was the look of someone who had made a mistake and now it was time to pay the price.

She stared at me from what seemed like a million miles away, "Are you from Northern or Southern California?"

"Southern," I replied. "I'm from Redondo Beach."

"No!" she said way too loud as she started moving toward me. "You were rejected; you shouldn't be here. YOU'VE MADE A MISTAKE!"

It took only a nanosecond for me to understand the entire story. A split second to realize there had been two Howard Wrights applying for admission, the worthy from Northern Cal and the loser from Southern Cal. Washington University had mistakenly pulled the wrong card from the index box and wrote down the Redondo Beach address on the acceptance letter posting it to Southern California instead of Northern California. That is why I never received any information concerning dorms or tuition. I never was accepted in the first place.

I enjoyed being a wrestler in high school. I wasn't a state champion like my brother, but a decent varsity wrestler in a division that was as competitive as they come, and while I lost as many matches as I won, there was one thing that every grappler who stepped on the mat knew to their very heart; when that referee said "wrestle," the game was on.

"No," I retorted through clenched teeth. "You made the mistake."

I threw open my briefcase, whipped out the acceptance letter and holding it aloft like a flag of victory declared, "YOU MADE THE MISTAKE!"

The receptionist moved forward as anger raged in her eyes. Bending across the desk she stretched to snatch the paper from my hand only to have me pull the document out of her reach.

Holding tight to the letter, I leaned forward, our faces moving to an inch apart. With as much power and defiance as I could muster, I looked her straight in the eyes and told her, "I just drove 3000 miles from central Mexico where I was going to medical school and I will not be turned away."

There was silence.

The receptionist composed herself, straightened her starched blouse and standing tall said, "Dr. Ring will handle THIS. He's the Admissions Director. Leave and be back at nine."

I left the building and walked the handful of blocks back toward the hotel. I stopped by a small florist shop and purchased a single white rose for my sister.

Joanne smelled the rose, "Thank you, Howard. How is it going at your new school?"

I looked at my sister as she combed her hair getting ready for the day, "Everything is fine. I just need to clear a few things up is all."

Dr. Ring arrived exactly on time at nine; I had arrived at eight-thirty.

I waited patiently, my briefcase on my lap, my hands folded neatly atop the case. I tried desperately to ignore the piercing stares of the administrator and her assistant as they glared daggers at me from across the room.

At about nine-thirty, Dr. Ring came out and asked me to follow him into his office.

"Please take a seat," Dr. Ring said as he settled himself behind his large desk, open applications and stacks of papers spread wide on its large surface.

Dr. Ring looked like a middle-aged Santa Claus as he fiddled with his pen and unconsciously rubbed his snow white beard. It was soon after wrapping his arms around his rotund stomach that he sat back and with a welcoming smile looked up and said, "We'd like to offer you a spot in this year's dental school class."

"I accept," I said, elated. After a short pause I went on, "But, if you don't mind, I would like to ask you a question."

"Go right ahead," Dr. Ring agreed, smiling genuinely, "ask away."

"These three applications," I said pointing to the open files on his desk, "they are stamped 'ACCEPTED.'"

Dr. Ring, embarrassed for allowing me to see inside other student's records, immediately closed each file, stacking them neatly to the side.

I continued, "The first had a 3.1 GPA and a dental admission test score in the 75th percentile, the second had a 2.9 GPA and was in the 82nd percentile and the third had a 3.2 and was in the 72nd per-centile."

Looking at him, not angry but confused, I asked, "I had a 3.56 GPA and was in the 96th percentile. I had strong recommendations from both dentists and doctors." I then leaned forward, shifted my briefcase to the floor and asked, "Why wasn't I accepted?"

"Well, let's see," Dr. Ring answered, curious.

Taking my folder from a tall stack of files, he turned it in his hand, opened it wide, and adjusting his glasses, read, "Here it is. It says you were rejected for medical reasons."

"Medical reasons? There is nothing wrong with me. What kind of medical reasons?"

"Not medical reasons," he said with a slight frown. "It says you once applied to medical school."

"Medical school? My mother insisted I apply. I wanted to be a den-tist; she wanted me to be a medical doctor. Is that why I didn't get accepted? Is that why I was rejected from every dental school in America?"

He held up the recommendations from Dr. Webber at UCLA and Dr. Rodrigues, the dentist I worked with in East Los Angeles. Both were still sealed in their original envelopes.

Replacing them carefully deep inside my file he closed the folder and set it aside.

"I'm sorry," Dr. Ring said as he shook his head slowly. "I am sorry, we never even considered you. Neither did any of the other schools."

"Thank you for accepting me now," I said with a smile.

"Oh," Dr. Ring continued. "I've good news. The other Howard Wright goes by his middle name, Ron."

We laughed. I shook his hand.

"Howard," Dr. Ring said as he looked at me sternly, "can I give you a piece of advice?"

"Of course," I replied.

"You may want to drop by our local florist shop and get Mrs. Ryan, our admissions secretary, a bouquet of flowers. She's as angry as a hornet and seeing that you're going to be working with her for the next four years, it would be a nice gesture."

My first stop after leaving the office was back to the florist shop where I did just what Dr. Ring asked. Yellow roses, a dozen.

# Chapter 11:
# The Proof is in the Pudding

*"My most brilliant achievement was my ability to be able to persuaᵢe my wife to marry me."*

Winston Churchill - Prime Minister
of the United Kingdom

I got married between my sophomore and junior year of dental school. My father told me it was a mistake. He told me that I wasn't ready and that I should wait till I had finished my education, my dental office was set up, my loans paid off and my life was in order.

"You should 'pin' her Howard, give this Vicki girl a pin from the dental school. Don't get engaged, give it some time, tell her you want to pin her. She'll understand."

Vicki, a devout Christian, stands six feet tall, is athletic, beautiful and not to be trifled with. I met her just weeks after arriving in St. Louis at a prayer meeting they were having on the campus of Barnes Hospital. She was attending the nursing school while I attended the dental school.

I had been advised by a friend's wife that the best way to meet a girl is to tell any potential dates that you're not looking for a girlfriend. So, during the prayer group's introductions I offhandedly suggested that I was new in town, a student at the dental school and wasn't looking for a girlfriend. It worked like a charm.

Our relationship grew slowly in the beginning, but with time, I fell deeply in love with Vicki's charm, wit and determination. We dated, frequently taking walks through nearby Forest Park or visiting the world-famous St. Louis Zoo. The date that ultimately convinced me that Vicki was my true life-partner, was when we went on a canoe trip down the Black River with her family.

I had never been canoeing before so it was really an adventure for me. The float, as it was called, was a fairly large extravaganza with Vicki's entire family, including uncles and aunts in attendance. We paddled two to a canoe, me in the back, Vicki in the front. At our feet lay snacks, a camera, sunscreen and drinks.

It was a beautiful warm summer day on the water. All around us, the tree-covered Ozark hills lay green, the warm clear water bubbling as it flowed gentle over the pebbly smooth river bottom. It was amazingly peaceful, until suddenly my breath was stolen from my lungs as I watched the largest spider I had ever seen, crawl into our canoe. It was a wolf spider, its black body the size of a silver dollar, its hairy legs nearly as long and thick as my fingers. It looked like a tarantula, but was faster, hungrier, more ominous.

Vicki didn't see the creature as it crawled up the towel that lay inches behind her. She didn't see it as it slowly crept over the canoe's gunnel and made its way toward the bottom of the boat. She was facing forward, paddling, unaware that the monstrosity had moved over the edge and was now less than half an arm's length away.

I leaned forward in the unbalanced canoe and tried to draw the towel toward myself in an attempt to pull the spider away from her, but it quickly became clear that my approach only forced the spider to move forward, closer to Vicki. I couldn't help but think of my four sisters and how they would react seeing the brute. They would throw themselves into the water; they would scream in terror.

Steadying my voice, I called out as calmly as I could, "Vicki, I need to tell you that…"

She turned, her beautiful smile clear and light, "Yes," she said softly.

It was then, as she looked back and down, that she saw the furry behemoth. I steadied myself both mentally and physically as the huge arachnid crawled toward her. It was at that moment, when she looked down on the monster, that I expected to hear her let loose the blood curdling scream, the primordial shriek. Instead what I saw was a flash of movement.

Like a ninja, Vicki shifted her weight and in a swirl of motion slid the oar from the water, raised it above her head and focused on the poor beast. She looked like Xena: Warrior Princess as her gorgeous blue eyes turned hard and she glared at the unsuspecting spider.

It was over in a nanosecond. Like some kind of atomic weapon decimating one of those precious islands in the South Pacific, the oar dropped with a loud crash, annihilating the bug into vapors. The huge creature one second happily crawling around the bottom of the canoe, the next obliterated as if it had never existed. I didn't know whether to applaud or run away.

"Yes, Howard," she said unfazed by the crushing of the mammoth spider, "did you want to say something?"

I caught my breath and slowly pulled my eyes from where the spider once was and simply replied, "Well, yeah, it sure is a nice day."

I've thought about that afternoon with Vicki and the spider and how she refused to be afraid. How she didn't act irrationally by screaming at it or screaming at me. She simply dealt with the situation.

I decided then and there that I would marry her.

I spoke to her often of my plans for the future and my hope that she would be my wife. I told Vicki what my dad said about being "pinned." I conveyed the idea with a smile, but with an undercurrent of seriousness. "What do you think? Want to get pinned?" I was sort of joking, but she didn't see the humor.

"You're crazy if you think I would ever be PINNED," she scowled, her red hair aflame, "and waiting to get married until you get your life together is ridiculous. We develop our lives together. I'm not some kind of…. afterthought."

My dad was incredibly smart, was accepted to both MIT and Caltech, (he chose Caltech) was a veritable genius when it came to engineering, but when it came to women and a slew of other things, my dad was as clueless as a box of rocks.

Vicki's mom, on the other hand, didn't want us to put off any wedding plans; she was against the relationship altogether. She would look at me with disdain and say I was too hyper, too short and more than anything, too "California."

"All they have in California is fruits and nuts," she would repeatedly call out from across the room, "Which are you?!"

But time changes all things, and in our case the change came in the course of a single Fall day, the transformation propelled by tragedy and the pain of seeing a loved one die.

It was late in the afternoon on a beautiful October day. Vicki and I had been seeing each other for about six months, and while we had hoped to get together for a date, she had committed to watching her three youngest siblings while her mother and father went out for dinner and a movie. Vicki and I were sitting on a wooden picnic table in her parent's back yard, fall leaves spread thick at our feet when suddenly the screaming started.

Vicki's youngest sisters were nine and eleven, her brother thirteen, and as they burst from the back door of the two-story house, it wasn't just the tears that coursed down their cheeks or the grief that painted their faces that told us a tragedy had occurred. No, it was their shrieks. They were gut-wrenching. The kind of cries that only come from a deep pain; not the "she took my toy" or "he hit me" yells, but the kind of shrieks that erupt when someone slams their fingers in a car door or when a leg is fractured. It was a primordial howl that pulled Vicki and I from our quiet conversation and without a second's hesitation, we ran to the children.

"Sandy!" they screamed. "It's Sandy!"

Sandy was not just a dog; she was part of the family. Vicki's parents acquired the beautiful golden retriever when it was just a pup and over the years it had become as much a part of the family as anyone.

"Sandy's dying," the kids sobbed. "She's dying."

Vicki's home was on a busy street on the outskirts of St. Louis County. Seeing the horror on the children's faces and having watched over the last few months as car after car rocketed down their winding street, I knew that Sandy must have been hit and hit hard.

"Where's Sandy," I asked. "Where is she?"

Through trembling sobs, Vicki's young brother answered, "She's in the house... in the kitchen."

Dogs, when they are hurt badly, will often run to a safe place and hide while they rest, licking their wounds until they either recoup or die. Sandy it seems had moved to the kitchen and that was why the kids were in shock. Sandy was, in all probability, now bleeding all over the kitchen and was now dying. With the kids following close behind, Vicki and I burst through the back door, bolted through the living room and entered the kitchen expecting the worst. What we found was something entirely different; there was no grizzly scene, no writhing dog, no stench of blood. Sandy was lying on the kitchen's tile floor unmoving, like she was resting. Looking closer, however, I quickly realized that the beautiful golden retriever was the furthest thing from asleep.

Sandy lay on her side, stiff as a block of concrete, her soft coffee brown eyes open wide with a stark pained look that screamed of shock. Her back was bent tight in an ugly contorted twist; her head, once so beautiful, now arched back as if she were looking to the sky; all four legs extended straight, rigid like wooden legs of a stout chair. But the most gruesome caricature, the grizzliest aspect was Sandy's mouth.

The skin that covered Sandy's muzzle was pulled taught showing her teeth in a pained grimace, her tongue extending rigid from the side of her mouth. But it was the color of the tongue that forced me past my own shock.

The tongue was a striking royal blue, a brilliant blue that I had only seen in medical books. It was then, as I focused on the blue tongue, that I understood that Sandy was dying of asphyxiation, seized in the constrictive grip of a grand mal seizure.

I looked at the dog trying to grasp just what was going on, trying to comprehend why every neuron in its entire brain was firing over and over again. I stared at Sandy, trying as hard as I could to narrow my focus, to block out the children's crying and get inside its pain and violent muscle contractions and understand what had caused the seizure. Most important, I struggled to determine what I could do to stop them when, SLAP. Vicki hit me hard across the arm.

"Do something!" Vicki yelled.

"Quiet," I answered back, never taking my eyes off the dog as I forced myself to fall deeper and deeper into the mind of the dying Sandy. "I am doing something."

As I looked at the dog, I concentrated using the skills I had taught myself to visualize what was going on deep inside Sandy's brain. In my mind's eye I tried to envision every synapse firing at once, struggled to see the nerves as they spewed an unrelenting series of impulses to every muscle in the body. If only I could quiet the synaptic junctions, get them to listen to the neuro-controllers and in some way force everything to stop and sleep.

I got an idea.

I lifted Sandy gently, propped her up on her peg legs like some kind of oversized stuffed dog and slowly closed my hand into a tight fist. I looked at the once beautiful and happy dog, her sad eyes pulled wide, the blue of its oxygen deficient tongue turning an even deeper azure. I then reached back, shifting my weight forward and with all my strength punched Sandy square in the head, hitting her as hard as I could.

WHAM!

Sandy flew back, careened hard against the lower kitchen cabinets only to crumple like a rag doll onto the floor. The children, who had quieted to a silent sob, now returned to their screaming, joined by Vicki. The sight of me knocking their precious dog senseless was in-comprehensible.

I watched as Sandy lay unconscious, her breathing now smooth and regular, her tongue turned a healthy pink. The ridged seizure-clad body that a moment ago was suffocating Sandy, was now relaxed, her eyes gently closed in sleep.

Thinking fast, Vicki went directly to the phone book and called the nearby twenty-four-hour animal hospital and explained the emergency.

"Had the dog gotten into any poison or maybe dug around the garage?" the veterinarian asked.

Vicki responded immediately, "Oh no," she groaned. "Just this morning my father put poison out to kill the moles in our backyard. I'm sure that's it."

"Strychnine," the vet said. "I'm sorry, but there's nothing you can do."

In the late 1970's, there was no internet and so we were dependent on the veterinarian to offer us even the simplest of suggestions for how to help Sandy, but he offered none. Vicki and I, refusing to give up, turned to her nursing book for answers. The bad news was that strychnine was indeed lethal in high doses; the good news was that strychnine was water soluble. If we could keep the dog alive, most of the poison would be urinated off in just under ten hours.

It was then that Sandy started to wake up.

In the beginning it was only a minor blinking of the eyes, a slight wag of the tail, but with time she started to improve. After a half hour, she was able to uncomfortably lift her head and drink from an offered bowl of water; clearly things were looking up. The kids sat around Sandy and gently petted her until the phone rang and all hell broke loose.

It seems that the grand mal seizures that are associated with strychnine poisoning are set off by sudden noises or movements; any stimulus that could bring about the cascade of unbridled nerve impulses.

We watched again in horror as Sandy lay rigid under the grip of her second seizure. Only after her tongue regained the deep cyanotic hue of a royal blue did I slam the dog hard upside the head forcing it again into a deep sleep.

Remove all stimulus: sound, light, motion.

We immediately pulled the receiver from the phone and in whispers and tiptoes, emptied the large closet adjacent to the kitchen. Lifting the still unconscious dog with the gentlest of movements, we placed Sandy inside the closet with a large bowl of water. Then stepping back, closed the door with the quietest of clicks.

Every hour, on the hour, we would open the closet and check on Sandy. After the first sixty minutes we saw that she had awakened and was able to slightly move her head. After the second hour she was drinking water and wagging her tail, after the third she could lift herself partially on her front legs.

It was around ten in the evening when Vicki's parents came home. There were no cell phones or pagers to prepare them for the sight of their beloved dog lying poisoned on the floor of the closet. No preparation for the sight of their daughter and three youngest children traumatized by the sight of having seen their dog undergo repeated seizures and my own brutal attempts to quiet them.

Vicki explained everything. There were no jokes from Vicki's mother about California's "fruits and nuts." No harsh comments about me being hyper or odd. No snide comments about me being shorter than their daughter.

Vicki's father called the vet and after a brief discussion decided to take Sandy to the animal hospital. I told them it was a mistake, that the journey was too long and placing the dog in a car would precipitate a series of seizures I wouldn't be able to stop; but the dog wasn't mine and the decision had been made.

Sandy died in the emergency room moments after we arrived at the veterinarian's office. I had tried everything I could to save her, but it wasn't enough, the trauma was too great.

"Who <u>are</u> you?"

It was Vicki's mom. She was sitting in the waiting room of the vet's office. It was well past midnight and we had just heard Sandy had passed away.

"Excuse me?" I asked confused.

"Really, who are you?"

"Just a guy in love with your daughter."

Six months later I asked Vicki to marry me and she agreed. A year later we married.

Curious as it may seem, Vicki's introduction to my own mother and father also involved another animal dying, only this time, it wasn't a dog.

I gave Vicki an engagement ring on a Friday night in the summer of 1980 and by the following Saturday we were invited to a dinner party at my cousin's house where we would celebrate the wedding plans with the rest of the family. It was a large affair with candle-lit tables and sparkling lights spread wide across their large open patio, a low brick wall separating the home from the beautiful desert to the east, the lights of the San Fernando Valley spread wide to the west.

The night was relaxed and wonderful, my brother, four sisters, aunts, uncles and friends having a spectacular evening. Everything was wonderful, everyone getting along swimmingly until, in the low light of the desert evening, the tranquility was interrupted by the distinctive SHHHHHHHT of an angry diamondback rattlesnake.

It was terrifying how ominous and unmistakable the sound of a rattlesnake can be. How the quick buzzing rattle can awaken the most powerful of basal fears that dwelt in the deepest crevices of the mind.

The grayish diamond patterned snake, having come from the desert and fallen into the patio enclosure, was now as mad as a hornet. It was huge, at least six feet long with a body as thick as a clenched fist, its dense girth shifting and sliding as it coiled and uncoiled on the soft dirt of the planter. Most remarkable was its huge triangular head that was raised high ready to strike, its coal black eyes and ribbon-like tongue unmistakable.

Between the shouts and the quick retreat of the entire party, my father stepped up and asked for a shovel with which he hoped to spear the monster. My father was raised in Panama and having spent a quarter of his life in the jungle, had no fear of snakes.

Moving toward the diamondback, my father raised the long handled shovel high into the air and thrusting down hard, hoped to sever the snake's head.

However, the fight was not about to end quickly.

It seems that my cousin, in an effort to spruce up the garden area, had tilled the dirt so soft that the stab by my father only succeeded in burying the snakes head, the rest of its body now writhing madly in midair. The situation had just moved from bad to worse as the snake's body, like some kind of thick demonic tentacle, sung wildly in every direction.

Everyone took a step further back as my father held the snake's head pinned underground, its thick body squirming and thrashing in every direction. Suddenly, dressed in a flowered sundress, Vicki ran forward and attacked.

In her right hand she held a steak knife snatched from a dinner place setting, with her left she reached out and attempted to grab hold of the rattler's writhing body. Vicki looked like some kind of backwoods Daisy Duke as she fought to secure the flailing snake tail.

"Hold tight Dad," Vicki called out to my father. "I'll cut it in two."

In unison, everyone screamed, "No!"

My sister Joanne, unable to contain herself, yelled out "Oh my God, Howard, you're marrying an Amazon!"

My father leaned harder onto the shovel and pressed the snake's head deeper into the earth as my cousin stepped forward with a garden hoe. "No, please, not the knife. Use this."

Taking the hoe, Vicki stepped back and raising the sharpened blade into the air, buried the tool into the snake over and over until it no longer moved.

From that moment on, my family had a healthy respect for Vicki's strength and unwavering commitment to step in no matter how intense the situation.

# Chapter 12:
# The Other Howard Wright

*"We cannot solve our problems with the same thinking we use*
*when we create* them."*

Albert Einstein - German-born Theoretical Physicist

My son, Tom was born in June 1983, just weeks after I graduated from dental school. My twin daughters, Angela and Jessica were born two years later. Between those two blessed events my world was rocked to its foundation.

My children are amazing, clearly the highlight of my entire life. My son so much like my wife, my daughter Jessica much like me, and my daughter Angela (the twins were not identical) a combination of the two of us.

If it weren't for these most wonderful children and my ever-patient wife Vicki, I doubt I would have made it through the trials that God laid at my feet over the next twenty-four months.

Ron Wright, "the other Howard Wright" (the one who actually was accepted to dental school) and I became close friends. Because of the way the dental lab at Washington University was laid out, the students sat alphabetically along long uninterrupted lab benches, Ron Wright sitting to my left, Lynn Yamamoto to my right.

For two years Ron and I sat side by side making crowns, setting up the teeth for dentures and cutting cavity preps. We worked a foot apart day after day, all the while talking about our hopes, dreams and long term goals. Ron Wright wanted to open a practice in downtown St. Louis while I hoped to join the Air Force.

By my fourth year in school, Ron had convinced me to abandon my dream of going into the military as a dentist, and to instead open a dental office in downtown St. Louis. He told me he liked my work ethic, my determination and asked me if I would consider being partners with him in his "dream office" downtown.

"We'll call it Saint Louis Dental," he said. "Locate it downtown, right where they are revitalizing the buildings."

Ron Wright put together a hundred-page prospectus that outlined office plans, traffic patterns and detailed demographic studies. He said it would be a ton of work and cost a lot of money, but working together, we couldn't lose. He said because of his advanced business degree and the fact that he had built and managed a number of dental offices in Northern California, it would be a win-win opportunity.

I sat down with Vicki and explained what Ron wanted to do and how sold I was on the concept of working downtown. We discussed the idea of partnering with Ron and building one of the premier dental offices in the Midwest. Vicki said it seemed like a lot of money, but, if I thought it would be alright, she wouldn't hold me back.

Next, I discussed the business idea with my parents. It seemed that Ron wanted my parents as part of the deal just as much as he wanted me, maybe more. In order to build the office, it was going to take over three hundred thousand dollars for everything: lease hold improvements, equipment and working capital.

Ron promised that if my parents could finance one half of the project, his parents would be willing to finance the other half and together both families would share in the tremendous windfall that would surely follow. My mother and father flew out to St. Louis to meet with Ron and after hearing his plans, agreed that it was a great opportunity and committed themselves to the project.

Six months later I graduated with honors and passed the national boards easily. Ron had found what he thought would be the perfect location, finalized the office design and purchased eight full operatories of equipment. I was twenty-seven years old, in business with a guy who I had known for four years and was now in the process of borrowing a ton of money in order to complete the project. Back in the early 1980's, a nice two story, four bedroom house cost a little over a hundred thousand dollars, so the idea of spending three times that amount building a dental office meant spending real money.

Ron had it all planned down to the smallest detail. He reminded me often how he had a degree in business and extensive experience starting and running two separate dental offices in Northern California, so I shouldn't be nervous. He was right. I shouldn't have been nervous; I should have been terrified.

Ron Wright had hired an architect to design the office. He had ordered custom furniture to go along with the custom desks for the custom operatories. He had ordered cloth wall coverings throughout, a circular reception desk and eight operatories, each with large floor to ceiling windows that overlooked St. Louis's Gateway Arch. The office was on the 18th floor of the Executive Office Building in downtown St. Louis, and according to Ron, would be the grandest office within four states.

While the dental suite was being built, I began doing dentistry at a friend's office to try to hone my skills while offering free cleanings to promote my new business and establish a patient base. With less than twenty active patients, I wasn't making any money drilling, filling and billing. To make ends meet I worked for both the State of Missouri placing tooth sealants on inner city kids and reading X-rays for the local military base.

The work on the office was proceeding at a glacially slow pace and with cost overruns, rent and equipment bills piling up, we were running through the working capital quickly. Ron, up to this point, hadn't treated a single patient and seemed personally offended whenever I pressed him as to when he would start doing dentistry. Often times he would leave town for days at a time, always responding with the same curt answer, "I'm working on something important for the office. Quit bothering me."

The way Ron had structured the dental office financing was to have our parents put up a total of $150,000 each and in return be paid a great interest rate with all loans paid back in less than five years. My parents committed to invest cash, while Ron's parents agreed to put up their house as collateral for a joint loan Ron and I were securing through a local bank.

The building was nearly finished with the $150,000 my parents had loaned largely already spent, while Ron's parents' loan for $150,000 was still with the bank. Now that the paperwork had come through for the bank loan, the only step left to obtain the second half of the dental office's financing was for both of us to sign the loan papers.

It felt strangely odd signing the bank's loan papers. We were in the small apartment Ron and his wife rented, seated at a small kitchen table, just the two of us. Despite all the planning and preparation, something seemed wrong.

Ron was giddy, not concerned. He acted like he had just won the lottery while I felt like I had just taken the weight of the world onto my shoulders.

Despite my ill feelings, I signed the papers.

Placing the pen onto the table, I asked Ron how he saw the influx of cash being used. Would we focus on settling past due bills or would we make a payment to the construction company that was finishing up the office?

"I'm not about to tell you how this money is going to be spent!" Ron shouted. "My parents put down the collateral for this, so really, it doesn't involve you."

"That's not true," I corrected Ron. "My name is on that loan same as yours. That money is to be used to fund the office. I have as much a voice concerning how it's spent as you do."

"You're wrong," he spat through gritted teeth. "That money is going into my account and I'll spend it on whatever I want."

I had known Ron for four years. During that time, we worked and studied together, and now all of a sudden it was as if a veil had been pulled back exposing a totally different person. I didn't know what caused the dramatic change, but I was not about to let him run unchecked with money I guaranteed with my name. I stared at him, shocked with the realization that I had just signed a promissory note for $150,000 and handed it to a complete stranger.

I decided to do what I should have done months ago. I called around to dental supply houses, followed up on rumors I had heard and checked with anyone and everyone who might know something about Ron Wright. It took me the better part of six hours, but by the end of the day, it all became clear.

Ron Wright never did graduate from business school, hadn't opened any dental offices and lied about having managed them. Most troubling of all, however, was when I learned the true reason why he kept disappearing out of town.

He was building another dental office with another dentist and using my money to fund the endeavor. He never intended on us growing an office together. He was just using me to get my parents' money and me to cosign on his parents' loan.

I called Vicki and after serious prayer and reflection, we agreed that our only option was to interrupt the financing by begging the bank to stop the already approved loan. We understood that this would put an end to Ron and my partnership and drive what was left of St. Louis Dental into near bankruptcy, but it had to be done.

We arrived at the bank five minutes after it closed, but noticed while peering through the glass window that a single individual still worked at a desk toward the back of the office. We banged on the glass until the bank employee approached the locked door.

"We're closed," he shouted through the tinted safety glass.

"You have to stay open," I pleaded through the glass. "I signed a loan paper and it has to be stopped."

"Impossible," he shouted, "we're already into the next business day. Everyone has left."

"You don't understand," I screamed. "My business partner is a fraud. If you complete the loan it will destroy me and my family. I swear, if we don't undo this thing, you'll never get your money back. Never."

He looked at us standing on the sidewalk for a very long time and then unlocked the door.

Vicki and I stepped inside.

We followed him through the darkened office, past empty cubicles and around desks until we arrived toward the back of the closed bank. The lights were off, the interior of the offices illuminated by a single lamp from his desk. After learning my name, he searched through stacks of documents until he finally stopped.

"Here it is. Your loan was approved today. The check is supposed to go out tomorrow," he announced as he pulled the thick ream of papers from a stack of about a dozen completed loan applications. "Howard Wright and Ron Wright. Are you brothers?"

"No relation," I answered tersely.

"So, what's the story?" the bank officer asked.

"This Ron Wright. We were gonna be partners, pool both our money and our time to build a downtown dental office. I just found out that he's building another office in Kansas City using money from this project. I never agreed to that."

The banker looked at us, "So, what does this have to do with me?"

"This new loan," I say, panic in my voice, "it is earmarked for St. Louis, but I know he plans on diverting the money and using the funds for his project in Kansas City."

Vicki looked at the banker, dread etched across her face. "You need to stop the loan."

The loan officer considered Vicki and I as he slowly shook his head. "You know this is all very wrong. These are signed legal documents."

I reached over and took Vicki gently by the hand and then turned back toward the loan officer, "If you let that go through, you will never see that money ever again."

He stared at us long and hard and then, after what seemed like an hour, walked over to a large trash bin and tossed the file in with a smirk, "I guess it got lost in the mail."

Ron Wright was furious when I told him what I did. He said there was no law against opening two offices. He said I had no right to cancel the loan, yelling that he wasn't bound to me and that he could spend as much or as little time in St. louis as he wanted. I showed him our contract and how we agreed to work full time on growing the St. Louis practice, but he just screamed back.

Then it got worse. I should have known Ron would go straight to the bank and steal the remaining money we had set aside for working capital and construction completion. He emptied our bank account, pocketed nearly thirty thousand dollars and went on to sue me for another nine million dollars for breach of contract. I countersued for malicious prosecution, breach of contract and abuse of process. It cost me tens of thousands of dollars to defend myself in court. Money that I didn't have. Money I was forced to borrow from my parents to win the case, but I did win.

My mother and father were livid. They said I had ruined their lives, destroyed everything they worked for and despite my promise to get their money back, they never relented in their condemnation.

"Where's the money? Where do you have the money?" Those were the first words out of my mother's mouth as she burst through the front door of the small house we were renting. Then she stopped dead in her tracks.

Vicki and I had lived in a very modest rental for two years and still had barely any furniture. The rental had a living room, but it was empty; the family room had only a small sofa and old used coffee table. We had a refrigerator we bought for twenty dollars from a guy at church and a kitchen table that was given to us by Vicki's mom.

"What have you done with the money? What have you spent the money on?" my mother hollered as she went room to room looking for some proof that we had squandered the funds they had loaned us.

"It's in the office, every penny."

My mother and father just looked at me with both contempt and disbelief.

I didn't know what hurt me more, the idea they thought I was totally incompetent or that they thought I was a liar. The idea that I was cheated by an unscrupulous partner never seemed to enter their mind.

My parents spent a week in St. Louis trying their best to understand the mess I made. Spent a week going through all my receipts, contracts and papers, while not missing a moment to remind me how I had destroyed their lives. My apologies went unheard and my explanations ignored as the loans, lease obligations and liabilities were laid out hard and cold across a yellow oversized ledger pad.

Once the amount of debt and legal obligations were tabulated, my mother and father sat down next to me, scrunched on our cheap couch in our nearly empty living room with Vicki relegated to a folding chair off to the side. Item by item my father laid out the way things would proceed from now on.

Reading from a list of demands he held clenched tight in his hand, he began. "We will give you more money," my father spat, "to keep your lousy dental office running but we want 14% interest on all loans, old and new and we expect them to be paid back in full."

"Fine," I replied.

"And we want half of the profits as long as you're in business."

"Fine," I replied.

"And we set your salary."

"Fine," I replied.

"And all the accounts will be handled through us."

"Fine," I replied.

"And if you ever try and sell this place, we get half of everything."

"Fine."

"NO WAY," Came a voice from the side.

It was Vicki. She had kept quiet during the entire ordeal and then, out of the blue, she interrupted. "No way."

"That's not acceptable." she said standing up glaring down at my parents. "This isn't fair, not by a long shot, so I am telling Howard we are going bankrupt. It's over. Goodbye."

"Don't tell us what we will and won't do," my mother shrieked.

"You two were duped by Ron Wright just like we were," Vicki continued. "We will pay you what we owe with interest, but using Howard's love for you in order to get what you call, 'a piece of the action,' is wrong."

They came back the next day with a new proposal, 14% interest on all loans while agreeing to forgive nearly $100,000 of past interest on unpaid past due interest debt we had already accumulated. Any unpaid interest from now on would be tacked onto the note at 20%.

We agreed.

When it was all said and done, I had bills of over eight thousand dollars a month: half I owed to rent and equipment payments, half I owed to my parents as interest payments on loans.

At the time, I had only enough dental patients to keep me busy three hours a day, four days a week, generating just enough money to make the most basic of payments. Vicki quit her job as a nurse and started working part time at the dental office bringing our young son Tom with her to the office. I stayed employed by the State of Missouri while desperately trying to grow the practice by working health fairs, doing free oral cancer exams and giving away free cleanings.

It was then, while walking past a park feeling like the entire world was falling in on me, that I saw a group of homeless men huddled against a low wall. It was winter and they looked miserable in their tattered clothes and worn out shoes. They looked lost and dejected; their heads hung low against the frigid wind. Suddenly I had an idea that changed everything.

# Chapter 13:
# The Homeless

*"When you confront a problem, you begin to solve it."*

Rudy Giuliani - American Politician, Attorney

Reverend Larry Rice was a preacher who, along with his wife and about fifteen volunteers, ministered to many of the homeless in downtown St. Louis. He worked primarily from a large four story brick building just nine blocks west of where my failing dental office was located. From that dilapidated venue, Reverend Rice provided well over a 150 individuals with decent food, clean clothes and a place to sleep at night.

I am not certain why I entered the shelter on 14th and Locust. I don't remember feeling particularly benevolent that day. Perhaps it was when I saw that group of homeless guys huddled together, destitute and forlorn, that I realized there was actually someone else in this world that was in worse shape than I was and decided to reach out. Maybe it was because, knowing how crappy I felt about my life, seeing someone in an even deeper pit of despair made me feel oddly gifted and, in a small way, in a position to give back.

I entered the center, walked up to a guy who was slowly pulling used shirts from a donation pile as high as a small car, and asked him if he knew where I should go to speak to the person in charge. Wordlessly, he swiveled and pointed a deeply nicotine-stained index finger past rows of folding chairs to a small door to the far left. I thanked him and made my way across the worn linoleum, starting to piece together a plan.

I had to, in some way, make lemons into lemonade. I had to on some level, stop seeing dentistry as the worst decision in the world and instead embrace it for what it could achieve. I had to and start creating something great from the flames of my bad decisions. I had to remember why I became a dentist in the first place.

"Hello, Reverend Rice. My name is Dr. Howard Wright and I am a dentist. I was hoping to volunteer and treat some of these guys, make dentures, remove abscessed teeth, get them out of pain. That kind of thing."

Reverend Rice stood up, walked around his desk and approaching me asked, "What do you need from me?"

"All I need is a room. A space large enough to fit a dental chair, some instruments and an autoclave, a sterilizer."

Reverend Rice, with his thin build, medium height and collegiate haircut looked amazingly like the nerdy Tom Hanks in Forest Gump. "When did you want to do this dentistry?" he asked, his voice picking up speed as we climbed a set of stairs to the second floor.

"Friday mornings, eight till noon."

He led me down a rickety hallway into a derelict studio apartment that had served as a storage catchall for the last twenty years. It was a fairly large corner unit with windows on two sides. Against the east wall was an ancient looking stand-alone sink while swinging from the ceiling hung a frail ceiling light.

"Do the plugs work?" I asked as I throttled the sink's hot and cold water taps.

"Most of them," Reverend Rice answered with a smile.

With one last look around at the peeling paint and ragged floor tile, I brushed the dust (that seemed to cover everything) from my hands and turning toward the Reverend nodded my head with a smile. "It's perfect."

There were three dental supply houses in St. Louis, and I called each one personally in hopes of scrounging some instruments to help me do my volunteer work. I explained that I planned to serve the homeless by mainly pulling abscessed teeth and placing simple fillings and that I would work out of the New Life Evangelistic Center down-town.

Two of the supply houses said they might have some old forceps and handpieces stuck in storage somewhere, maybe even an old dental chair, and that they would see if they could find them and call me back. I appreciated their willingness to help and made a note to follow-up in a couple days.

Late that same afternoon I got a call back from the third supply house. A call that set me reeling, a call that reminded me of the man in the tan suit who told me in the lonely park during my freshman year of college that "I was not alone."

"You need to get out here now. Right now. You have no more than two or three hours."

It was Patterson Dental Supply and it seemed that they were in the middle of some kind of warehouse reorganization program. I arrived and was quickly told to drive my old minivan to the rear-facing parking lot and that I would be met there by one of the warehouse managers.

It was strange pulling around the side of the building and seeing an older man, sleeves pulled up, his tie thrown over his shoulder as he leaned over the edge of a large industrial sized dumpster.

"I'm Joe Schumacher," the gentleman called out as I made my way to the row of large gray trash bins. "I run the warehouse here. You must be Dr. Wright."

"Good afternoon," I replied with a smile. "What's going on?"

"Well, you must have some pretty powerful friends in high places, Doc," Mr. Schumacher commented as he waved me closer.

"I've been praying for direction," I replied as I bellied up to the waste cans, "I just didn't expect to end up at the bottom of a dumpster."

"Four days ago, the president of the company decided that we should clear out all our old dental equipment," Mr. Schumacher explained. "This stuff has been accumulating for forty years and now, right after we just finished hauling it all out, you call asking for these exact same supplies."

I leaned out way over the ledge of the dumpster not knowing what I was looking at as I stared down at the pile of trash. There were stacks upon stacks of bent and folded cardboard boxes from dental manufacturers, some split open, others intact. Suddenly I understood what I was seeing. These were display sets of discontinued lines. Entire assortments of brand-new dental instruments that had been given to Patterson years ago, left unsold. Now they were being thrown away, cleared out.

The warehouse manager looked at the unbelief in my eyes and chuckled. "Most of these companies went out of business decades ago. The big boss decided just a few days ago to reorganize the warehouse and throw all the unsold displays away."

I reached deep into the dumpster and grabbed one of the boxes and opened it slowly, as if it were Christmas morning. Inside the damaged and discolored cardboard containers were meticulously crafted stainless steel forceps, elevators, syringes and root tip picks, each glistening brand-new in their individual compartments. They looked like precious gems the way they sparkled in the late evening dusk.

"Can I have these? I mean, there must be $10,000 worth of instruments here."

"More like $100,000 worth," he said looking over my shoulder, "and sure you can you have them. Our pleasure, but the trash truck gets here at around five, so you have about an hour to grab whatever you want before they get here."

Between all three dental supply houses we ended up getting enough donations to equip two clinics. With the support of local churches, I had plenty of volunteers to help with everything from charting to assisting, from cleaning to completing health histories.

When I started doing charity dentistry on the homeless, I didn't know what I expected from God, and I definitely didn't know what God expected from me. What I did know was that there is no such thing as "luck."

In the Old Testament, the book Ecclesiastes talks about "throwing bread upon the waters." For some people, that scripture seemed confusing and convoluted, but for me, being an avid fisherman, it always made sense. When you give back, even with a token morsel as tiny as a crumb of bread, it is amazing what is often brought to the surface.

Word spread quickly about the clinic, and by the end of the second month I had patients lined up and down the hallway looking for relief from their dental problems. It was tough working at New Life. During the summer it was oppressively hot and during the winter downright freezing.

It was on one of those particularly hot and humid days in St. Louis when a young man entered the clinic with a badly infected upper molar. It was so hot you could actually feel the humidity cling to you; it was as if someone took an old army blanket, soaked it in hot water and threw it over your head. It was a 100 degrees outside and a 110 inside with a forecast of thunderstorms in the evening.

I was dressed in green full length long-sleeved surgeon's smock, mask and my ever-present glasses, sweating like a pig as I tried desperately to pull an abscessed upper second molar. It wasn't going well.

After twenty minutes of wrangling with the tooth, I stepped back for a second to rest my hand. Suddenly I noticed a large pool of water on the floor. I stepped back and quickly realized that it wasn't just the floor, but the young man's T shirt was also drenched along with his shorts and half his leg.

My first thought was that we must have spilled a cup of water on him or perhaps the old dental chair had sprung another leak. Rubbing my forearm across my head, I then realized that it wasn't a spilled cup or broken water line that had drenched him, it was me. I had dripped sweat all over him, puddles of it, and he hadn't complained, hadn't whined one bit.

"I am so sorry," I apologized grabbing a paper towel to dry him off. "I had no idea."

"You're ok, Doc," he mumbled, his gauze-filled mouth twisting into a contorted grin, "you're doing great. It's all good."

I don't know how many teeth I pulled while volunteering at the New Life Center, how many dentures I placed or how many cavities I filled. I tried to do my best for each and every patient that walked through our door. On one occasion however, my best wasn't good enough and I've had to live with the pain of that mistake every day since that warm autumn morning when that young child entered the clinic.

I remember it was in the fall because of the dress the large middle-aged woman was wearing. It was a bright orange and hung from her shoulders like a gigantic tent, making her look like a huge overripe pumpkin. It would have been funny if it wasn't for the anger and hatred that burned in her eyes. I heard her coming long before I actually saw her as she bullied her way through the line of waiting patients and volunteers.

"Don't tell me I have to wait," she yelled at our triage nurse. "I have an appointment with the court later today. Get out of my way!"

It was barely ten o'clock in the morning and we had already treated a handful of patients with at least another half dozen people already lined up down the hall. The patients earn their place in line, not by arriving early, but based on the severity of their dental problem. Patients with a serious abscess or extreme pain received treatment first. On the other hand, if someone needed a denture adjustment or had a chipped tooth, they got worked on last. This pushy woman and the small child she dragged in tow obviously didn't care one snip about our procedures or the nurse in charge and pushed herself to the front of the queue.

"Hey! HEY! My WARD has a broken tooth," she yelled as she poked her sausage-like fingers into the youngster's mouth, "See? She needs attention now."

I looked up briefly from an elderly man's wide-open mouth and the split tooth I was slowly working to extract. He had endured the broken tooth for months and now was in the middle of having the tooth removed.

"Can I help you?" I asked tersely through a stark white surgical mask.

My dental assistant, Carol, a housewife who volunteered at the clinic, stood unmoved, shocked at the absurdity of the intrusion. Beside her another volunteer named Judy, a part-time nurse at the local hospital, stepped up to intercept the advancing woman.

The irate woman stood toe-to-toe with Judy and glaring with contempt bellowed, "I've been waiting fifteen minutes!"

I looked at the woman and the child she was whipping around by the arm and shook my head in frustration. Suddenly, up-stepped Rodney, a mountain of a man over six feet six and built like an armored truck. Rodney had been a street person for years, but now worked at the New Life Center full time.

"Is this woman giving you trouble, Doc?" Rodney asked as he took a step forward, relieving Judy of her role as sergeant at arms.

My mask shifted as I smiled. "I don't know, Rodney. Maybe you should ask her yourself."

Rodney leaned forward, his hands on his hips, his voice low and menacing, "Are you giving the Doc trouble, lady?"

"No," she answered sheepishly.

"She's not going to give you any trouble, Doc." Rodney scowled.

All of a sudden, the little girl, her arm still grasped tight by the large woman in orange, bent down and squatted like she was sitting on a low toilet.

"Oh hell," the lady grunted, "she's got to crap."

The woman bit her lip with disgust, slung the young girl around by her arm and spat. "This is Betty, and she's deaf. She can't hear and she can't speak. Damn girl is up and retarded." Then, shaking her head with a repulsive sigh, the ignorant woman went on and said, "When she squats down that means she has to crap."

Looking at the deaf girl, I could tell she felt embarrassed and humiliated squatting down in front of us.

Years ago, I had worked as a volunteer at a summer camp for special needs kids and while there, learned that the American Sign Language "bathroom" sign was the letter "T" (the thumb stuck between the middle and index finger) and then twisting it. Looking at Betty I squatted down low and shook my head an emphatic "NO." Then, standing tall, I made the letter "T" with my gloved hand and twisted it.

I figured that if Betty was a special needs kid, the sign language would be a difficult concept to understand, but I couldn't have been more wrong. Raising herself up tall, she straightened her dirty ill-fitting dress and with a gorgeous smile made the "T" with her hand and twisted it.

This girl wasn't "retarded" as the crass woman had ignorantly expressed, not by a long shot. Betty understood immediately what I was trying to convey, what the sign meant and how to use it.

"Judy," I said as I returned to my work finishing the extraction of the man's tooth, "If you have a second, can you take Betty to the ladies' room?"

In the fifteen minutes that Judy and Betty were gone, we had completed the extraction, cleaned up the work area and had given an injection to our next patient, a middle-aged man who needed a large filling. I had just put on a new pair of gloves and mask and was about to begin removing the decay from the new patient's tooth when I looked up and was completely taken completely aback.

Betty had undergone a complete metamorphosis. Moments before she looked like a small drowned rat, her thick auburn hair a matted mass of tangles that hung thick over her face. Her hands and cheeks had been heavy with dirt and grease, all of which made her look no older than twelve. Now I realized she was at least sixteen, maybe older.

As she walked into the room, Betty looked completely different, a genuine glow emitting from her amazing smile. Judy had combed her hair, tying it loose behind her head. Her once filthy face had been washed, revealing a beautiful complexion and her hands had been cleaned of what must have been a month's worth of grime. However, it was her eyes that had changed the most. Betty's eyes shown bright, like it was Christmas morning: happy, beautiful and keenly intelligent.

I assured Betty's custodian that I understood she had to get to court and that I would repair the young girl's cracked tooth just as soon as I finished the patient I was currently working on.

I used my dental drill to remove the decay on the man's tooth, occasionally glancing over to see an amazed Betty. She watched every move my assistant Carol made as she suctioned the water from the patient's mouth and passed instruments to me as I worked.

It was now time for the relatively simple procedure of filling the tooth. It was then that Carol proposed a most interesting suggestion.

"Let Betty try and assist. I'll guide her along."

"You sure?" I asked with a smile.

"I got a good feeling about this," Carol stated as she waved to Betty, signaling for her to follow.

Carol and Betty moved off toward the room's storage area and after a short period of rummaging, came back with Betty draped in a clean dental smock, gloves and mask. What was moments ago, a ragamuffin learning how to say 'I have to go to the bathroom' in sign language, was now a confident young woman excited beyond belief.

I thought Betty, all decked out in her dental garb, would be nervous or timid as she approached the dental patient, but she walked up like she had been in health care her entire life. Patting the patient gently on the shoulder, Betty lifted the suction from its cradle and stood ready to assist, her eyes beaming with delight.

Betty was amazing and I wasn't shy about telling her "stepmother" how fantastic she was, I could see more and more of Betty's personality coming out with each moment that passed. The way she communicated with the patient with just a touch, the way she anticipated which instrument I would need and the dexterity with which she moved.

Shifting my attention toward Betty's foster-mother, I asked, "Has Betty been to school? When was the last time she was tested?"

"She's never been to school," the foster-mother called out, excited. "Do you know someone, anyone who could help? It would be wonderful."

"I have friends who are social workers." I explained. "I could set something up."

"The court wants us to come back next week at the same time," the foster-mother said giddily. "Can we meet here at nine o'clock next week? Can we do it next Friday? I could bring some of the things Betty has made. She is a great artist."

I had misread this woman entirely. She wasn't mean or hateful, she was simply frustrated and saddened by Betty and her inability to hear or speak. I had seen the look of disappointment in my own mother's face whenever I would stutter over my words or failed another test. Betty's foster-parent wasn't evil, she simply felt helpless, but that was going to change.

I completed the repair of the middle-aged man's tooth, popped Betty into the dental chair and started the examination while her health history form and contact information were filled out.

Betty had a very large cavity on a lower premolar that had fractured months ago, leaving the inside of the tooth exposed and infected. It was a simple extraction. Betty was a saint and in no time, I
had the foul tooth removed.

With all of Betty's and her foster mother's contact information in
hand, I immediately reached out to my friend at Missouri Family Services, a guy I knew who would be able to help.

He returned my call two days later. It was early Monday morning,
so I took the call in my office at St. Louis Dental.

"Howard," he said, a sadness to his voice, "what are you doing? You
know, this is just going to break your heart."

I was confused by his statements. "Break my heart, what are you
talking about? Wait until you meet this girl."

"You don't understand," he continued. "The contact information
you gave me, there is no such address. And the phone number, well, it
was made up."

"You just be there Friday, 9:00 am. This girl is gonna knock your
socks off."

On Friday morning, my social worker friend sat patiently behind
an old writing table. Before him lay government forms and brochures
splayed across the gnarled desktop. He arrived at 8:30 and now it was
close to noon. He watched me work doing dentistry, made a few calls
and sighed each time I looked up whenever someone came through
the open door.

"Let me explain," the social worker grimaced. "That woman has
probably three, maybe four children at home, each just like Betty. She
gets upwards of three hundred dollars a month per child to raise
them. Most foster parents are wonderful, but some... Let me just say,
the last thing that woman wants is for Betty to go to school and become independent."

"Are you saying Betty's trapped like some kind of domestic slave
and I let her slip though my fingers."

"Did you check her foster mother's ID?"

I shook my head, "No."

"It's not your fault; its hers," he said as he collected his materials. "Next time remember the adage, 'when in doubt, call them out.'"

As he started to leave, he turned back, and with a pained frown told me, "I will keep searching both the Missouri and Illinois data banks for the girl; Caucasian, deaf, twelve to seventeen years of age. I'll get back to you with what I find."

I thanked him.

He never found her.

Nearly every day for months I searched for any sign of Betty and her foster mother. I checked the courthouses, called police stations, looked everywhere, but never heard a thing. I don't understand why God would torture me like that; allowed me to be touched by such a wonderful child and then snatch her away just as fast. I know God has a plan and that I am just a bit player, but the pain and guilt I felt having let her slip through my fingers hurt me through and through.

The British writer Lawrence Durrell wrote, "Guilt always hurries towards its complement, punishment; only there does its satisfaction lie." Maybe that is why I worked so hard trying to find Betty; punishing myself for the guilt I felt for having lost such a precious soul to that horrendous witch of a woman. My only hope is that in the short time she was nurtured by Carol and Judy, that she saw the larger world outside and maybe found the courage to escape.

All in all, the patients at New Life Evangelistic Center were fantastic. I worked on both children and adults; gangbangers and homeless, all without charging a penny. It wasn't just the patients I worked on that were tremendous. The people I worked with, the dental assistants, prep nurses, prayer partners, they all made my time at New Life Evangelistic Center wonderful.

Many people thought I was being generous by giving my time to care for the homeless, but actually it was the exact opposite. For every moment I spent working on the poor, I received ten times God's graces in return. I came to realize, standing side-by-side with people who had absolutely no possessions, that a person's worth wasn't measured by how much you can accumulate, but by how much you can give back.

# Chapter 14:
# Taking it to the Streets

*"If you hear a voice within you say, 'You cannot paint,' then by all means paint, an• that voice will be silence•."*

Vincent Van Gogh - Dutch
Post-impressionist Painter

One of the keys to any company's growth is expanding its customer base, and by that I mean appealing to different kinds of customers. Widening the base is critical because as different classes of customers demand your products, the more stable your product becomes.

Disney did this by first establishing itself in fun parks, then children's retailing, then films and now in cruise ships. It doesn't matter if you're selling whistles, dental fillings or Mickey Mouse, by diversifying into new areas of distribution, it is possible to both generate more income while "trend-proofing" your product.

There are many techniques to generate a wider customer base. One common approach involves product diversification where the parent company mutates its product into new areas. Starbucks did this when they started selling their coffee in grocery stores and Ensure, a dietary supplement originally meant for older adults, is now marketing their product to underweight children.

For me, the easiest and least expensive approach to growing the dental office was to simply listen to our customers and find out what they wanted. That explains why so many of the large retailers make it a practice to ask their clients, "Did you find everything you were looking for?"

Thankfully, six months into my time at my floundering dental office, I got a call from a prospective patient who not only demanded I diversify, but guilted me into it.

"I broke my denture and I can't eat," the patient complained, "and with my bad leg I can't get out. You're the tenth dental office I've called. Isn't there somebody who can do a house call?"

It was a question I had never heard before and I had to kind of roll it over in my head before I answered. At New Life Evangelistic Center, I learned to do most any kind of dentistry with a minimum of equipment. Furthermore, we are not talking about doing brain surgery; it's just fixing a denture. I didn't need suction or x-rays, just a steady hand and some quickset dental glue.

"Where are you? Where do you live?" I asked, literally not really knowing where this was headed.

"Fenton," she said. "Probably half an hour from your office."

"Yeah, but that is only ten minutes from my house," I thought out loud.

"Wonderful," she cheered over the phone, sounding truly delighted. "How much do you charge?"

"How much?" This was uncharted waters. What do you charge someone for going to their house, working for less than an hour and then going home? My price sheet with all the insurance codes and fees didn't have a section for "house calls."

All of a sudden, I thought back to some point of reference, a time when I had heard those same words. In a flash I remembered back to the garage door repair man I hired not more than six months ago. That guy showed up two hours late, left a mess and charged me thirty bucks just for the house call.

Channeling the snarky garage door man, I blurted out, "Thirty dollars for the house call. And depending on what needs to be done, and I won't know till I get there, probably fifty to repair the denture assuming there's no missing teeth."

I squinted my eyes thinking she would hang up, but, amazingly, she agreed.

I scheduled the appointment for the next evening which would give me time to put together a mobile dental kit. I thought of all the things I might need: quick set acrylic, polishing stones, an electric handheld drill, gloves, a couple masks. I didn't know what to expect walking into somebody's home. I pictured myself like some kind of eighteenth-century doctor delivering a baby on the kitchen table. Would the patient be alone or would the entire family be present? Realizing the multitude of risks involved, I then considered one last question. Should I be bringing along an assistant?

I try to never be alone with a patient. First and foremost, an assistant's job is to be there to hold a tongue back, hand you an instrument and take care of the patient between steps in the procedure. Secondly, and just as important, an assistant is there so in case the person says you stole their wallet or claims you smacked them upside the head, you have a witness.

I considered involving my dental assistant, but she was too expensive, so after a lot of hand wringing, I decided to drag in my sister-in-law Jean to accompany me. She was a freshman in high school, aspiring to be a nurse some day and was cheap; I paid her "babysitting wages."

After I swung by Vicki's parents' house and picked up Jean, we headed off to the patient's residence having no idea what to expect. The house was only a couple miles away but trying to find the address in the dark with only a map from a gasoline station was nearly impossible. A half hour later we pulled up in front of an older single-story brick home, grabbed our equipment and headed to the front door.

I knocked, and after what felt like a million years, a squatty old man answered the door clearly inconvenienced by the task. He was dressed in a stretched out T shirt, sweatpants and looked at us like we were from Mars. "You the dentist?" he asked.

"Hi," I introduced myself. "I'm Dr. Wright. This is my assistant. Is there a Mrs. Ortega here?"

"Yeah, I'm her husband." The man announced, his protruding stomach stretching his shirt to the point of breaking. "She's in the back."

We walked down the narrow hallway to the rear of the house with the husband, every-so-often glancing back to make certain we were following. Clearly seeing we were uneasy with the whole house call ordeal, he asked over his shoulder. "So. How long you been doing house calls?"

"First time," I answered with a chuckle.

"Wonderful," he said.

Jean and I followed the husband as he slowly walked through the home, passing lamps centered on doilies and countless photos of family gatherings covering the walls. The house had the smell of cooked dinner and old furniture. We ended up in the kitchen where Mrs. Ortega sat, a crumpled napkin loosely held in her folded hands.

"I thought you were going to be here at six?" she grumbled.

"We got lost," I answered. "Didn't you say you were off Gravois Ave?"

"I said it was near Gravois."

I shook my head like I understood, but didn't. "Is that the denture?"

"Yes," she replied gruffly, her hand covering her toothless mouth. "I haven't been able to eat for nearly a week."

Placing my briefcase/medical bag onto the table, I pulled on a set of latex gloves and took the denture. It was in three pieces.

Fixing dentures is not all that different from fixing a car's dented fender, only the denture is smaller and a heck of a lot more slippery. Lucky for me, I spent part of a summer working for a worn-out whiskey-smelling auto mechanic named Mr. Houser. I worked for the often drunk Houser for seven weeks cleaning distributors, changing brake pads and fixing dented fenders. Who knew it would help me years later in Mrs. Ortega's kitchen piecing together her mangled denture?

It was my dad's idea that I work for Mr. Houser. He figured I needed to learn the valuable skills surrounding the keen art of auto repair. Clearly my father was indeed paying close attention during all those parent teachers conferences and realized my hope of attending college was somewhere between zero and none.

Work with Mr. Houser started at eight and ended at a little after five. In exchange for my nearly two months of hard labor, Mr. Houser agreed to give me a very seasoned pickup truck he had parked on the back lot, promising that I could spend the last week of my internship using my new-found skills to revive it.

Mr. Houser had me do everything from rebuilding starters to tearing down and cleaning carburetors. I learned to pull out dents, weld motor mounts and lay a pretty good coat of paint. However, the most important thing I learned that summer was to never trust an alcoholic over-the-hill mechanic named Mr. Houser who promised to give you a cool old truck for a half of summer's worth of work.

Two weeks before the start of school, I reminded Mr. Houser that it was just about time to start working on the truck, but he felt it was smarter if I finished replacing a transmission on a car that was just towed into the shop. Three days later he had another job for me and then another. By the end of summer, he was struck by an amazingly profound case of selective amnesia with me ending up with nothing but a handshake and a keen knowledge of the "real world." I did however learn the ins and outs of body work which was now coming in handy in an old lady's kitchen ten years later.

It took me thirty minutes to finish Mrs. Ortega's denture, once again made whole with the help of skills taught by Washington University School of Dental Medicine and Mr. Houser, the sandbagging auto mechanic. I was paid the $80 and gave Jean ten dollars in appreciation for the fact that she spent her evening watching me grind, build up and polish a smelly fifteen-year-old denture.

Over the next six months I had performed at least a dozen more house calls visiting patients all over the St. Louis area. On most of the appointments I was accompanied by Jean. On one particular assign-ment I went alone, and in this particular instance it was a good thing I did. If Jean had been there, she may not have made it out alive.

I was called about an older lady that had a loose tooth in the front of her mouth, so loose, according to her daughter, that it prevented her from eating. We organized a time on a Saturday around noon and because Jean was busy, I was forced to go alone.

I arrived at the all brick home in South St. Louis, took up my doc-tor's bag and approached the house. I had found out quickly that you could learn a great deal from the home before you entered. How neatly the shrubs were trimmed and how close the grass was cut spoke volumes about the owner long before you knocked on the door.

The house was one of those "shot gun" kind of houses where from the front door you can look down a long hall all the way to the back of the house. Bedrooms, bathrooms and closets all shot off from the center corridor like branches from a tree.

The middle-aged woman who answered the door was tiny, stand-ing no more than five feet three and weighed less than a hundred pounds. She introduced herself as the patient's daughter and as she led me past a row of closed doors to an open kitchen, I soon found myself standing in a small nook where the patient reclined asleep under the cleanest white sheets I had ever seen.

Typically, when you visit the elderly, there is the ever-present odor of urine, disinfectant or the odd smelling food that can literally reek. But this was different. This patient looked as flawless as the front lawn, her hair brushed meticulously, her fresh clothes adjusted impeccably. The only sound I could hear was the slight wheezing breath of the patient and the low GRRRRR of the window air conditioner as it fought to oppose the near triple digit heat wave sweltering outside.

Bending low, the daughter touched her mother on the shoulder and as she did, you could see the slightest of movements as her mother slowly awakened.

"This is the dentist I told you about, Mom," the daughter remarked softly. "He's here to help you with that loose tooth."

The woman's eyes flickered slightly, then closed again.

I set my doctors bag on the floor, reread the patients chart my staff filled out from an earlier phone call and put on a pair of gloves and mask. Sitting on a sturdy wooden chair, I examined the woman and felt a simple extraction was in order.

"Is there anything you need?" the daughter asked.

"Actually, yes," I said, looking at the stark white bed covers pulled up to the patient's chin. "There might be a few droplets of blood. Do you have any towels I can drape so as not to soil these sheets?"

"I know just what we'll use," she said with a smile and disappeared down a side hallway.

It was then, just as the prim and proper daughter disappeared to the right in search of a towel, that a door midway toward the front of the house swung open. It was odd how it opened, uncontrolled, flung the way you would if your hands were full and you had to kick the door wide with your foot.

I watched, curious. I didn't know what I expected to see as I sat back in the old wooden chair, my arms crossed loose on my lap. Suddenly, I was startled by something large that slowly rose from what must have been the basement. At first I wasn't certain what I was looking at until it turned and faced me.

He was a mountain of a man, young, maybe twenty, and obese. He was bare chested with low slung jeans and no shoes. He must have been at least six foot six and every bit of three hundred pounds. His skin looked a sickly milky white, the sweat that poured down his torso soaking the top band of his jeans.

In contrast to his anemic, almost blue looking skin, his hair shone jet black, long and unkept as it draped soaking wet down his face.

"What are you doing to my Grandmother?" he growled like some kind of wounded ogre.

I stood and faced him with my hands raised in a reassuring gesture, but despite my attempt to calm him, his eyes showed confusion and fear. "What are you doing to my Grandmother?" he yelled louder.

I called down the hall, "I'm not doing anything to your grandmother, I'm just the dentist. I'm here to help."

Now he was moving fast, arms pumping as he ran towards me. "WHAT ARE YOU DOING TO MY GRANDMOTHER?" he screamed as a look of blind aggression filled his face.

I looked behind me for an exit, any exit, but the window behind me was sealed tight with one of those large window-mounted air conditioners. I turned once again to the advancing madman and saw with perfect clarity that he wasn't stopping. I lifted the chair by its twin heavy back stiles, raising it high above my head like an ancient Viking battle axe.

"Stay back!" I screamed.

I stood stock still as I pictured myself first swinging high and then slamming the heavy wooden chair straight through his knees, breaking both his legs.

The monster from the basement was now a scant ten feet from me when, like some kind of blessed angel, the daughter appeared between us.

"Andy!" she screamed. SLAM, she swung her fist into his chest, "I told you to stay in the basement." SLAM, she hit him again.

I could see the rivulets of sweat flow down his face, the rage now quieting as the young woman hit him again and again, the perspiration erupting off his chest with each blow.

Slowly the monster of a man backstepped, hanging his head low. With a confused grimace, he marched back down the hall and descended the stairs until he finally disappeared beneath the floorboards.

The daughter attempted to act unfazed as she secured the basement door, her hands trembling as she locked it closed with a simple latch and hook. She then turned to me, straightened her apron, smiled. "It's ok. Go ahead, finish up."

I stood unmoving with the chair still raised high over my head. I replayed what I had just seen over and over in my mind. I still had my gloves on and my mask pulled down below my chin as I returned the chair to the floor. Settling my nerves, I searched from amongst my instruments, and finding a pair of straight forceps, drew them from the bag.

Turning toward the old woman, who mercifully had slept through the entire ordeal, I bent low, grasped the tooth and plucked it from the inflamed tissue as quick and easy as snatching an electric plug from a wall socket. I positioned a sterile gauze in place of the tooth, and stuffing my soiled tools into a Ziplock bag, made for the door.

"My office will bill you," I called out as I hurried out towards the street.

House calls are not always terrifying, often they are simply mystifying. It was winter, and I had received a call from an older woman named Martha who wanted to know if I could perform a dental cleaning on her sister Anne. It seems that Anne had been bedridden for a very long time and was in dire need of a good tooth cleaning.

I agreed, informing Martha that it was difficult to properly clean teeth in the home setting and that there would be minimal polishing, but we could try and do our best. I arranged for Jean to be my assistant, blocked out the time and scheduled the appointment.

After getting lost for the five-millionth time, we pulled up just after dark in front of an old, all brick house in an area of South St. Louis called Dutchtown. Dutchtown is a small, mile-square township located about a quarter mile from the banks of the Mississippi River and was a center of mass German settlement in St. Louis in the mid-1800s. The neighborhood is nice, old and simple.

We walked up the narrow sidewalk, keeping our heads down as the cold winter wind swept snow across our faces. Moving carefully up the icy driveway, we shuffled up the snowy steps and knocked on the door.

Through the sealed door I could hear a voice. It was old and raspy. "Who is it?" the wavering voice asked, the locked door unmoved.

"I'm Dr. Wright and this is my assistant. We're here to do a dental cleaning," I answered as I shuffled my feet trying to keep warm. "Are you Martha?"

The door opened mere inches, held taught by a small chain.

"Show me your card," came the response.

I fumbled my freezing hands out of my pockets, fished for my wallet and passed her one of my business cards.

The door closed.

After what felt like an eternity, the door opened with a clank of loosed chain and we were allowed to enter. Martha was short and frail. Her deep wrinkles and uneven voice making it seem as if she was well into her eighties with her coarse gray hair and bent hands.

The interior of the house was dark, nearly impassable. The only light glowed from red votive candles that burned along each wall. Jean and I moved slowly into the living room as our eyes adjusted to the cheerless gloom and found it empty of any furniture, the flicker of candles illuminating a bare floor, the windows covered with thick blackout curtains.

On the walls I could see paintings, underneath each was the ever-present prayer candles housed in a ruby red glass. There were pictures of Jesus, Mary and Joseph, all displayed in grand fashion on nearly every surface imaginable. It reminded me of one of those old fifteenth century monasteries you see on late night TV, the way the dim shadows flickered against the statues of the saints that graced nearly every corner and nook we passed.

Jean looked at me with eyes that screamed, "This is crazy!"

We followed closely as Martha navigated the gloomy hallways until, after one final turn, we entered a large, nearly empty room. It was a bedroom, again lit with candlelight, a single hospital bed centered against the far wall. Just above the headboard, a life size portrait of the Holy Family hung prominently.

Despite the darkness, I was able to see a small child no older than six or eight asleep in the bed. The bedridden youngster was facing away from us, its face twisted toward the far wall, its hands hidden deeply beneath the covers that lay neatly folded just beneath its chin.

"This is Anne," Martha announced, her voice thick with kindness and love. "She is my older sister."

"Older sister?" I asked. "But isn't she a child?"

Martha shook her head with a sad smile. "Anne developed scoliosis, curvature of the spine, when she was ten. By the time she was a teenager she was completely bedridden. It was when she was in her late twenties that she quit speaking and she has been silent ever since. She has not moved for over thirty years; she has not spoken for over fifty.

"Your sister hasn't spoken for fifty years and you have been by her side the entire time?"

"She is my sister," Martha said humbly. "What was I to do?"

I was awestruck by both the dedication of the sister and the enormity of the task at hand.

There are few things as gross as cleaning a person's teeth who, for the last fifty years, has lived on a liquid diet while being unable to brush her teeth. But despite the fact that it was indeed the zenith of disgusting, I wanted to help in any way I could.

"Anne, Anne," I swooned as my hand instruments emitted the oddest KRRRRR sound as I scraped decades of tartar off her teeth. "When we are done, you are going to look like a million bucks."

Jean rolled her eyes as she held the flashlight and, using a small square gauze, wiped the goo from the working ends of my periodontal curettes.

"As a matter of fact, Anne," I joked, trying desperately to ignore the putrid smell as I held back her limp lips to expose her sludge-encrusted teeth, "you probably think this cleaning is going to cost fifty bucks. But I'm sorry, no. After this, you're going to want to go to Nordstrom's and buy a dress and get you hair done. And when the mailman sees you, well, you'll have to get new shoes."

Martha laughed, and Jean, accustomed to my weak attempt at humor, simply shook her head with the most tired of smirks.

"The way I see it, this cleaning will cost you a couple hundred bucks if you figure in lipstick, getting your nails done..."

Suddenly Anne stirred.

She moved her head ever so slightly, her eyes opening for just a moment and then closing again.

Seeing the slightest of blinks, I supposed I must have hurt her, slipped while trying to dislodge a chunk of tartar and gouged her gum causing her to jerk in pain.

"I am so sorry, Anne," I stepped back. "I didn't mean to hurt you."

"Did she move?" Martha asked startled, a sting of panic mixed with hope weighing her words. "Did you see that? I think she moved!"

In the light of the flickering candles and the glow of Jean's flashlight, Anne slowly blinked her eyes open while, inch by inch, she gradually turned her head away from the wall and toward me.

Jean stepped back, as the flashlight wavered in her hand.

"You said she hasn't woken up for years," Jean called out. "You said she hasn't moved for decades."

"She hasn't," Martha gasped, her hands drawn to her lips, "not for over fifty years."

Anne's eyes seemed to focus and then with a kind of fitful swivel of her head, looked from me, to Jean, to Martha and then back again. In the eerie light of the darkened room we watched, stunned, as Anne, having spent most of her life in an unconscious comatose stupor, slowly woke.

Anne stared at us silent and still, her wide open eyes taking in the entire room, until the bedspread that lay tucked just beneath her chin started to move.

It was as if something was on her chest pressing up, sliding every so gradually on its way toward her neck. The sheet rolled upwards in the same way that a ship's sail would billow in a soft wind. The bulge in the sheet just under her chin looked like some kind of snake shifting and slithering beneath the thin covers and I remember stepping back, afraid.

I heard Jean gasp as a bundle of bones rolled from beneath the bedcover. It was a withered hand, only just recognizable in its contorted, claw like state. It moved slowly until it gradually poked up from beneath the bedcover; the nails dark and curved, the arthritic joints frozen at odd angles.

"Oh my God, oh my God," I heard Martha cry out.

Bit by bit the gnarled hand pulled itself free of the sheets, the anemic digits flexing as the index finger began to extend, pointing toward me like some kind of harbinger of death.

Martha, in whispered prayer, asked God for protection as Anne continued to stare at me, her crooked neck wobbling contorted, the upraised hand unmoving as it pointed unremittingly in my direction.

And then Anne spoke.

Her voice was haunting, her speech dry and raspy in the oddest, most shrill whisper I had ever heard. It was like some kind of strange sound you would only expect from the Wicked Witch of the West, but in this case, it was delivered with the softest and most hushed of murmurs.

"You are a strange man," she said, her index finger slowly moving closer and closer to me, my mask now pulled beneath my chin, my hands crossed in front of my chest. Then after a very long pause, "But you are a good man."

Anne returned her hand to beneath the bedcover, her eyes slipping closed, not to be reopened.

Martha and Jean were crying, overwhelmed by what they had just witnessed. I was overcome myself realizing that a woman who had not spoken in over fifty years had just broken her silence to tell me I was "strange. Good, but strange."

I understand why dentists don't do house calls. They are exhausting, dangerous and time consuming.

The stress and difficulties inherent in performing dental house calls came to a head one late-night when I went out on a home visit to treat an elderly woman just north of St. Louis in a town called O'Fallon. I had just finished a ten-hour day at work and was now driving alone back and forth in the dark, my trusty Michelin map spread across the empty passenger seat.

I was frustrated, exhausted and completely lost creeping along at ten miles an hour on what I figured was a discontinued railroad access road looking for a cross street that clearly didn't exist.

This was the last straw.

"I don't know why I'm doing this, the patients don't care," I hissed through clenched teeth. "If they cared AT ALL, they would give me directions that actually took me to their houses. But it's not worth their while. They'd rather have me drive in circles for hours rather than take fifteen seconds to figure out where they live."

I took another turn to an area that had at least a few streets lights, pulled over and once more compared the directions I received over the phone to the map that I now was crushing in my fist.

"The patients don't care that I'm away from my wife," I called out. "They don't care that I miss my children and by the time I get home they'll be asleep. They don't care that I'm going bankrupt."

As I pulled from the curb, I muttered out through the windshield to no one in particular, "All they really want is someone to talk to. I ask them which tooth is bothering them and they go into their life story. These patients don't even realize the risks I'm taking. Nobody cares, even God doesn't care. If he did, this wouldn't be so difficult. I wouldn't always be so lost."

Fifteen minutes later I found the apartment building, sat in my car and fumed. "This is the last house call," I said to myself. "Nobody gives a rat's ass that I've spent the last forty-five minutes driving in circles and am now on the third floor of what looks like a crack house in the middle of nowhere."

I climbed the three sets of stairs, walked down the dark hallway to a battered and dented door and stood there, exhausted.

I knocked on the door and heard a distant, "Come in."

Cautiously, I turned the knob and threw the door wide to what looked like the apartment of a serial hoarder. The smell overwhelmed me as I looked across stacks of tattered magazines and piles of filthy clothes. In the distance, across the sea of filth, I noticed a huge woman as she sat in the corner, her obese frame overfilling the La-Z-Boy re-cliner she had clearly not lifted herself from for hours, if not days.

"Hello," I recited hollowly, "My name is Dr. Wright. So, which of your teeth is giving you the pain?"

She looked at me from her throne and pointed to a dented metal folding chair. "First, let's talk."

My head dropped to my chest, "Listen, ma'am, if you can just tell me where it hurts and for how long…"

"Sit down," she said with a soft smile. "I need to tell you something before we get started."

I reluctantly followed her instruction and threw the pile of yellowed newspapers that covered the chair onto the ground and took a seat. Like a hockey goalie preparing for the start of a game, I shifted my feet back and forth and cleared the debris from around the chair.

"So, what do you want to tell me?"

"I know what you've been saying to yourself," she remarked leaning forward, looking at me with the look of some kind of mystical prophet. "You don't think your patients appreciate you. You don't think anyone cares that you are away from your wife, and that by the time you get home your kids will be asleep. You think we give you bad directions because we don't care about you getting lost."

I leaned forward shocked by what I was hearing.

"Dr. Wright," she goes as gentle as a lamb. "I know how hard it is on you right now with the money you owe your parents, the debt collectors and nowhere to turn. I know how much it frightens you going to the houses of people you don't know and don't trust."

I lifted the dental bag into my lap as tears filled my eyes, "How do you know this?"

Her expression intensifies, "I know you just swore that this is the last house call you will ever answer. I just want you to know that we do care, and we do appreciate how you miss your family and all the frustrations you are feeling. We do care, and I want to assure you, SO DOES GOD."

Tears poured down my face. I felt guilty for giving up, not trying harder. Then, as I raised my head up, I looked back at her perched on that silly worn-out chair and saw that she wasn't judging me, wasn't upset with how I felt, wasn't accusing me of being weak. She just wanted me to know that I wasn't alone.

I ended up spending nearly two decades as a dentist and during all that time never once refused a house call.

# Chapter 15:
# Dr. Allen

*"An investment in knowle•ge always pays the best interest."*
Benjamin Franklin - Printer, Writer, Scientist,
Inventor, Statesman

My father, Harvey Wright, had a number of sayings he would throw into conversations as often as he could. Sayings like: "There is no greater memory than a two-inch pencil," or "Don't just stand there with your bare face hanging out." Another was, "It's better to remain silent and thought a fool than speak up and remove all doubt." Then there was "Wake up and die right."

My favorite, however, was the adage he used on only "special" occasions when things got rough, when the ebb and flow of life was holding you down to the point of drowning. "If you find yourself being hit and hit hard and you don't know which way to go, just pick a direction and move. If it gets worse, turn around and go the other direction, but above everything else, you must keep moving." I had been in business for just over fourteen months, and after being hammered relentlessly, I was indeed drowning. It was time to change directions and move.

It was the summer of 1985. I had just turned twenty-eight years old. My wife Vicki had recently given birth to our wonderful twin girls, Jessica and Angela. I owed a little over $450,000 to creditors at 14 % interest and it was getting worse by the day.

Despite the fact that I was working six days a week while moonlighting two extra jobs and performing the odd house calls, I was still falling further and further behind on my payments. I was making only incomplete "minimum payments" while the interest-on-interest was compounded on to the backend of the loan at a rate of nearly $6000 a month. It was killing me and for the first time I was seriously considering bankruptcy.

As a struggling student at Whittier College, I used teacher's assistants and mentors to help me excel in school. Now as a struggling dentist, I decided to search St. Louis for a business advisor who could mentor me and show me how to dig my way out of my financial crisis.

In an attempt to get help, I signed up with SCORE, an organization run by the U. S. Government's Small Business Administration that helps new and struggling businesses hook up with expert business mentors. My counselor was indeed experienced and knowledgeable about keeping your costs down and expanding your market share, but my level of debt was so huge, the basic measures of cost savings my advisor was suggesting were simply not enough.

What I needed was someone in the dental community that really understood what it meant to run a dental office. Someone who could look at my accounting books and with real world experience, decide if it was truly time to throw in the towel.

It was while I was dropping off a payment at the local dental supply house that I was given advice that changed my life.

"You should talk to Dr. Ed Allen," Henry suggested from across his catalogue-strewn desk. "Dr. Allen taught business at St. Louis University Dental School, has been around forever and is really a great guy."

Henry was the executive director of one of the large dental supply houses in St. Louis and for the last fifteen years, had become acquainted with nearly every dentist in the community. Sitting there talking to Henry, I realized that I had foolishly spent too much time trudging in one direction, losing ground with each step. It was time to change course and move in a new direction.

Henry leaned forward and rested his elbows on the table, "You know, there's a number of people around town, both dentists and businesspeople, that are literally betting that you'll be declaring bankruptcy within the next six months." Sitting back, he laughed, shook his head and smiled, "Personally, I've got a hundred dollar marker that says you'll make it."

"Well," I cringed, "I'm betting a lot more than that, so let's see what Dr. Allen has to say about everything."

I contacted Dr. Allen's office and made an appointment to see him before the end of the week. What I had hoped to achieve with the meeting was basically to show him where I stood financially and find out, once and for all, if there was any way I could make St. Louis Dental work.

I was shocked as I entered Dr. Allen's dental office and followed his assistant past the reception desk, file room and rows of dental chairs. Everything was beautiful. The office took up a quarter of the eleventh floor and from the crown molding to the stunning oil paintings, everything screamed "old money."

Seated in a luxurious leather chair in his private office, I waited for a little over ten minutes as I mulled over what I was going to say. I decided to be completely honest and neither hide anything nor overplay the level of debt. I was going to just lay it out exactly as it was and see what he had to say. It was then that Dr. Allen burst into the room with a hearty, "Good afternoon!"

Dr. Allen was twice my age and stood no taller than five foot seven, his classic light blue zipper front dental smock pressed tightly against his portly build. He had meticulously-styled steel gray hair that looked very military and proper. In contrast, his smile was infectious, making you think someone had just told him an old joke. He sat down behind his large desk and got right down to business.

"So, what is going on?" Dr. Allen asked with a smile. "How can I help you?"

"I'm in trouble and I don't know what to do," I answered as I handed him a thin sheath of papers that explained my debt, income and expenses. "I am in way over my head and I am about to lose my dental office."

"Where's your office located?" he asked as he looked over each page, finally stopping on the profit and loss statements.

"Downtown on Sixth and Olive, five blocks from the Arch. I have eight operatories on the eighteenth floor."

After about three minutes of studying the numbers, Dr. Allen tossed the financials onto his desk and leaned back slowly in his large swivel chair.

"The way I see it, what you need is an experienced dentist to move into your office and show you how to actually treat patients. A dentist who knows all about dental insurance, employees, purchasing, labs, everything."

"Yeah," I agreed, "that would be great, but right now all I have is a sinking ship and no one I know is willing to hop aboard. The rats jumped ship about a month ago."

Dr. Allen leaned forward and continued, "What you need is an experienced clinician working with you who has a large enough patient base to justify throwing you at least an additional four to five patients a day so you can grow the practice. An experienced dentist with enough income to keep you afloat for the next year until you start making some money."

"Well, that sounds great," I answered back sarcastically, "but the only problem is, where am I going to find someone foolish enough to risk everything on a practice that is weeks from losing everything?"

Dr. Allen stood up and walked around his desk to face me.

"Ever since I got your call, I've been doing a little checking up on you: asking around to learn as much as I can about who you are, what you're all about," Dr. Allen remarked as he looked at me closely. "I've heard what you've been doing with the street people, the house calls. How you have been struggling."

I looked up at him as he stared down on me. I didn't say a word.

"Two days ago," Dr. Allen continued, "my leasing manager, the guy who runs this building, walked into my office and told me they are raising my rent by nearly double. He told me my lease is up next month and that I can either pay him the increased rent or find a new place to work."

I couldn't believe what I was hearing; could Dr. Allen actually be considering joining my practice? I felt a rush of excitement, then immediately tamped it down. This was the same type of elation I had felt when I walked into the front entrance of Washington University Dental School, the same exhilaration I felt until I was told I didn't belong and that, "I was the wrong Howard Wright."

Never too high, never too low.

I shifted myself back further in my chair and shook my head no. "Please, don't toy with me. I am at the end of my rope and I don't appreciate being teased."

Dr. Allen rested back against his desk and continued, "The arrogant ass in the leasing office told me, 'Seeing that I'm too old to relocate, I had better prepare to pay up.'"

"So, what are you going to do?" I asked with a restrained smile.

Dr. Allen looked at me deep in thought. "Let me sleep on it. I'll get back to you on Monday with a proposal."

I often considered what would have happened if I had never approached Dr. Allen. If I had not reached out when I did. Would I have just fallen deeper and deeper into debt and then lost everything, becoming a disgrace to my parents, to my family, to my wife?

On the other hand, perhaps I should have called Dr. Allen earlier; but then again, without the timing of the landlord's arrogance, would Dr. Allen have been motivated to consider joining forces with a debt ridden upstart like myself?

In Hebrews 10:36, the Bible says, "You need to persevere so that when you have done the will of God, you will receive what he has promised." What I came to understand was that I had to keep going and never give up. I had to remember that God loves me and has not abandoned me. I remembered back to the man in the tan suit and bland tie that approached me in the park outside of Whittier College. "You are not alone."

The Scriptures promise us both hardship and love; pain and forgiveness. We must persevere and know that we are not alone in our trials because God is with us.

I didn't volunteer at the New Life Evangelistic Center and treat the homeless to earn God's favor, and I didn't go out and engage in house calls as some kind of *qui• pro quo* scheme with Jesus so I could "give something to get something." I just tried to do my best and treat others how I wanted to be treated. Now, whether the events were connected or not, Dr. Allen was considering joining my practice.

Clearly, I prayed for God's help and without a doubt I pleaded that God would lift me from my debt. But my intent was never to change God's mind or try to convince him to do something special for me. I prayed that God would change my mind so that I could do something special for him.

Dr. Allen's offer involved me buying his practice for a price of $200,000, payable at a rate of around $4000 a month starting in five years, with no interest. He wanted forty percent of his gross sales and he would pay his own lab fees and insurance. He said there was no room for negotiations, take it or leave it.

It was a fair offer and I jumped at it.

Within a month Dr. Allen moved in with his three staff members and nearly ten thousand patients. More than anything, what Dr. Allen brought into the office was a sense of hope, a confidence that was amazing.

In May of 1955, Jonas Salk tested his polio vaccine on himself, his wife and his three sons. When asked where he got the courage to do this he answered, "It is courage based on confidence, not daring, and it is confidence based on experience." From the moment Dr. Allen stepped into the office, our office, he brought with him a confidence based on nearly fifty years of time-tested dental experience and with that experience my entire world changed.

The first stepping-stone to success that Dr. Allen taught me was the importance of knowing the day's schedule. By being acutely aware of the schedule I could plan my time, anticipate possible conflicts and, as silly as it may sound, stay on time. Dr. Allen taught me that being on time was the key to staying relaxed, never being in a hurry and above all looking professional. One of the quickest ways to show someone you are inexperienced and unorganized was to make them wait.

Dr. Allen's second lesson involved the importance of truly listening to the patient's problems and concerns. Only after a patient's problems were completely understood could a dentist know how to treat them.

Nearly every day we worked through lunch rewriting fee schedules, employee manuals and service timetables for the dental equipment. We met with insurance salespeople to obtain the best and least expensive malpractice, property and key-man insurances. I had never heard of key-man insurance before, but quickly came to understand that, in the event that either he or I died or became disabled, any debts we may owe one another would be covered by insurance.

A critical aspect of running the office also dealt with patient payment options, accounts receivable and billing. Dr. Allen and I discussed and came to agreements on payment protocol, how we would handle copayments, which staff member would review the patient's dental insurance and what kind of credit cards should be accepted. We reviewed the American Dental Association's insurance codes and made certain that procedures were written down properly so our patients received the benefits they deserved.

The most important facet of working with Dr. Allen, though was his willingness to step into my operatory and give his advice on the best way to bring back a patient's smile. In dental school they taught exacting techniques to repair teeth. Dr. Allen taught me to do much more than that. He showed me how to save a person's smile for a lifetime.

At least once a day, he'd call me over to look at one of his more difficult patients and ask me what I felt was the best approach to treating the patient. It was amazing working with such a great dentist and educator. Dr. Allen, having been an instructor at the esteemed Pankey Institute, was an expert in treating occlusal imbalance, temporomandibular joint disorders and dental implants.

Dr. Allen and I had worked together for a little over three and a half years when one evening after a hard day of work, he pulled me aside and told me the back pain he had been having was not from arthritis or muscle strain. He explained that he had visited a doctor and the results had just come back. Dr. Allen had an advanced, aggressive form of bone cancer. The news brought me to my knees. He was more than a mentor to me, more than a friend. He was like a father.

Dr. Allen's pain increased quickly and within less than two months he went from my vibrant partner in St. Louis Dental to being admitted into the hospital until eventually he was transferred to hospice care at home.

The dental office became a hollow workplace without Dr. Allen's dynamic personality. Despite the fact that I struggled to fill his shoes, many of his patients were unaccustomed to a thirty year-old upstart and decided to leave. It was difficult to see them transfer to other dentists, discouraging to see the business that we had built up so far falter, but what came next was even more devastating. A below the belt hit I never saw coming. A blindsided smash that I would have never expected in a million years.

"He doesn't have much time," the new Mrs. Allen declared over the phone. "You better have a check for $200,000 dollars ready for me once he dies."

"Mrs. Allen. I understand his dental office needs to be paid for," I explained, "that is why Dr. Allen and I purchased the special key-man insurance from the start, for instances exactly like this."

"No, that policy is mine," Mrs. Thana Allen screamed over the phone. "You owe me $200,000 for his practice, that insurance has nothing to do with you." The phone line slammed dead.

It had been fifteen years since Dr. Allen cheated on his wife, Judy, and divorced the amazing woman who bore him his wonderful children. He told me his affair with Thana was a mistake, that he was a fool for leaving Judy the woman he loved for so many years, in order to find "something more exciting."

It was six months before he became ill that Dr. Allen sat me down in his office and shared with me the details of his divorce. His eyes tearing as he pulled an aged letter from his top drawer: a letter from Judy begging him to stay married; to leave the flight attendant Thana and return home.

Dr. Allen, again acting as a mentor to me, confessed how selfish he had been, choosing to remain in the sordid relationship, not believing Judy could forgive him since he was unable to forgive himself.

Now, with Dr. Allen on his death bed, I had to deal with his new wife, Thana. The "New Mrs. Allen," and she was out for blood.

I called Dr. Allen at home hoping he could explain to Thana the reason we set up the key-man insurance. I thought that if he could tell her himself and clarify the purpose for key-man insurance and why we obtained it, she would understand.

I knew he was very ill, but was nonetheless shocked by the frail voice that answered the phone. I needed Dr. Allen to explain to

Thana that there existed two insurance policies: one owned by St. Louis Dental that was key-man insurance earmarked to settle my debt with him, and the second insurance, a half million-dollar life insurance policy, which he had just for her.

"Yes," Dr. Allen answered the phone, his raspy weak voice barely audible.

I pressed the receiver hard against my ear as I spoke urgently into the phone, "Dr. Allen, I am so sorry to bother you, but I have a terrible problem. Your wife, Thana, says I owe her the $200,000 dollars for the practice. I don't have the money."

"That is why," Dr. Allen coughed, "that is why we got the key-man insurance. She knows that."

"Thana called me just yesterday." I tried to explain, "She is saying that she gets your life insurance, the $500,000 and the $200,000 from the key-man insurance and an additional $200,000 from me. Thana told me she is going to sue me..."

"No," Dr. Allen wheezed, "the key-man was to pay the debt for the office."

Suddenly I could hear a voice in the background. It was Thana and she was screaming at him. "Is that Dr. Wright on the phone? I told you not to talk to him! Hang up! Hang up that phone right now!"

"I have to go," Dr. Allen's voice wavered. "I am sorry."

I sat stunned. Dr. Allen was on death's door and now I was being attacked by a greedy selfish witch. Dr. Allen wasn't going to be able to convince his wife to back off. Thana could taste the money and she didn't care if it ruined me and my family to get it.

I went home and told Vicki what Dr. Allen's wife, Thana said and explained how she planned to sue us in order to force us to pay.

Vicki cried, "What are we going to do? Where are we going to get $200,000?"

Then I had an idea.

Missouri law states that in order to legally record a phone conversation, only one of the parties participating in the phone conversation need be aware of the recording. It is against the law to set up a wire-tap and walk away, but if one person that is actually on the line knows the recording is taking place, it is not only legal, it is admissible in a court of law.

I jumped into my car and headed straight to the local electronics store, a Radio Shack. I didn't know what I would find when I got to the store, didn't know if they sold telephone listening devices or if they even worked. I was surprised when, standing in front of the display, I had a choice of three models. I took the expensive one that plugged into my cassette tape recorder. I figured it wasn't the time to be cheap.

The phone recorder was an odd device, basically a microphone inside a dime sized suction cup that you stuck to a telephone's handset. I tried it a couple of times calling the operator, and once I figured out how it worked, planned out my approach to calling Dr. Allen.

My idea was to call Dr. Allen when his wife wasn't around. I knew Thana had a job as a flight attendant and after thinking about work schedules and when Dr. Allen would be most attentive. I decided to call around ten o'clock in the morning.

Wetting my finger, I dampened the suction cup and attached the listening device to the phone and started the cassette recorder.

"Hello, Dr. Allen, I am sorry to bother you. This is Dr. Wright, can you talk?"

Dr. Allen's voice was muffled and tired. "Yes, how are you doing?"

"Not very well, Dr. Allen. I have a problem. I need your help."

I had rehearsed in my mind what I was going to say. I thought of how Thana's attorneys would accuse me of leading him on, how they would accuse me of putting words in his mouth. I carefully chose my words, "Dr. Allen, the key-man insurance, what was that for?"

"I told you before," he answered in a strained, gravelly voice, "it's for when I die. We got the key-man insurance so if one of us die, it will pay the cost of the practice."

"Your wife is saying it is life insurance for her and has nothing to do with the practice."

"No no," Dr. Allen answered back, "Thana has her own life insurance. The $200,000 key-man is different it's..."

Suddenly I could hear yelling in the background.

"Is that Dr. Wright on the phone? You hang that phone up or I swear to God I will never wipe your ass ever again. You will lay there and never get another meal. You will starve..."

Dr. Allen spoke again in a shattered fearful voice, "I need to hang up now. I am sorry, Howard."

It was the last time I heard Dr. Allen's voice. He died a week later.

It wasn't even a month after Dr. Allen was laid to rest that Vicki, my attorney and I were forced to sit at the end of a long wooden desk at the law offices that Dr. Allen's new wife, Thana had hired. We were there to settle the estate and as the attorneys strutted in and took their seats, it was clear that they were cocksure and looking for a big score.

Next to us sat Judy, Dr. Allen's first wife, along with her two attorneys and a court stenographer. I didn't know Judy was going to be there. Truth is, I didn't know what to expect at all. Somewhere in the back of my mind I thought Judy would look homelier, more like a gray-haired old spinster, but what I saw was an amazingly caring and lovely woman. I could see clearly why Dr. Allen married her and hadn't a clue why he left.

A moment later Dr. Allen's new wife, Thana, entered the room with a snide confident sneer pressed tight across her face. She took a seat and after a short-whispered discussion with her attorneys, they began the attack.

"The most current 'Last Will and Testament' available is dated May 1973, signed four years before Judy and Ed Allen's divorce. This will take a fair amount of discussion, so if it is alright, we will start with Dr. Wright and the matter of the money owed on the dental practice.

Everyone agreed.

"St. Louis Dental owes our client $200,000, payable in twenty days for the purchase of Dr. Allen's dental office, pursuant to this contract you signed three and a half years ago." It was Thana's head attorney and he was wasting no time in laying down the law.

I felt my heart beating in my chest as I shook my head no, "The policy you are talking about is a key-man insurance policy that was put into effect for this very reason. It was taken out by Dr. Allen and myself and I have his testimony saying exactly that."

"There is no such documentation," the attorney rebuffed with a smirk.

I reached into my pocket and removed the small cassette tape, "This is a recording of Dr. Allen where he states unequivocally that the $200,000 insurance policy was key-man insurance and was established to pay this debt."

"When was the recording made?" the attorney for Dr. Allen's wife asked mockingly.

"I called Dr. Allen a week before his death. I asked him about the key-man insurance and he confirmed it was to pay off the practice. The recording is a little scratchy, but if you listen carefully, you can even hear his wife in the background. She can be heard telling Dr. Allen that if he talks to me again, she will stop feeding him."

I placed the cassette tape onto the dark table in front of me. You could hear a pin drop.

"Dr. Wright," it was one of Judy's, Dr. Allen's first wife's lawyers. He was both shocked and elated. "Don't you worry about that tape.

There are companies in St. Louis that can clean that tape spotless so that the words will literally ring like a bell."

Thana looked like she had been kicked in the stomach, her face losing all color as she stared at me like she wanted to rip my heart out.

Without hesitation, her attorneys fell into heated deliberation. It took only a moment, no longer than a single minute, for the pathetically arrogant attorneys representing Thana to make me an offer.

"We are prepared to accept those key-man funds as payment for Dr. Allen's stake in the office. Agreed?"

I looked at my attorney who was smiling broadly, shaking his head happily.

"Agreed," and with the strike of a pen, it was over.

I worked alone for the next four years trying my best to create beautiful smiles while paying off loans and supporting my family. Despite my efforts, the high interest rates I was paying my parents made it impossible to make any headway against the debt. Vicki encouraged me to refinance the high interest loans, many being interest on interest, but my father emphatically reminded me that it was illegal to refinance loans between family members. Vicki disagreed, pressing me at every turn to "look into it."

Finally, after being unable to rebuff my lovely wife's persistence any longer, I called the bank that was on the ground floor of our building and asked if they could do a refinance on a father to son loan.

"Of course, there's no law against that," the bank manager answered. "Is this Dr. Wright from upstairs?"

Yes," I answered, both confused and upset that my father had misled me about a possible refinance. "I'm the dentist."

"Right, you've been making deposits here for the last eight years. How much do you need?"

I was flabbergasted. "I am thinking of a business loan for $250,000. When do you think you can get back to me?"

"Later today. It should be easy; we have all your numbers." He hung up while I stared at the receiver trying to understand what had just happened and why.

I was at the end of lunch when my receptionist popped her head into my office and handed me the envelope from the bank. My father assured me that he was my only source of money and that I couldn't refinance the high interest loans, but here was this envelope sitting on my desk. I closed the door and, getting Vicki on the phone, started reading the bank's loan proposal.

I have heard the amazing way compound interest can make you a lot of money. How, for instance, if you make ten percent on your investment, you will double your money in just seven years. I just never pictured what it would look like if I was on the wrong side of the equation, making somebody else rich. Up until that moment I had been paying my parents well over six thousand dollars a month, all of it as interest, and had been doing so for the last ten years.

Holding the phone between my shoulder and my ear, I opened the envelope and, sifting through the pages, read Vicki the proposal.

"It says here payments of thirty-eight hundred dollars a month on a seven year loan."

"Seven years," Vicki exclaimed over the phone, "are you saying they are lowering our payment by nearly half and we can have everything paid off in seven years?"

"Exactly. If I am reading this right, we are about to save over three thousand dollars a month."

I was speechless. Everything paid off in seven years, and if we paid double premium payments, we could have the office paid for in less than five years.

Vicki's only response was, "Told you so."

I called my father with the good news.

"You're a goddamn selfish ass," my father hissed, "You'd rather pay a bank than your own family. You're pathetic."

The words hurt, but I didn't back off. The voice on the other end of the phone wasn't my father, it was my seventh-grade teacher who told me, "If it was up to her, she would have held me back," it was the receptionist at the dental school, the teachers in Guadalajara, Ron Wright, Mrs. Thana Allen.

"What I need is a final number, Father. I just want to pay you back like I promised."

"Fine," my dad fumed, "I'll give you a number," and he did.

My father put together a final bill that included bills from accountants that went back years, airplane tickets, lawyer fees, food and hotel bills. By the time it was all said and done, the final tally was closer to $290,000.

According to my accountant, over the duration of the loan with my parents, I paid out upwards of $950,000 in interest alone.

I signed the loan papers and sent my father the check. Vicki and I paid the money back to the bank in less than four years.

Despite my father's initial reaction, my relationship with him improved. He wasn't a bad guy. He never held a grudge at least none that I could see. After that initial reaction on the phone my father never spoke of the loaned money ever again. It was as if it never existed.

My mother was delighted when I paid the money back but more importantly, she was thrilled by my success in business. My mom seemed genuinely proud of me.

# Chapter 16:
# Understanding the Market

*"Creativity involves breaking out of establishe• patterns in or•er to look at things in a •ifferent way."*

Edward de Bono - Maltese physician, psychologist, philosopher, author

It was two years later that Vicki and I, along with our three children, took part in a family reunion on a cruise ship to Mexico. There must have been thirty of us on board. Cousins, aunts, uncles, parents, the entire family. The vacation was great, but it was what happened in the first few hours of the cruise, that changed so many people's lives; because it was on that cruise that the underwater whistle was rediscovered, reinvented and came back to life.

Ever since the tragedy surrounding the sinking of the Titanic, Maritime law states that every cruise ship must, within twenty-four hours of departure, muster the passengers and instruct them on the location of the exits, the whereabouts of the lifeboats and the proper use of life preservers On our particular cruise, we had to don our personal flotation devices, move out onto the deck directly opposite our assigned lifeboats and line up women and children first. Our family, being good soldiers, followed the instructions to the T.

Standing on the windswept deck wearing my bright orange personal floatation device with the attached mirror and whistle, I was reminded of something quite by chance. A funny little invention I created when I was a boy.

"You know, Vicki," I yelled from the back row of the queue, "these whistles they have here, they won't work when they are wet. If this

149

ship ends up sinking, it doesn't matter how hard you blow, it won't make a sound. It'll just fizzle."

"What are you talking about?" she called back. "What good are the whistles on an ocean liner if they don't work when they're wet?"

"They are useless," I cried out, holding the orange plastic whistle by its lanyard. "But don't worry, when I was a fourteen, I invented an underwater whistle. If we sink, I can blow it and we can signal one another as we slowly descend to the bottom."

"Really?" Vicki smiled back laughing out loud. "That's wonderful."

"Well, not really," I confessed. "Who on earth needs an underwater whistle? Flipper? Jacques Cousteau? The Creature from the Black Lagoon?"

The ship's whistle blew to mark the conclusion of the exercise, and as everyone went their separate ways, Vicki walked over and asked me again about the underwater whistle.

"So, let me get this straight. This whistle you invented works underwater. Right?" she asked, a strong seriousness in her voice. "How about above the water? Does it work above the water, in the air?"

I thought back to the whistle I made from cheap fragments of my sister Claire's toys. "I think so, maybe. I don't remember ever using it anywhere but underwater."

Vicki shook her head like she was explaining ice to a three-year-old. "Don't you see, if it works both above and below the water, then you didn't invent an underwater whistle, you invented an all-weather whistle. A waterproof whistle. If it only works underwater, then it would only be of interest to divers, but if it also works above the water, then it could be sold to hikers, boaters, hunters, the military."

"Yes," I agreed, "an all-weather whistle. We can mass produce it, sell it all over the world as the first all-weather whistle. When we get back, I'll see if it works. If it does, I'll try and get it manufactured."

It was then that Vicki did something she had never done before. Something that knocked me back on my heels so fast and so hard it made my head spin. She stepped up to me and looking me straight in the eyes said, "Talk's cheap."

"Talk's cheap?" I repeated appalled.

I couldn't believe what I was hearing. After everything we had been through, the years of fighting through debt, the death of Dr. Allen, the deceit of Ron Wright, everything, she still didn't trust me. I glared at Vicki and she glared back while the hardwood deck of the cruise ship shifted under our feet.

Strange as it may sound, as Vicki and I stood an arm's distance apart like gunslingers ready to fire, all I could picture in my mind was an incredible young girl and a story I had heard about one of America's greatest sports heroes of all time.

It was on August 3$^{rd}$, 1984, during the summer Olympics in Los Angeles. Mary Lou Retton, gymnast for the United States, was sixteen years old and stood just four feet nine inches tall. She was in second place for the woman's individual all-around behind the Romanian gymnast Ecaterina Szabo.

The vault was the last event. No woman outside of Eastern Europe had ever won a gold medal and this was Mary Lou's chance; but in order to win she had to score a perfect 10 on this last event.

Before performing the vault, the gymnast tells the judges which maneuver they will perform and then executes. Mary Lou chose one of the most difficult maneuvers, the full-twisting layout double Tsukahara. As she prepared to make her run down the long track, hit the springboard and fly off the 'horse', she looked past the mat, all the way across the gym floor to a lone television camera.

Seeing the distant camera, knowing full well they would never be able to hear her, she mouthed four words to the entire world. At sixteen years old, realizing that this was the most important moment of her life and that people from over a hundred countries were watching, she ran, vaulted off the springboard and stuck the landing, scoring a perfect 10.

In that one moment, Mary Lou Retton became the first American woman to win a gold medal in women's gymnastics.

Years later, in an interview with the press, she was reminded of the four words she mouthed to the camera moments before her amazing win. In all the time since that life changing spectacle, no one had asked her what she had said to the camera. What she had said to all of America, all of the world.

Thinking back, Mary Lou smiled at the reporter as she pictured in her mind the four simple but powerful words she had spoken. "You just watch me!"

Standing on the deck of the cruise ship, Vicki having just laid down the gauntlet by challenging me with the words, "Talks cheap," I looked her right in the eyes and replied, "You just watch me!"

There is an old story about a man from the city who, while driving down a narrow country road, slid off the pavement and landed his car deep in an irrigation ditch. The driver, having noticed a farm about a half a mile back, rolled up his sleeves and walked the twenty minutes to get help.

A farmer greeted him at the gate and willingly offered to use his plow horse, Butch, to pull the car back on the road. Once the harnesses were attached and the reins made secure, the farmer called out loud to the horse, "Come on Betty! Come on Betty! PULL!"

The horse didn't move.

Then, just as loud, the farmer once again shouted, "Hank, Pull, Hank. Let's go, Hank."

Again, the horse didn't move.

Now the farmer in a quiet but stern voice commanded, "Hey Butch! Yup, Butch! Pull!"

As powerful as a locomotive, Butch the plow horse, standing seventeen hands high, dug in and yanked that car onto the road as easy as one, two, three.

The city slicker was delighted, shook the farmer's hand and offered him money for his trouble, which was summarily refused.

"Can I ask you a question?" the driver asked as he settled himself in his car. "Why did you call out Betty and then Hank? What was that all about?"

The farmer laughed, "You see, Butch is blind, as blind as a bat. He's a good horse, but without somebody standing beside him, pushing him, well, he doesn't work very well. I've learned that if I call out the other names and make him believe that there are other horses around it makes him want to show off a little. Once I get him motivated, he works better than any workhorse I've ever had."

Did I know Vicki was just egging me on to motivate me? Yes, but she had always been my best friend, as well as my wife, and the fact that she wanted me to succeed and knew how to motivate me to succeed was all that mattered.

As soon as I got back to St. Louis, I pulled out one of the old underwater whistles from a box of junk and began testing. The good news was that it worked in the air, not just underwater. The bad news was that, with all the coverings that encircled the whistle to make it waterproof, the whistle became muted; the only sounds created were both weak and muffled. I realized right then that if the all-weather whistle was going to work, I would have to redesign it to be powerful both above and below the water.

With the same understandings that I had as a boy, I started building whistles. My goal was to keep the sound-producing opening protected and free of any water while at the same time recontouring the whistle's walls so that it could produce as much sound as possible. It was a difficult task made easier now that I was a dentist.

When I was a kid, I would cut plastic and weld it back together again using old Christmas candles and razorblades. Now, working at night in both my downtown dental office and basement back home, I had access to high speed drills, lathes, grinders and modern glues to shape and mold my designs. Before I would hijack supplies from my sweet unsuspecting sister, now I was able to go to the local hobby store and get pretty much any materials I needed.

Despite the improved working conditions, I found it largely impossible to increase the sound output of the waterproof whistle. I studied wind currents, air density and the venturi effect, but despite all my trials, I was unable to increase the whistle's loudness.

Hoping to accurately measure any increase in the whistle's efficiency, I visited the undergraduate physics department at Washington University and borrowed a sound level meter to precisely gauge the different whistle designs and document the sounds they created. Despite six months of hard work, I failed to improve the loudness of the whistle. Sure, it worked underwater, but above the surface, it was no louder than a soft yell.

"But Daddy, you said you'd save lives."

It was my daughter, Jessica. Blonde hair and blue-eyes, she sat disappointed in me at the kitchen table, a small bowl of ice cream held tightly in her small eight-year-old hands. I had just come up the stairs from the basement after spending the better part of the evening designing and redesign the whistle to no avail, a pair of well used earmuffs hanging loose around my neck.

"What I am trying to explain to your mother is that it can't be done. You can't place a bowl over the top of an alarm clock and expect it to be just as loud. I'm finished with this foolish project."

"But Daddy," Jessica muttered between bites of vanilla, "you can't quit."

"Aren't you supposed to be in bed?"

"You promised," Jessica droned.

Vicki watched with a not-so-sympathetic smirk as I tried to save face in front of my daughter.

"I will try again tomorrow, but then enough is enough."

Our basement was unfinished, the gray concrete walls and floor looking particularly stark under the twin fluorescent lights that I hung from the aged wooden floorboards overhead. For the last half year, I had performed all the tinkering, cutting and gluing on a pair of small folding tables, the sound level meter with its large analog dial numbered zero to ten was centered before me. At the far end of the room, the sound meter's microphone pickup sat on a small throw pillow, its thick cord running out a good 25 feet. Strewn across the tables lay test whistles, some I built, some I bought.

I had been working since after dinner and now it was past ten. I picked up a standard police whistle and blew it. It registered a three on the sound level meter scale. I then took an expensive Fox 40 referee's whistle and blew that; it registered a four. Finally, I took hold of my latest version of the all-weather whistle and blew it hard. It registered a dismal two point five. "Ugh." I was running out of ideas.

Shifting the thin plexiglass walls of the underwater whistle inward hoping to funnel the air flow into a tighter swirl, I, for the thousandth time, put it to my mouth and blew.

"WHEEUW!"

The scream of the whistle was so loud, it felt as if I had just been kicked in the head. The trill bore clean through my ear protection, the needle on the sound level meter pegging past ten.

I didn't move. Not one muscle.

One thing I had learned as a dentist is that every event has a cause. When you hear a noise in the backyard, it's never "nothing." It may be inconsequential, it may be all the pizza you've been eating causing your ears to ring, but something clearly happened. Even when you think you saw something and there was nothing there, synapses in your brain fired; every event has a cause. There may be more than one cause, but there is always a cause.

When the whistle that I held in my hands emitted the earsplitting alarm, I knew to my very soul that something had just happened; somehow everything had just lined up. This was the moment when I had the opportunity to either create something special or dismiss the event as inconsequential. After all my work, all my trials, I wasn't about to do that.

Maybe I had discovered the exact design to make the whistle scream by pure luck, maybe it was a gift from God. I don't know. All I knew was, I couldn't let it slip through my fingers.

"Vicki, come here!"

I didn't need to call her twice, she was already halfway down the stairs. "What was that?" she called out.

"The whistle!" I shouted. "Help me freeze it into position. Get the hot glue gun off the far table and seal every joint you can reach." I held the parts together without moving my hands in the slightest. Only after Vicki had globbed hot glue over nearly every surface of the whistle did I tell her to stop.

The whistle looked like a gigantic ball of clear snot with only the slightest nub of the mouthpiece sticking out.

I removed my ear protection and took up the police whistle, blew it, the meter registered three. I then blew the referee's whistle and again it registered a four. I then carefully placed my lips to the mouth-piece of the first all-weather whistle and blew. Vicki was forced to cover her ears as the whistle pegged the sound level meter's needle well past ten.

We had done it.

# Chapter 17:
# The U. S. Patent

*"Our business is infeste• with i•iots who try to impress by using pretentious jargon."*

David Ogilvy, Advertising Tycoon

With a functional all-weather whistle in hand it was now time to secure true patent protection, not some letter sealed in a post-marked envelope and then hidden in a desk drawer, but real patent protection.

Truth be told, a patent is really not that different from a twenty-year land lease. It is a piece of paper, guaranteed by the U.S. Government, that outlines your territory so, in the off chance someone trespasses on that land, they can be successfully sued, kicked off and/or allowed to stay at a price. The main difference between a land contract and a patent is that, instead of controlling actual property, you have dominion over intellectual property, a design or an idea.

Unfortunately, unlike when some intruder happens to walk across your front yard, when it comes to protecting intellectual property, it's a lot more difficult to tell when someone's trespassing. Identifying the intellectual territory on an idea like a whistle that has been around for hundreds of years is tough. This is where the patent attorney comes in. It is their job to determine if an idea is new and if it is, to create a legal document that describes the unique design's parameters so clearly that anyone and everyone who reads the patent knows exactly where your idea starts and finishes.

I asked around to friends and dental patients and found a law firm in St. Louis that handled patents and, between doing fillings, dentures and cleanings, made an appointment.

The prospect of talking to a professional about the whistle was incredibly exciting. By consulting with an experienced patent attorney, I would be able to determine if the idea was practical, if it would be easily "knocked off" and if it was financially feasible. Most importantly, the patent attorney would be able to tell us if the idea was either novel, already patented or, heaven forbid, in the public domain.

Something that is in the public domain is something that is basically acknowledged as being common knowledge. The pencil, for instance, is common knowledge, you can't patent what everyone already knows about. But a pencil with a special grip that reduces fatigue may be novel enough to earn patent protection, but only for a period of twenty years, and the government won't actually fight for your rights, they will only attest to your ownership of that right. After the patent's twenty years is up, the patent protection disappears, and the idea falls into the realm of public domain with all the other common knowledge ideas.

I signed in with the law firm's receptionist, carrying under my arm a set of simple drawings, one prototype and a list of the whistle's features and benefits. It felt odd waiting in the busy lobby, wondering what all this toil and trouble would create. My goal was to save lives, same as it has always had been since I was a kid, and maybe, if things worked out, make a few dollars to help pay for the kids' colleges. I glanced at my watch and noticed the time. I had been waiting over thirty minutes.

I lifted myself from my chair, walked over to the reception desk and, as politely as possible, asked the receptionist if there was a problem. She looked at me as if I were the most impatient person in the world and told me that the lawyer would be down straight away.

As a dentist, Dr. Allen taught me the importance of being on time. Every second a patient remains in the reception area and waits, the more they get nervous, feeling abandoned and forgotten. If there was ever an instance where a delay did occur and a patient had to wait, I made it a priority to pop my head in the waiting room and apologize making certain the patient knew why I was late, how much longer I would be and, ultimately, offer the patient the option to reschedule.

Another thirty minutes went by.

All the excitement I had felt an hour before had now turned into frustration as I returned to the receptionist.

"What's going on?"

"Mr. Jones didn't have you on his schedule," she said nonchalantly. "They are looking for another attorney."

"Why didn't you tell me this an hour ago?" I asked.

She thought I was being rhetorical (I wasn't) and ignored my question, "The attorney will be with you in a moment."

After another ten minutes, a ruffled rather unkept young attorney showed up, apologized for having made me wait, handed me his card and started asking me questions about my invention.

"So, what do you have?" he asked, gesturing to a chair in the reception area as he took a seat on the overstuffed couch.

"I thought we would be meeting in your office."

"This is fine. We can talk here."

Irritated, I looked around the circle of dated chairs and, despite my reluctance, foolishly took a seat. He was young with a strange appearance that reminded me of a youthful blond Charlie Chaplin. I gazed uncomfortably at my hands, dreading the idea of holding this discussion in the lobby of such a busy building, but then gave in and started to describe what I had built.

"It is the loudest whistle in the world," I explained as I presented the handmade prototype. "This box here holds an air pocket that

makes the whistle waterproof while at the same time it acts as a res-
onator that focuses the sound waves amplifying their power. It is totally waterproof, even works underwater, and is twice as loud as any
whistle in the world."

"Great," he smiled. "I will start a patent search, work on getting the
drawings up to U.S. Patent and Trademark specifications and away
we go."

"Do you think it is patentable?" I asked. "Does it seem like a good
idea?"

"Sure," he nodded his head, "sounds like a great idea."

"How long do you think it will take before we receive the patent?"

"Well, unfortunately the patent office is backlogged, but if we can
get the patent papers submitted soon, it shouldn't take any longer
than a year and a half, maybe two years."

"Two years?" I repeated, clearly discouraged by the long wait.

"Two years if you're lucky," he said, "but don't worry because you
don't have to wait till you get a patent to market your product. Once
the paperwork starts, your idea is considered to have a 'patent pending.' Once you get that patent pending you can market and sell your
product all you want. The only thing is, while you're in the patent
pending status, you won't be able to sue for damages if someone sells
a "knock off" of it, but on the same token, they can't steal your idea.

"Ok," I said, feeling better about everything. "How much is all this
going to cost?"

The patent attorney looked at me and leaning forward answered,
"The patent search will cost around fifteen hundred dollars. The artwork another thousand and with filing fees another five to six hundred. All in all, the cost will be around five to seven thousand dollars."

"What do you need from me? How do we get things started?" I
asked shell shocked from hearing the cost of doing business.

"Send me twenty-five hundred dollars, a list of what makes your
whistle special and the most accurate drawings available and we can

get the wheels rolling."

I shook his hand and stupidly, felt better about everything.

I spent the next three weeks working on the whistle in the small lab in my dental office, designing and redesigning the shape. I wanted it to look easily identifiable and new, while retaining its unique ability to be both extremely loud and waterproof. I next added flowing ridges on the back of the whistle to make it easy to hold with either bare hands or gloves.

As a final modification I changed the mouthpiece making the whistle easier to hold with not only your lips but just your teeth and added a rough patch on the sides to help with the grip. Most importantly, however, was how I adjusted the all-weather whistle's tone.

The larger the whistle chamber, the lower or deeper the tone; the smaller the whistle chamber the higher the tone, but determining which sound functioned best as an alarm to be heard in the most difficult of situations was still not clear. I decided to call the world authority on whistles, the Acme Whistle Company located in central England. They were established in Birmingham in 1870 to provide police whistles to the constables and had made some of the world's finest whistles ever since.

"Hello, this is Dr. Wright from America. I am doing a study on whistles. I just wanted to know why you chose to make Acme's most popular whistle with what I consider to be a relatively low tone?"

"One moment please."

I waited on hold until I was greeted by an elderly gentleman, his thick British accent making him sound like the ghost of King Henry VIII, both old and proper. After introducing myself, I asked him the all-important question.

"Why, for over a one hundred and fifty years, have you made nearly all your whistles with that same low tone?"

There was a long pause until eventually the elderly man answered, "That is the way they were always made. We've never changed the tone from the first whistles made back in the turn of the century."

"So, you haven't done any studies?"

"No studies I've ever heard of," the Brit replied, "that's just the basic tone we have always made."

I hung up the phone and considered for the first time, what sound emergency alarms and sirens make; I mean really make. I decided it was time I researched emergency alarms, who manufactures them and what noise is the best.

The Europeans outfit their ambulances with undulating tones that are more of a BEEP BOOP BEEP BOOP ; high low, high low alarm, while in the United States the emergency vehicles produce a siren that slowly progresses from high to low. The international governing body of SOLAS (Safety of Life at Sea) has strict guidelines and demands that marine vessels and personal floatation devices have three tone whistles or a whistle with a pea that causes the whistle to trill.

The All-Weather Safety Whistle has a single tone that is warbled with the help of a rotating pea, so now all I had to do was to find the proper frequency that would be most easily heard.

It took me about ten hours of digging through the internet, but sure enough, I discovered that in 1973, the U.S. Government appointed a million-dollar study to investigate air raid sirens. They were commissioned to determine what frequency was most efficiently heard through walls, over long distances and above the noise of machinery, music and cars.

The conclusion after the government's yearlong study. 3,150 hertz.

Returning to Washington University Department of Physics, I borrowed an oscilloscope that would show me the wave frequency produced by the all-weather whistle. After I hooked it up and recorded the exact tone of the whistle, I got a disappointing and un-welcome answer.

4,300 hertz. The frequency was way too high.

I struggled to rebuild the whistle larger so it would produce the desired 3,150 hertz. It took me weeks of work to adjust the size of the whistle and tune the sound generator to that 3,150 hertz frequency. What I ended up with was not only the loudest whistle in the world, but also the most easily heard whistle in the world.

There was, curious enough, one additional finding in the government report that caught my attention. Tuning the frequency to 3150 hertz would also enable the sound to be heard through most types of glass windows.

I completed the design of the all-weather whistle, keeping in mind the goal of manufacturing a safety and survival whistle that could be used in freezing cold water, icy snow slopes and the worst sandstorms imaginable. I needed a whistle that would work efficiently on the top of Everest while functioning just as well on the sea floor. I wanted a safety whistle that would fit in your hand yet be powerful enough to not only be heard from a half mile away, but also penetrate glass. It was exactly what I had hoped for.

Having created the exact model of the all-weather whistle I wanted to patent and mass produce, I went to Vicki's father, Gus Hoernschemeyer, to make the drawings. He was an accomplished civil engineer and had years of experience rendering drawings of everything from some of the largest sugar mills on the planet to the tiniest of motors. He was perfect for the job.

It took my father-in-law a full week of evenings to finish all the drawings, but when it was all said and done, they were beautiful, drawn to an exactness of one hundredth of an inch. I summed up the features and benefits of the whistle along with a check for twenty-five hundred dollars and placed all the items requested into a large manila envelope and sent the entire package to my attorney.

The check cleared in a matter of days.

I read books on taking your product to market, creating long lists detailing what I had to do and what to expect. I studied articles on everything from branding to marketing, from pricing to packaging.

Through all the studies however, I was always hesitant, wondering if my idea was really new. Would my attorney show up suddenly and say his patent search found some person in Madagascar or Siberia who had already thought of the idea forcing me to abandon my project? It had been over six weeks since I had sent the materials to the patent attorney and despite having left over a half dozen messages with my lawyer, I'd never heard back.

Finally, late one Friday he returned my call.

"Howard, I've got good news. There is no previous art, your idea is new. We can start the patent process."

"That's fantastic!" I yelled over the phone. "Let's do this thing."

"Sounds good," the attorney replied, "I will need another two thousand dollars for filing fees and my time spent."

"All right," my voice cracking at the thought of another two grand being paid out, "I'll put it in the mail."

We were good to go.

Four days later the check cleared.

It killed me spending so much money on the whistle. In the back of my mind I could still hear my father telling my mom that it was just a silly toy, but my children, Angela, Jessica and Tom believed in me and so did Vicki. I pressed on.

All my friends in Missouri, save one, said it was foolish to try and bring an all-weather whistle to market. But it was my brother Ken who was most outspoken concerning the idea.

"That old underwater whistle of yours?" Ken yelled across my mom's dinner table. "You are still working on that? You're crazy. You know what you should do? I know what you should do."

"Tell me," I replied impatiently as I shook my head, "What should I do?"

"This is what you should do," my older brother shouted as he stood up and waved his arms over his head. "You should take the money you're going to spend on this silly idea and throw it out a high window."

I looked at Ken as I tried to wipe the frustration from my eyes, "And why would I do that?"

"Because it will be more fun watching the people down below scurrying to pick up the cash, than for you to waste your time and money trying to manufacture that stupid whistle."

Vicki just whispered for me to ignore him. I tried but couldn't help but take his comment to heart.

With so many people telling me how foolish the whistle was, I realized it was time to seek professional advice and determine if the all-weather whistle invention was really worth anything. I had determined that my target market was SCUBA divers and, with that in mind, decided that it was in the SCUBA industry that I would see if the all-weather whistle was truly marketable.

As a kid, *Skin Diver Magazine* was the coolest publication in the world. It had stories of exotic places where the coral reefs were beautiful, the fish were enormous, and the water was clear and warm. It had new product reviews, tips on diving safety and amazing pictures. Spread throughout this magazine were advertisements for every gadget and tool you could dream of and it was those new product ads that I was most interested.

I went to the local library, grabbed the most recent copies of *Skin Diver* and started to read. What I learned quickly was that people buy dive gear from dive shops and the dive shops purchased the vast majority of their dive gear from one of two places: Sports Divers Distributors in Florida or Trident Diving Equipment in Southern California.

I had to visit them. I had to sit down with professional dive distributors and see if they really saw a market for the underwater whistles. I called both Sports Divers and Trident and made appointments to meet with each of them, one on the East Coast, one on the West; the meetings were to take place in less than six weeks.

# Chapter 18:
# The New Product Pitch

*"Don't let the fear of losing be greater than the excitement of winning."*

Robert Kiyosaki – American
Businessman and Author

Having just made appointments to meet the two most powerful SCUBA diving product distributors in the country, I suddenly realized that I had just taken my invention and, in the same way a gambler places a large bet in Las Vegas, "laid it on the line."

I worried that these experts wouldn't take me seriously. That they would fail to take the time to understand what I had developed or, worse yet, I would bungle the trial just like the Dive n' Surf experience off the coast of Catalina Island decades before. More importantly, what if they, like so many others, simply said that the idea of an all-weather whistle was foolish and a waste of time?

Shaking my self-doubt aside, I decided that the first order of business in preparing my whistle for its big unveiling was to get the prototype looking less like a glob of half chewed bubble gum and more like a dependable life-saving device.

Before computer aided design (CAD) or stereolithography (SLS), in order to obtain an exact sample of an invention, expert craftsmen were hired to work from blueprints to create the prototype. Unfortunately, these handmade models were incredibly expensive and took months to complete. I didn't have the time or the money to make that happen, so I needed to find another way.

It was two days later while I was having my brown bag lunch at my desk that my dental office manager popped her head in and asked if I had anything else to send to the lab. Looking up, I said "no," but then seeing one of my handmade whistles lying on my desk, I told her to wait.

I had an idea.

Three times a week, the local dental lab sent a courier to visit our office to pick up the half-dozen boxes of dental impressions, broken dentures and orthodontic appliances that needed attention. A good dental lab will manufacture everything from precision gold and porcelain crowns to dentures, ortho appliances and mouthguards. Lab technicians are amazingly creative and are able to produce beautiful works of art using porcelain, gold, chrome alloys and high impact plastic.

Taking up one of our lab prescription pads, I wrote a note asking the head technician, Karl, if he could do something special for me. What I was looking for was for him to rework the rough looking, hand-crafted whistle I made in my basement and make it look sleek and cool. I needed him to straighten out the lines, smooth out the curves and basically make the whistle that I patched together with Plexiglass and super glue look like a precision, mass-produced safety device. I rubber-banded the note to the original hellish looking proto-type and sent it out with the other cases.

It was two hours later that I got a call from Karl. He had inspected the special job I had asked about and was giving me the verdict.

"I got your whistle," Karl remarked with his thick German accent. "So, you want me to make it look store bought?"

"Exactly, Karl," I said with a smile, "store bought. Can you help me?"

"That is what I do for a living," Karl joked, "make you doctors look good."

"And you do that very well," I chuckled. "How long do you think it will take? How much will it cost?"

"With my schedule, I can have it done in two or three working days. Let's say, twenty dollars to finish it up."

I was flabbergasted. Three days and twenty dollars!

"Karl, what if I sent you three home-made whistles," I asked nervously, "all looking as bad as that one I just sent you?"

"For three I'll need a week and the cost will be fifty dollars."

"Great!" I exclaimed over the phone. "Please start on the one you have there. I will send over two more later this week. Just be careful and don't touch the inside of the whistle, just the outside. Make it look wonderful."

I hung up, elated.

Days later the lab dropped off the three refurbished whistles at the dental office. As I spun the whistles with their ribbed backs, elongated mouthpieces and smooth curves in my hand, I was amazed. It looked beautiful, and despite the fact that it had the sick, pinkish color of an upper denture, it was perfect. I put the whistle to my mouth and blew it gently. It rocked the house.

Now I needed a name. Something that would be both short and powerful, while on a deeper level, represent the purpose of the whistle. I wanted a name that was both easy to spell and easy to pronounce in most languages. I had always disliked my own name, Howard, because it sounded so weird. Half the world didn't pronounce the **H** so when people from places like South America, Europe or England saw my name they would call me "Oward."

I finally settled upon the name while at a family picnic at my brother-in-law Mike's house in St. Louis. Mike's dog, Stormy, had gotten out of the back yard and was running around the neighborhood with Mike chasing after him screaming "Stormy come here! Storm, Storm! Hey Storm."

Storm was a pretty cool name and as soon as I returned home to my computer, I checked the patent and trademark website and found it wasn't trademarked for whistles. Vicki agreed with the idea and the kids loved it.

I called my patent attorney the next day, leaving a message to secure the rights to the name, "Storm."

Having a prototype in hand and a name, I now needed to determine what I would charge for the whistle. Finding the right price for the Storm whistle was difficult, and with all the convolutedness inherent to establishing what a customer would pay, not to mention the complexities of talking about distributor pricing, wholesale pricing, retail pricing, cost-plus pricing and markup pricing, made the task all the more difficult.

Hundreds of articles and books have been written about pricing a new product and with every publication there are strategies that justified the usefulness of each approach. A key to all of the different pricing strategies centers first around establishing the cost of both building and selling the product and then adding a sufficient profit margin. A second aspect of setting a compelling price involves adjusting the markup so that the product remains cost competitive and is not priced out of the market.

A final factor, and in many ways the most critical aspect of establishing a price point, involves setting a price that makes a statement as to what the product represents. For most customers a higher price means higher quality, (consider everything from wine to clothes), a factor that should not be ignored.

Working with Vicki, we listed our expenses including everything from the cost of the whistle, the cork-ball, and the split ring, to figuring in the price of packaging and postage. Added onto those costs we tacked on the cost of insurance, labor, telephones and marketing. As a last step we calculated the price of the big money items like the patent and the injection molding tool that were critical to bring the product to market.

The injection molding tool is an expensive block of steel about the size of a lawnmower that contained intricate cavities in the shape of the twin halves of the whistle. It is within these steel cavities that molten plastic is pressed and ultimately forms the whistle halves. Once hardened, the plastic parts are then ejected from the steel cavities, cleaned up and eventually welded together to become the plastic whistle.

Having added all the costs, we then had to decide how many whistles we would most likely sell to offset the fixed cost of the patent and the injection molding tool. The patent and trademark would cost around seven thousand dollars and the tool probably another fifteen thousand. Totaled together, that represented twenty-two thousand dollars that we would need to spread over three years. If we assume that we sell ten thousand whistles a year, we needed to add seventy cents to the cost of each whistle just to break even.

Up to this point we calculated that it would cost sixty cents to build the whistle, seventy cents to pay for the tool and patents, (assuming we sell ten thousand whistles a year for three years) and a dollar a whistle for profit. That put the distributor price for Sports Divers and Trident at $2.30 each, the wholesale price at around $3.00 dollars and the store's retail price to consumers at $5.98.

Sitting at a fast food restaurant, Vicki and I wrote down the numbers for the thousandth time, and after a moment's reflection and my recounting of a bizarre dream I had the night before, decided on a distributor price of $2.38.

To help me establish the final, or retail price of the whistle, I used another tactic that was not so much mathematical, but instead more of a hands on, real world kind of approach. This technique was dependent, not so much on our costs, but instead relied on what people thought in their hearts the Storm whistle was worth.

To do this I went to the local mall and, armed with a clipboard and one of the slick prototype All-Weather Safety Whistles, walked up to people asking two simple questions:

"Hi, this is a new product. It's the loudest safety whistle in the world and it is totally waterproof. What is the most you would spend for something like this? What is lowest, cheapest price you would ever find this selling in a store?"

Surprisingly, nearly seventy-five percent of the people I approached gave me their honest opinion.

"I wouldn't pay more than seven dollars and it would be a steal at three."

"Four dollars would be a good price, but if it really is the loudest, I would pay as much as nine dollars."

Over and over I asked the questions and over and over people gave me their best guesses. In the course of a single Saturday afternoon I had statements from upwards of a hundred people: men, women and kids with nearly everyone giving me a serious answer. At the end of the day I sat down, took out a piece of graph paper and diagramed the high price average, $8.00, and compared it to the low price average, $3.50. Using those parameters, I knew that a retail price of $5.95 was golden.

I had everything I needed and after a fretful night's sleep, flew to Florida the next morning to meet the owners of Sports Divers Distributors.

"Yes?" The woman called out as she hunched over a cardboard shipping box, a bright orange razor knife held loose in her hand. "What do you need?"

I had just walked into the non-descript warehouse, and after checking the address once more asked, "Is this Sports Divers Distributors?"

"Yeah, Sports Divers," she replied.

The woman was young, wearing worn out jeans and a tank top from some Heavy Metal band I had never heard of and despite her thinly veiled graciousness, she clearly didn't appreciate my intrusion. She looked up for only a second and then returned to her work rifling through a case of red and white dive flags, a yellow invoice held tight in her free hand.

"I am looking for Paul. I have an appointment," I interrupted.

"He hasn't told me anything about any meeting." she said from the corner of her mouth.

"I called about five weeks ago," I said persisting. "I just flew in from St. Louis."

Dropping the flags back into the box and scribbling a note on the invoice, she stood.

"Fine, I'll see if I can find him," the girl said irritably. "He's around here somewhere."

It was ten minutes later that a young man walked into the disheveled show room, his open Panama shirt and Bermuda shorts screaming South Beach casual.

"Hi, I'm Paul. Did you say you called and made an appointment?" he asked, confused.

"Yes," I said. "My name is Howard Wright. I called about a month ago and told you I invented the loudest whistle in the world and that it works underwater. You said I could meet you here and discuss its marketability."

"Well," Paul said as he pushed his dark hair back behind his ears, "as long as you're here, let's see what you got."

Moving to a glass showcase, I cleared some space, placed my briefcase on the counter and brought out the prototype. It looked beautiful. Two weeks before, my dental assistant's husband, who made a living detailing boats, painted the prototype a bright safety orange. It looked stunning.

"We call it the Storm All-Weather Safety Whistle. Storm for short."

Paul took the whistle, hefted it in his hand and placed it to his lips and blew.

"Oh, my Lordy," Paul cried out, "what the …"

"Sorry," I lied, "I meant to warn you."

Paul rolled the whistle in his hand, "And you say this works underwater?"

"Yes. Not as loud as up here, but yeah, it works."

"There is a hotel across the street and down a block. How about we jump the fence and try it in their pool. You cool with that?"

I paused for a second, remembering back to when I was a kid and Dive n' Surf messed up the underwater test of my first whistle off Catalina. "I want to go with you," I said, "you have something I can wear?"

Paul smiled, "No problem."

Ten minutes later, we were walking through the parking lot of the small two-story horseshoe-shaped hotel, me in a borrowed bathing suit. As we walked, we were talking about how I came to invent the whistle where I grew up and how long I would be in Florida. We laid our towels on a nearby table and, without hesitating a second, jumped in the water.

I figured Paul would take his time trying the whistle out, seeing how it felt in his mouth and making sure it was easy to hold. But no. After blowing the whistle a few times underwater and hearing me blast it from the far end of the pool, we were done. All in all Paul and I were in the water for just under a minute. Moving to the shallow end, we climbed out.

Drying off his hair he looked at me and asked, "So, what is the cost?"

Playing it cool I answered, "Your distributor pricing is $2.38. I'm figuring the wholesale price is around $3 with the retail price at just under $6."

"How's it going to be packaged?"

"Small Zip lock bag with a header. STORM on one side and a loudness warning on the other."

Paul handed me back the whistle and then asked a question I had not expected. A question I clearly was not prepared for. "What's your minimum order."

Minimum order? What do I say? I stood, stunned. I had hoped he would give me advice on whether or not it would sell. I thought he was going to tell me what I had to change in order for it to work. But no, he actually wanted to buy it.

I quickly went through my options. Should I go low? I don't want to scare him away. Or should I really try to find out if the Storm whistle actually blew his socks off?

I looked him straight in the eye, "Two thousand five hundred."

Paul nodded, "Ok, sounds great. When can you deliver? Who pays postage?"

Oh no I thought! Two more questions I had no idea how to answer. It felt like I was in school again.

"Four months and you pay postage," I guessed.

"Nice. I'll write you a purchase order."

I changed back into my regular clothes, thanked him for the order and hurried back to my rental car before he could change his mind. I couldn't believe what I had just done. I sat and did the math in my head, 2500 x $2.38. Nearly $6,000.

I called Vicki from the first pay phone I could find.

Vicki was as astonished as I was.

The next week I flew to Southern California and met the owners of Trident Diving Equipment. Trident was different than Sports Divers in nearly every way. At Trident the building was new, spacious and well lit. Trident's catalog was nearly two hundred pages long and organized down to the smallest detail. The receiving dock was immaculate, the inventory computerized with sales to over a hundred countries. More than anything, Trident was expecting me, and for the first time in my life, the people I was supposed to hook up with didn't make me wait.

I gave my pitch to both owners and, like Paul from Sports Divers, they wanted to see it work underwater. Luckily, one of the owners had a pool at their home, so I didn't have to "Dip and Dash" like I did in Florida. After a short fifteen-minute drive and a two-minute swim, they wanted to make a deal.

"Ok, the pricing sounds good," the owner agreed, "what is the minimum order?"

I was ready this time, and without hesitation I answered. "2500 whistles with delivery in four months."

"Perfect," the owner said. "Let's go back to the office and I'll write up an order form."

Again, I hurried to a pay phone and called Vicki.

I couldn't believe it. In just two weeks I had sold five thousand whistles. Now, all we needed to do was to have a tool built, find an injecting molding company, manufacture 5000 Storm whistles and package and deliver them all in a time span of just under four months.

What I didn't realize was that I had just bitten off a lot more than I could chew.

# Chapter 19:
# The Injection Tool

*"The way to get starte· is to quit talking an· begin ·oing."*

Walt Disney - American Entrepreneur,
Animator and Film Producer

Four months to build five thousand whistles. Sixteen weeks, and I naively thought I could actually do it. The realization that the task was nearly impossible hit me as soon as I got back to St. Louis and met with one of our local tool and die shop owners who took me on a tour of the facility.

Tool and die maker: "So how many cavities will your tool need to have?"

Howard: "I don't know."

Tool and die maker: "How many ton press are you going to need? How big is your mold?"

Howard: "I don't know."

Tool and die maker: "What kind of plastic do you plan to use?"

Howard: "I don't know."

Tool and die maker: "What kind of gates are you going to use? What kind of steel?"

Howard: "What is a gate?"

Tool and die maker: "How much are you planning to spend?"

Howard: "Fifteen thousand dollars."

Tool and die maker: "You're crazy! Don't waste my time. Any tool worth its weight will cost you no less than $45,000."

I felt my heart sink. Talk about getting in over my head, I wanted to find a hole to crawl into and just disappear. I can't believe I went so far out on a limb and didn't realize how hard it was to actually mass produce the whistle. All I really wanted to do in Florida and California was to see if they liked the whistle. It never really entered my mind they would actually step up and buy them.

Back in 1993, we didn't have 3D computer measuring machines to copy a prototype or computer driven lathes to magically cut a block of steel into a perfect mold shape. There were only metal files and drills, grinders and lathes all handled by die makers, men and women, who designed and cut molds from blocks of steel using nothing more than hard work, experience and stacks of mechanical drawings.

A tool, also called a mold, is the heart of the plastic manufacturing process. The tool can be as small as a loaf of bread or larger than a dinner table. Made of hardened steel, the tool contains anywhere from one to as many as thirty hollows or cavities. These cavities are cut using precision drills and grinders in the hopes that when filled with quick setting thermoplastic, they will produce parts over and over again, identical to the original design.

Attached to these cavities are tubes called gates that carry the molten thermoplastic to the cavities. The molten plastic is pressed under tons of pressure into every corner of the cavities, hardened with cooled water and as a last step opened like a clam with the fin-ished product ejected like a candy from a PEZ dispenser.

There were well over a dozen tool and die shops in St. Louis, all of them different. Some were immaculate where tile floors were so clean you could eat off them. Facilities where senior mold makers wearing spotless coveralls oversaw apprentices as they worked behind gleam-ing drill presses and shaped and polished intricate blocks of steel.

Other tool and die shops looked more like a hoarder's garage where the workers, dirtier than a coal miner's boot, would labor with ancient drill presses and grinders forming cold steel into polished works of art. Always, laid out in the center of the stacked confusion, sat the design drawings, soiled and barely readable, but key to the entire endeavor.

Having visited a number of these tool and dye shops, I came to the realization that I once again required the help of a mentor: an older craftsman experienced in all aspects of the trade that could show me a way out of this confusion and direct me on which way to move forward.

I called back a few of the tool and die shops I had visited and asked them if they knew of any tool and die makers who I could sit down with and just talk, maybe someone retired or a person who was between jobs. After hearing nothing for nearly a week, I received the name of an elderly tool and die shop owner who had recently sold his company and was willing to speak with me.

The retired tool and die shop owner was named Robert, and he lived in Ladue, one of the most fashionable areas in all of St. Louis. It was a beautiful Saturday morning and after pulling into his circle drive, I gathered up my set of drawings, the prototype whistle and a full page of questions.

I was nervous as I sat in the car and collected my thoughts. This meeting was crucial. I had established both a price and a timeline with two of the largest distributors in our market, all based on foolish and naive assumptions and now I would learn the truth. It was here that I would find out if I would have to double my price, double my delivery date or cancel everything.

I stepped from my car, said a quiet prayer. and walked toward the house.

He came to the door, showed me in and directed me to a beautiful living room that overlooked his gigantic backyard. We had just gotten seated when he quickly started talking about his grandkids. He had three. A half hour later he started reminiscing about his wife who happened to be shopping and then spoke of his love for sailing.

I sat patiently and listened to all his stories for well over an hour, a legal pad filled with the all-important tool and dye questions lying flat on my lap. I asked about his life, the age of his grandkids, where he learned to sail and how he met his wife. We had a very enjoyable conversation, but suddenly he seemed to catch himself and his demeanor changed.

Robert shifted forward and smiled a hard, super serious kind of grin. It was as if I had passed the test, paid the price of admission and now I was accepted into the "inner sanctum."

"But you didn't come here to discuss all of this. What is it that you want to know?"

I told him my story, showed him the whistle and laid out the drawings.

He studied the diagrams one by one, slowly, and then, without the slightest air of superiority or haughtiness sat, back and pointed to my notepad.

"Write these things down."

For the next forty-five minutes, Robert told me what I had to do to succeed, describing the process in a very point by point kind of format.

"One - Use C-7 Steel. Demand it. Two - Start with a two-cavity mold, one cavity left half one cavity right. Three - Make sure you have three water cooling lines running to each cavity. They will tell you it's overkill, but you demand it. Four - Ask for references and call each of them. Five - Don't be afraid of the small outfits, they are some of the least expensive and the best. Six - ..."

By the time we were done I had filled at least a dozen pages with notes detailing just how I was to proceed. The great weight of utter confusion which had been weighing me down for the last week was now replaced with a kind of yoke of responsibility, a burden that seemed to thrust me forward rather than press me down and hobble me.

It was ten days later that I found Pete Buckert of Buckert Mold and Machine. He had his tool and die shop in a large warehouse building ten minutes from downtown St. Louis where he worked with two other machinists building molds for medium to small products. I told him what I was looking for over the phone and, being receptive to what I was trying to do, agreed to meet the next day after work.

Pete was middle aged, slender in build and of average height. He was a serious man with a quiet demeanor who wasn't afraid to laugh at himself. I liked him immediately. Sitting with Pete, my drawings spread wide on his well-organized desk, I went down the list. "We need to use C-7 steel and three cooling lines for each cavity."

"That is what I would have insisted upon." Pete agreed.

"And I need references," I said.

"I'll have my wife get you names and phone numbers," Pete replied with a smile.

"Alright," I said standing up, "if everything works well with the references, what are your thoughts on scheduling? How long to build the tool? How much will it cost?"

Pete remained seated and shifted the drawings as he leaned closer to a particular cross section. Then, writing down a list of numbers on a note pad, he slowly sat back.

"Unless something totally unexpected comes up, and I don't foresee any problems, I am looking at about ten weeks and nine thousand dollars."

It was wonderful news, "Excellent."

Never too high. Never too low.

It was three weeks later that I visited Buckert Mold and Machine only to have Pete inform me that they were bogged down on a previous job and hadn't gotten started yet.

Expressing my frustration, I sat down with Pete and we discussed the situation wherein he assured me that there was no problem and that within seven weeks he would complete the tool. Personally,

I hate being late and with a hard deadline just a month and a half away I felt particularly anxious at the thought of not being able to deliver on time to the diving distributors.

I stepped back from Pete for a week and started getting five thousand zip lock bags and card stock headers ready to be filled.

I called Pete early Monday morning and he said he had a few jobs to clear up and then he would start straight away. Six weeks till delivery, no problem.

I waited another week and on Monday morning called over to Buckert Mold and Machine. Pete said he was too busy and couldn't talk. Five weeks. Ugh.

It was then, totally frustrated, that I had an idea. I had been pushing Pete for the last month, trying to press him to get the mold finished, pushing him to get started. I looked at my watch and it was a little after eleven in the morning.

I stepped away from my dental patients, called Vicki and asked her to go out and buy three large pizzas and a couple of six packs of soda.

"Vicki," I asked frantically, "get the pizza and soda and please deliver them to Buckert Mold and Machine. Just drop them off."

An hour later I got a call from Pete. "Hey, Howard did you drop off some food to the shop?"

"Yeah," I told him. "Vicki dropped the pizzas off, I know you have been swamped and probably didn't get lunch, I figured I'd try to help out."

There was silence on the line until Pete finally responded, "We'll start tomorrow."

And he did. Five weeks later the mold was ready to go.

I watched as Pete placed the tool into the press, safety orange ABS plastic being injected through gates into a C-7 steel, side by side two cavity mold at 125 tons pressure. To finish the whistle off we had the side of the mold "burned" with the STORM logo so that each whistle had the name embossed on the side. It looked amazing.

We had Pete manufacture seven thousand whistles, five thousand for the dive distributors and an extra two thousand as stock for future sales and marketing.

We had one last task to perform in order to complete the manufacture of the whistle. We had to place a cork ball inside and then weld the right and left sides together, fusing the plastic walls so it would never fall apart.

We purchased the cork balls from a company in New York and, having never worked with anyone that far up the East Coast, I was unaccustomed to their unique way of doing business. My experience with the saleswoman was so offensive and uncomfortable, I nearly dismissed her and her company until I realized she was an absolute princess.

"Good morning," I greeted the gruff woman who answered the phone. "I am looking for pricing on seven thousand 3/8th inch cork balls."

"What do you want them for?" The elderly voice on the other end demanded. She seemed angry, like some kind of pissed off, cigar smoking prison guard who just missed lunch.

"Well," I answered, put off by the gruff reprimand, "whistles. I make safety whistles."

"Then you need only high-quality cork," she demanded. "I'll get the pricing."

"What about composite cork? I heard they're like, half the price."

"That is stupid!" she yelled at me, her voice coarse and raspy as it cackled across the phone line reminding me of the witch in "Hansel and Gretel. "Only an idiot would use composite cork in a whistle."

"And why's that?" I shouted back, feeling attacked.

"Because the sound of a whistle causes the resin in composite cork to turn to powder!" she yelled. "In a year, the ball will fall apart. Is that what you want? Is it? WELL?"

I suddenly realized she wasn't mean at all. She was honest and her affect, the way she was in my face, was that New York brusque I had heard about.

"All right, I shot back," just as short and aggressive, "I guess I do need the high-quality cork."

"I guess you do," she retorted. "When do you need them?"

"Yesterday," I replied.

"I can put them in the mail today," she screeched back, sounding oddly amused.

"Thank you very much," I shot back.

"You're welcome," she grunted.

"Have a nice day," I spat.

"You too," she grumbled, "and good luck on the whistles." Then she slammed down the phone.

Welcome to the Big Apple.

To finish the whistle, we turned to an assembly company. These are businesses that, either by hand or using automation, finish products so they are ready for market by either gluing, welding, sewing or wiring parts together. Pete knew of a couple small outfits he trusted and after visiting them and getting pricing and timelines, sent them the seven thousand twin whistle halves and the cork balls.

After seeing the whistle and how the parts came together, the assembly company suggested fusing the two halves using a technique called "solvent welding." Solvent welding involves dampening the open ends of the whistle halves with a dissolving solution, dropping the cork ball inside, and then bringing everything together using the alignment pins that stick up from the part. The whistle is then placed into a clamp, the halves held together until the sides are bonded as one.

We were nearly done, with one more step to complete. With thousands of brightly colored orange Storm All-Weather Safety

Whistles stacked neatly on the kitchen table, Vicki and I, along with the kids, spent the next three hours dropping them into small Ziplock bags and placing them carefully into large shipping cartons destined for Florida and California.

Robert Goddard, when asked by a reporter, "What is the hardest part of shooting a rocket to the Moon? Was it the vacuum of space? The distance? The tremendous forces?" The father of rocketry said, "The most difficult part of going to the Moon is making the commitment."

It took years to bring the Storm All-Weather Safety Whistle to market. It turns out that after all the delays, all the problems, we ended up a week and a half late for delivery. Trident and Sports Divers didn't complain, they were both impressed by the final product. Now that our first orders were completed, and the whistles were getting placed in dive shops across the United States, it was time to move on and begin marketing the whistle to a wider group of potential customers.

# Chapter 20:
# Marketing

*"One sometimes fin♦s what one is not looking for."*

Alexander Fleming – Discoverer of Penicillin

Vicki and I spent half the day cleaning out the basement of our small house in South St. Louis county to make room for our growing company. We hauled box after box of old clothes, used kids' toys and all sorts of things we would never miss, out of the dank space in a valiant attempt to make enough room to build the whistle company.

Into the now open space, we set up two large cafeteria-style folding tables, an old computer and printer along with a new phone and answering machine. Against the far wall we stacked the boxes that held the two thousand remaining Storm whistles, all of which represented the seeds we hoped to distribute, display and donate in hopes of winning the war for the mind and heart of the American consumer.

One of the last additions to the basement office was a large cork board. It was hung high, centered just above our twin desks. Push pinned into it, between pictures of kids and an old marriage photo, was a large flowchart illustrating our marketing plan. Above the flowchart was a banner with a message written in fist sized block letters. "CONFUSION IS THE ENEMY."

The goal of the marketing plan was to show potential customers why they needed the most powerful handheld whistle on the planet; why the Storm whistle was key to a person's safety and the benefits of owning one. Our marketing plan consisted of over 80 individual detailed steps we planned to follow in order to tell as many people as possible about the newest greatest whistle in the world. The block letter message written above it identified what I saw as the primary stumbling block to obtaining that success, CONFUSION.

In the mid-1990's there wasn't Twitter, YouTube, Facebook or Instagram, so getting the word out concerning some new gadget was tough. Without question there were advertising and public relations firms who, for a substantial fee, would put together an advertising campaign that would target a market, develop a strategy and then, after setting concrete goals, implement the program. However, a paid advertising campaign cost thousands of dollars and there was no way we could afford that.

What we did instead was become our own ad agency by utilizing a combination of Public Relations (PR), Public Service Announcements (PSAs) and direct mailers, all organized and executed through a technique that is known today as, "Guerrilla Marketing."

Guerrilla Marketing is simply an unconventional approach to getting the word out. The name is a spinoff of the term guerilla warfare, where instead of using tanks, you use tunnels; instead of guns you use sharpened sticks hidden in shallow holes. It can be very effective, but at a cost. Guerrilla marketing is very difficult, extremely time consuming and demands incredibly thick skin.

The amazing French Olympic skier Jean-Claude Killy said, "The best and fastest way to learn a sport is to watch and imitate a champion," and that is exactly what we did. We studied how the big advertising firms promoted their new products, analyzed how they put together their slick full-color brochures and "borrowed" their ideas for logos, slogans and photo layouts. Most important of all, we learned from their battle plans.

AdAge and Ad Week are journals for the advertising industry that love to dissect to the utmost degree just how the boldest and greatest companies market their products. From Coca Cola to Ford, these journals tell you specifically how the most successful advertising agencies develop their battle plans, implement that plan and ultimately evaluate their successes. Going to the library, I made every effort to read these journals and learn the mega-advertiser's tricks-of-the-trade and imitated them.

One of the first gems I learned involved Bacon's Media Directory and how it was the Bible of all that is marketing. Bacon's had the name, address, phone number and circulation for each and every publication in the United States. It gave the editor's contact information, how often it was published and the type of material the publication covered.

I learned that in order to make any kind of splash, I needed to send a sample, a press release and photo to ten magazines or newspapers per day for a hundred days. I realized that I most likely would only get one placement out of ten so that meant that by sticking to my schedule, I would eventually have the Storm whistle featured in a hundred publications. Which, in my mind, was considered a success.

By studying the journals, I came to understand that one of the best ways to convince a magazine to place your product as one of their free public service announcements or to include you in their "new product section" involved sending a pitch that included a three-pronged approach.

First and foremost was to give something away and "wow" them with it. The beauty of the Storm whistle was that it was unique, cheap to give away and easy to ship. Was it a bribe to give away an item that retailed for nearly six dollars? I don't think so, it was simply meant as a simple attention grabber, but if it worked as a bribe, fine. I'll trade a six dollar whistle for a five hundred dollar advertisement any day.

The second prong of the attack involved including a snappy press release. The books I read about public relations emphasized that the press releases should tell a story, be formatted properly, have a personal quote and be no more than one page.

I learned to try and cater the release to specific editors and to always use their name. I was taught to never use the words "amazing," or "great" and to keep in mind that magazine and newspaper writers are incredibly busy, and anything you can do to make their job simpler represented a direct conduit to convincing them to work with you.

I wrote five basic letters for the different genre of magazines and newspapers I was targeting. One release letter catered to sporting goods and outdoor editors while another was more tailored for general interest. I wrote a more serious safety and security letter for the travel and leisure editors while spinning a more technological piece for the more science and engineering type periodicals. In each case I made certain that I sent the appropriate cover letter to the right kind of magazine. I learned quickly that nothing pushed you into the trash bin faster than a press release that didn't match the editor.

Included in the letter was always a catchy title. "Dentist Invents Loudest Whistle in the World," or "New Underwater Whistle Toots its Own Horn." I wanted to make the magazine's job simple so if the editor was up against a hard deadline, they could just copy and paste everything right into the periodical.

Near the end of each entry I was taught to always include a call to action; some concrete instruction to move the reader one step closer to actually buying the Storm whistle. Toward that end, I added contact information into each letter with the all-important "just send $5.95 plus $3 shipping and handling to P.O. Box..."

The final step was the follow-up call.

During lunch at St. Louis Dental, between paying bills, organizing payroll and ordering dental supplies, I would sit at my desk and call each editor I contacted asking if they had received the press release I had sent. This communication was key, not only in order to "press the attack", but also the callback allowed me to receive feedback on what I was doing. Was my letter unclear or too long? Was the photo wrong or was I leaving vital information out that I needed to include? Lastly, I needed to find out if the editor even received my packet.

I would like to think it was my keen writing skills, my catchy title or the marvelous way Sears Portrait Studios captured the essence of the Storm whistle in our photograph that got me into so many publications, but it was actually the follow up call that had the greatest impact.

"Can I help you?"

He spoke just four words, and within that time I could already tell the person on the other end of the line was both supremely busy and supremely important. I had, over the last two months, sent out press releases to upwards of five hundred newspapers and magazines with great results. I had appeared in everything from Newsweek to Louisiana's Times-Picayune, from Popular Science to the Los Angeles Times. This particular call was a follow-up on a packet I had sent to Forbes, arguably the most famous American business magazine in the United States.

"Hello," I answered having no idea who I was talking with. "My name is Dr. Howard Wright and I just wanted to know if you received my Storm whistle? I sent a press release last week."

There was a pause and then, "Who are you trying to get hold of?"

"An editor," I answered. "I don't have a name. I have this new invention, a waterproof whistle..."

"Hold on a second," he interrupted, "You don't know who you're calling?"

"Well, no. I am kind of doing this in the blind," I confessed. "I got your address from Bacons' and they didn't have an editor listed so I just thought I would kind of wing it."

"Wing it?" He retorted, "What do you mean, 'Wing it'?"

"I don't have the money to advertise," I continued. "My wife and I are doing all this out of our basement, so I send out press releases and follow up over the phone during my lunch hour, I'm a dentist. So far I've sent out hundreds and hundreds of press releases and follow-up on each one a few days later."

"Take down my name and address," he replied with a laugh. "Send me one of your packets. One of your whistles."

What I didn't know at the time was that the voice on the phone was from one of the hardest hitting associate editors at Forbes, a writer who didn't just look at a company's profit and loss column, but instead looked for the story behind the company. Two weeks after my cold call, he phoned me.

"Howard, this is Fleming Meeks from Forbes. Any possibility I could meet you and your wife? I could visit you two in St. Louis and we could talk over dinner."

This was epic!

A month later Vicki and I met with Fleming Meeks at one of the nicest restaurants in St. Louis. We talked for hours discussing all aspects of the Storm whistle, Fleming taking notes on how we got started in the manufacturing business and where we dreamed of ending up. By the end of the long wonderful evening we were told a photographer would be sent out to take our pictures.

Vicki and I had never been in a serious photoshoot before. They told me to wear a suit with a lightly colored shirt and a simple tie and Vicki should wear a patterned dress. The photographer was a casual guy who looked like he would be more comfortable at a racetrack making bets than behind a camera. He brought with him two large carryalls with every piece of photographic equipment you could dream of and ended up using each and every piece.

We took photos for over an hour. Sometimes, I was asked to stand alone looking out the window, my hands rested, relaxed into my coat pockets while others were of Vicki and I together as closeups. There were photos of me behind my desk looking pensively at a whistle and there were photos of both of us looking serious, like oil barons or bank presidents. The photographer must have taken over a thousand pictures until, with a tired smile and a shake of the head, he thanked us for our time, repacked his gear in those cool black foam shipping crates and made for the exit.

Halfway to the door he looked back and stopped. Placing the equipment onto the ground, he pulled a small instamatic type mini camera out of his pocket and suggested we take one final snapshot, just for fun.

"What if we get you two sitting in your dental chair holding up the whistles," he laughed. "Just one shot, something wacky."

"Sure," we laughed. "Why not?"

"Hey," he smiled as he threw me one of my zip up dental smocks, "Take the jacket off and put this on and hold up a bunch of your whistles."

Relaxed now that the photo shoot was over, I laid back in the dental chair with Vicki sitting beside me, both of us holding whistles.

The photographer held his tiny camera loosely in his hand as he suggested we place the whistles in our mouths and pretend that they were really loud by covering my ears.

Like five-year-old kids, we did just what he asked. Laid back, stuck the whistles in our mouths like a bunch of goofballs and covered our ears. He took one single photo and chuckling, put his cameras away.

A month and a half later, we got an envelope in the mail. It was from Forbes and contained a copy of the magazine that would hit the streets in less than three days. As I opened the thick shipping packet and thumbed through the magazine looking for the article, I wondered what the article would say. Would it be a small, two paragraph piece in the back, or an actual feature article?

Suddenly I found myself staring at a two-page spread titled *Whistle Blower,* with the middle of the article featuring a gigantic full color photo. It was, of course, the "We are Midwest goofballs" shot with a single whistle in my mouth, two in Vicki's, our eyes wide and our hands held tight over our ears. Honestly, it looked great.

It was the steady stream of seven and fourteen-dollar checks that started to appear at our P.O. Box that told us the public relations program had started to work. We had sold or given away nearly twelve-hundred whistles. Now, after close to three months, it was time we focused more directly on getting into chain stores and catalogs that would not only put the Storm whistle on display for tens of thousands of shoppers to see, but also enable us to start seeing some return on our own personal investment.

To put together the brochure, we hired a retired graphic artist from church that helped us with our photos, our layout, and our slogan: "When Being Heard is a Matter of Life and Death." He retook the photos we sent to newspapers and used quotes from people who had tried the whistle and loved it. Lastly, he designed a cool logo that had a bright orange lightning bolt with our name, Storm whistle, centered over the top.

To get the attention of both catalogs and brick and mortar stores, we initiated a direct marketing campaign that included the new brochure, price list and the critically important whistle sample. The internet had just started making headway and by searching store and catalog names, I was able to get lists of buyers for outdoors, sporting goods and SCUBA diving.

One of our first orders and reorders was from the U.S. Navy. It seems that the Navy SEALS out of Coronado, California got hold of the whistle somewhere and had been using them in their training. They had ordered forty-eight whistles and now had reordered another four dozen.

"Vicki," I called out excited from the basement, "I just got another order from the military guys, the Navy Seals."

"That's great!" she called back down from the kitchen where she was stacking dishes.

"Yeah," I hollered back, "they say the MPs are stealing them from their lockers."

"The military police? That is amazing," Vicki commented as she descended the stairs. "Really, the MPs?"

"It's only forty-eight whistles, but they are reordering. That's what's important."

"No," Vicki said as she shook her head slowly, "What's important is the MPs, the police; that's what's important. The only way the cops are getting ahold of the whistles is by stealing them from divers. We have to stop looking at this as a waterproof whistle and start seeing it more as the loudest whistle in the world. We need to market more aggressively to other groups like the police."

She was right. I had fallen back into my comfort zone, back into seeing the Storm whistle as a diver's whistle and not as the loudest whistle in the world, the finest all-purpose safety and security whistle on the planet. I reworked my contacts and sent out another batch of promotional material, this time with more of a general appeal to women's groups, security officers and outdoor safety.

It wasn't even two weeks later that we landed our first big catalog named Early Winters. They were out of Seattle, Washington, with sales of twenty million a year and a circulation of nearly thirty thousand catalogs every three months. Early Winters was clearly a player in the outdoors industry with their first order amounting to well over three thousand whistles. A week after that we picked up Bass Pro Shops and L. L. Bean. It was time to increase production.

# Chapter 21:
# Manufacturing

*"My motto was always to keep swinging. Whether I was in a slump or feeling ba•ly or having trouble off the fiel•, the only thing to •o was keep swinging."*

Hank Aaron - Major League Baseball Player

From an amazing start-up the previous year, we began to pick up some real speed when it came to sales. Pete Buckert, the man who built our first tool and ran the initial seven thousand whistles on a small injection molding machine, called us into his office and explained how he was in no way, shape or form, able to handle our production.

"It's not what I do," Pete replied with a sad shake of the head. "I am a tool builder. The only reason I run an injection molding press is so I can evaluate the molds I build."

"We're starting to get some real orders, Pete," I said. "You can't help us?"

Pete leaned back in his old office chair and shook his head, "Making parts is not for me. There are too many deadlines, too much inventory to keep track of, too much to worry about. Sorry, you're going to have to find someone else to run the parts."

"Who?" I asked, frustrated. "What company has a press that will fit the tool you built?"

"That tool," Pete smiled through his clasped hands, "will run parts on nearly any press you slap it into." Then scribbling a quick drawing and writing down a series of numbers, he handed me a piece of oil-

195

smudged paper, "Call around and give them these specs. You'll find someone."

And I did. I don't know why I picked the middle-sized injection molding company on the outskirts of Herman, Missouri, to make my whistle, but I did. They seemed competent, had a dozen older presses and had been in business since World War II.

Despite a good first meeting with the owners, it was a complete and utter disaster.

"I'm trying to tell you your tool is messed up! It was built wrong."

He was the foreman in charge of injection molding and he had been screaming at me over the phone for the better part of five min- utes. His voice was that of an older man severely reprimanding a young boy, his German accent so thick the only way I could picture him was in lederhosen and one of those funny felt hats.

"I don't understand," I replied confused. "Pete Buckert ran both black and bright orange whistles and the tool worked perfect."

"Nope. The sides don't match up. This tool is no good."

"But you told me the black whistles ran great yesterday," I argued, "and now, this morning, you're saying the orange parts are wrong?"

"That's right, the orange parts don't fit together," he said defini- tively. "The tool has to be remade."

"Crap!" I screamed. "Ok, I will cancel my afternoon patients and leave here at noon. I will be in Hermann in two hours. Have some parts laid out so I can see what's going on."

My staff called my afternoon patients and apologized profusely for my absence as I raced down Highway 70 as quick as I could to see the extent of the damage. Because of the way the whistle tool was built, there were a number of delicate ejection pins and thin blades of steel that went into forming the part and if just one of them became bent or twisted, it would mean disaster for the tool.

I arrived just before two in the afternoon, the heat of the Midwest August day sending mirage-like shimmers across the parking lot as I pulled up outside their loading dock. I walked through the wide open warehouse roller doors where the molding machine lay quiet, a small mountain of orange and black whistle halves stacked on a small work-table nearby.

"I'm Howard Wright and we spoke on the phone about these parts not being correct."

"Like I said," the huge giant of a man commanded. "The tool was made wrong, the parts don't fit together."

"The parts made last week were fine. There must be something else going on."

The foreman stood at least six foot five, three hundred pounds and with his arms folded across his chest he looked like Wodan the Ger-man god of war. As he raised his voice, he took a step closer to me, "You don't know what you're talking about. The tool was made wrong."

I ignored the angry ogre and went directly to the table where the parts lay stacked. I picked up two of the black parts. Holding them to-gether the right and left halves lined up flawlessly with a snap. Re-turning the black parts back to the table, I then held two orange halves together and saw immediately that they were off by a quarter inch, clearly a mismatch.

Comparing the parts I looked at the foreman and told him the or-ange plastic, not the tool, was the problem.

"You don't know what the hell you're talking about!" He screamed. "You don't know anything about making parts. The black and orange plastics are identical."

"No," I said, maybe a little too loud, "the mere fact that one plastic is orange and the other plastic is black should make it clear to even the most foolish dolt, that the two plastics are not identical."

"The color of the plastic doesn't matter," he yelled as he clenched his fist an inch from my face. "I've been manufacturing plastic parts for thirty years and no pissant college puke is going to walk into my factory and tell me how to run a mold."

About this time, I looked around and found that nearly every worker in the plant was staring at us, mouths agape, as we argued toe to toe in the middle of the plant floor. They watched from catwalks twenty feet off the ground, from behind half-closed doors and from alongside stacks of wooden crates all with the same "I can't believe it," look on their faces.

I realized at that moment that people must not get into this Goliath's face very often and decided, despite the fact that my record in high school wrestling was pretty much 50/50, I should back off, but not before I asked one more question.

"Who makes your pigments? Who makes the colorant for the plastic?"

He leaned forward, his contorted flaming red face inches from my own, and shrieked, "3M."

In 1994 there weren't any cell phones, so I jumped into my car and sped off in search of a pay phone. Five minutes later I was in a gas station's parking lot speaking with the help desk at 3M plastics trying desperately to calm myself and sound coherent.

"Excuse me," I stammered, "I have a serious problem. We just ran our parts first in black ABS plastic and then in orange, but the orange parts don't fit the way the black did. It just doesn't make any sense."

"Let me guess," she said in the calmest, most angelic voice I had ever heard. "The orange pigment you are using is a bright, fluorescent kind of safety orange. Right?"

"Yes, it is," I answered, totally mystified by her statement. "How did you know that?"

"Because," she answered just as sweet, "when you add fluorescent orange, yellow and pink pigments to your ABS plastic it becomes incredibly heat sensitive. If you run the presses too hot by as much as just ten degrees, it will change the properties of the ABS, causing it to expand by ten to fifteen percent."

"If you don't mind," I asked gently, "what is the maximum temperature the brightly pigmented ABS plastics can be heated without expansion?"

"No hotter than 430 degrees," she responded. "You must keep the temperature of the ABS plastic under 430 degrees."

"Thank you very much." I told the lady, "Have a wonderful day."

"You too," she replied.

I hung up, got back in my minivan and headed to the factory. Walking through the open bay doors, I saw the foreman standing amongst the machines. I walked up to him and waited for him to look my way.

"So, tell me, what temperature are you running the orange plastic for the whistle?"

Looking at me like I was crazy, he shrugged his gigantic shoulders, "I don't know."

Staring at him straight in the eyes I asked further, "Come on, you must have a thermometer on the machines that tells you how hot you are running the plastic?"

"No," he replied, "I put my hand on the side of the housing and I can tell if it's the right temperature."

"Not in August in Missouri you can't. Not in this heat!" I shouted pointing out toward the shimmering parking lot asphalt. "The word from 3M is, 'If the maximum temperature of 430 degrees is exceeded by as much as ten degrees for orange, yellow and pink fluorescent pigmented ABS, you get a fifteen percent expansion.' It's not the tool that's broken. You're over-heating the plastic."

I then asked, in no uncertain terms, that his workers remove the tool from the press and put it in the rear of my van. I left the injection molding company in beautiful Hermann, Missouri, never to return.

Driving the two hours back to St. Louis with a hundred and fifty-pound tool in the rear of my van and a stack of unfilled orders at home, I knew my next order of business was to find another injection molding company that could successfully make my whistles without driving me crazy in the process.

To help organize my thoughts, I decided to make a list of the elements I felt were key to successfully building a consistently great whistle.

First and foremost, the company had to have a cutting-edge injection press, one that would consistently produce parts at the right speed, temperature and pressure. Secondly, the molding company had to be local so I didn't have to drive halfway to Kansas in order to check up on things. Lastly, I wanted a company that would help me be as successful as possible and not slow me down. A company that would show me how to be more productive, either through making my part better or by helping me market the whistle more efficiently.

After considering a number of different manufacturing plants, I found a company that was not only local and had modern machinery with computer-regulated temperature controls, but an establishment that also understood that there was more to making parts than just pressing hot plastic into a mold.

The company's name was Mueller Manufacturing and from the moment I walked into their offices it was clear they that understood, not just how to make parts, but how to make them better. Mueller Manufacturing showed me how, by spending a small amount of money modifying my mold, I could add ultrasonic weld lines into the parts that would enable them to be ultrasonically welded together as they popped hot out of the machine. This minor modification enabled a faster, more complete weld, was better for the environment and saved me money.

A week after moving the mold to Mueller, I approached Pete Buckert, our tool and die machinist, and asked him to start drawing up the plans for a new tool. This one, unlike our initial two cavity mold that ejected a single right and left part per cycle, would create four right and four left halves per twenty second cycle. This new mold would reduce the cost of making the whistles by nearly half and with the introduction of ultrasonic weld lines would enable us to make whistles faster and more consistently.

One more important change I made in order to adjust to the growth of the whistle company was packaging. The package we had been using was rather unprofessional and consisted of a Ziplock bag and a pale blue paper header. Now that we were in more stores and in greater demand, we opted to move toward a more protective, tamper-resistant blister package with its clear plastic cover hot pressed to a full color plastic-coated card. The blister package was important because it displayed the whistle clearly while still leaving enough room on the front of the card to explain how it was the loudest whistle in the world, totally waterproof and was easy to hold.

On the back of the card we included a picture of the inside of the whistle along with testimonies from a police officer, a camper and a nurse, all describing how they depended on the whistle for safety. Lastly, we placed on the lower left corner a warning about the loudness of the whistle and our UPC barcode.

The Universal Product Code or UPC is issued by the Uniform Code Council, a nonprofit organization that was setup to help grocers label their products, streamline inventory control and make purchasing at the checkout simpler, quicker and more accurate. Having a UPC barcode was a critical addition to the packaging if we were to be accepted as a vendor in big box stores.

We chose an experienced company in Chicago to manufacture the new cards and clear blisters but opted to have the individual packages assembled and sealed in St. Louis. The final act of actually bringing together the finished whistles in tightly sealed packages required the union of the blister card, a clear blister, a split ring, shipping boxes and the actual whistle. Because each of these parts were expensive and easily lost in transit, Vicki and I agreed to find a local company with both great inventory control and experience in consistently producing top quality thermal sealed packages.

The packaging company we found was Lafayette Industries, a sheltered workshop located a little over thirty minutes from our home office that specialized in packaging. Lafayette Industries had been doing product fulfillment and small product packaging since 1976 and had a reputation of doing great work. What sold us on Lafayette was how they supported the community by giving jobs and instilling pride in adults with developmental disabilities.

My Aunt Anne had Down Syndrome and it was while I spent time with her that I learned how precious individuals with disabilities are and how having a purpose can add so much to their lives and the lives of people around them. Vicki, having been a camp counselor for severely disabled adults, felt the same way, so the decision to have Lafayette do our packaging was simple.

The fact that there were less expensive packaging companies that could do the same job faster was of little concern when compared to the joy we saw on the faces of the employees at Lafayette. Vicki and I would stop by occasionally to drop off whistles, blister covers or printed cards only to be greeted by dozens of smiling faces as the employees did everything from running a machine to stacking boxes to sweeping the floor. Using a sheltered workshop for our packaging has been one of the best decisions Vicki and I have made throughout this entire process of bringing the Storm whistle to market.

# Chapter 22:
# Keeping the Ogres at Bay

*"Lea•ership is solving problems. The •ay sol•iers stop bringing you their problems is the •ay you have stoppe• lea•ing them. They have either lost confi•ence that you can help or conclu•e• you •o not care. Either case is a failure of lea•ership."*

Colin Powell - American Statesman and
Retired Four-Star General

It had felt like forever since my last conversation with my patent attorney and it was high time we talked. I was reluctant to call him because it seemed that each time I picked up the phone, it cost me another thousand dollars. Despite the cost, I needed to know how much progress we had made securing the patent and when would we move from the Patent Pending status to having a full U.S. Utility Patent.

"Hello, Mike," I said after sitting on hold for what seemed like an eternity, "this is Howard Wright. I am the guy with the underwater whistle patent."

"Oh yeah, Howard," he answered, sounding annoyed. "What can I do for you?"

"I want to know where we stand," I replied, exasperated. "When are we going to get the patent?"

"It takes time," he chuckled. "What's the hurry?"

"Well, Mike," I responded both impatient and frustrated. "I've been putting a lot of money and time into selling the whistles and I don't want it knocked off."

There was a pause over the line and then the voice on the other end turned deadly serious. "What do you mean you've been selling the whistles?"

"What did you think I have been doing over the last year? What do you think I am doing this for?" I asked. "Did you think this was some kind of academic exercise? I've sold over ten thousand whistles."

"Tell me!" his voice noticeably trembling over the line! "When did you start selling the whistles? How long has it been since your first sale?"

"I don't know. About a year."

"Tell me exactly," he shouted, "how long has it been?"

I put the phone down and moving to the basement, rifled through a stack of papers until I found what I was looking for. I returned to the phone. "Thirteen months. We sold our first whistle in October of last year."

"I can't be your attorney; we can't do business anymore."

"What is this about?" I demanded. "Tell me right now! What is going on?!"

There was a long pause until he finally answered, "It's the law," he mumbled. "Once you offer a product for sale, you have twelve months to submit a patent application to the USPTO and not a moment longer. One second past that one-year deadline and your idea, no matter how novel it may be, no matter how unique, is immediately considered public domain and you lose your right to any patent protection."

"Wait! Wait! The patent application hasn't been sent in? You haven't finished writing up the patent? It's not patent pending? What have you been doing for the last year?"

"I've had a lot of things going on and I haven't gotten to it."

"You're saying I can't get a patent because you've been too pre-occupied to send the paperwork in?"

"I didn't know you were serious about actually manufacturing your product."

"Serious? I gave you over six thousand dollars. That's how serious I was. What have you been doing for the last year, Mike?"

I waited as I heard only breathing on the other end of the line. "Now, you listen to me," I spat into the phone. "I may not be an attorney and I may not know a lot about patent law, but there is one thing I do know." I held my breath and tried to control my raging anger then continued through gritted teeth. "It's against the law for a dentist to abandon a patient, no matter how rough it gets. And if I remember correctly, that's also true for attorneys, so you can forget about this 'I can't be your attorney' crap. You're not abandoning me and my wife. I'm not going to let you kick me and my wife to the curb, so you better start thinking about some kind of way we can get past this."

"The only thing we can do, legally," Mike said sounding insulted and wounded, "is to modify the original idea using a "continuation" application. Concede to the patent office the all-weather whistle patent is in a state of flux and then change the claims to reintroduce a spinoff invention that can be patented with a new start date. That is the way patent trolls ambush a patent, they make a slight change to the patent to highjack the entire project and threaten everybody with a lawsuit if they try to contest it."

"Is it legal?" I asked, trying to understand the idea of high-jacking my own invention and basically having two patents on a single idea.

"Yeah, it's legal," he responded sounding offended. "In this case you'd basically be ripping off your own idea."

"Then do it."

It took my intellectual property attorney another three months to submit the paperwork for the new, revised continuation version of the All-Weather Safety Whistle patent.

I don't know why I didn't fire him right on the spot for sitting on my patent work for over a year. Maybe it was because I figured it was partially my fault. I should have known something was wrong. I should have checked up on him. I was just being an idiot. As Mark Twain said, "Denial ain't just a river in Egypt."

The other reason I kept Mike on was because I didn't want to start over again now that I was halfway across the proverbial stream; I didn't want to change directions after already investing thousands and thousands of dollars. I guess I just wanted to get it over with.

One thing I did do that was intelligent, however, was to get a trademark on the shape of the whistle.

A trademark can go a long way to protecting the uniqueness of a product and, as long as you pay the fees that are due every ten years, a valid trademark never expires. There are rules about what is considered an acceptable trademark, but if your product is considered compliant, a trademark can work wonders at keeping the competition away.

A great example of a trademarked shape is the Coca Cola bottle. Because of the trademark, no one can make a bottle with that unique kind of in and out shape of the coke bottle. One company that could not get a trademark was Owens Corning. They wanted a trademark for the color pink for insulation and make it illegal for anyone to make insulation in that light pink color. The U.S. Government decided that people did not see the pink color as critical in identifying the Owens Corning brand, so the application for a trademark on pink for insulation was denied.

In order for me to get the trademark for the All Weather Safety Whistle, I had to prove that people purchased the Storm whistle by looking for its special profile. I had to show that the customer identified the Storm whistle because of the "pregnant seahorse shape."

Fortunately, I had kept all the addresses from people around the country who purchased my whistle through the mail, and using those contacts, sent each one a letter asking them to write me back telling me how they liked the whistle and how they look for it because of its unique shape. I sent out two hundred letters and got back an amazing one hundred and fifty responses. I applied for a trademark and I sent copies of the hundred and fifty letters to the Patent and Trademark office. Incredibly, a bonified trademark for the shape of the Storm whistle was issued.

It was during that twelve-week period when the patent was being redone that I realized there was another way, besides having a patent, to help prevent my whistle from being knocked off. I had read a compelling business article that suggested, "If you are hesitant to come out with a new product because you are afraid it might pull sales from your primary line, don't worry, your competitors will do it for you."

I thought long and hard as to just what kind of whistle one of my competitors would build in order to win over my customers. If I could do it all over again, how would I make a whistle better than the Storm whistle? Vicki and I sat down and ran through all the complaints, criticisms and odd suggestions we had received over the last year from anyone and everyone that had ever seen the whistle. Their complaints typically consisted of, why is it so big, why so expensive, why so clunky looking?

I decided if a competitor was to try to build a better whistle, it would be a little smaller, cheaper and have a slicker, more modern feel. Vincent van Gogh wrote a hundred and fifty years ago, "Do not quench your inspiration and your imagination, do not become a slave of your model." It was time I rebuilt the Storm whistle.

It was thrilling configuring a new whistle, designing one that was less cubic and more "space-age." Vicki and I decided that rather than wait for a competitor to build a second-generation all-weather whistle, we would build it first. Three months later we had a new whistle that was smaller, sleeker and designed in such a way that it would be easier and cheaper to make.

For a name we decided to play off the original Storm name. After

Vicki, the children and I went through every possible name over pizza and ice cream, we decided that the new whistle would be called the Windstorm.

Generating a lower price point for the Windstorm whistle was a key feature we hoped to create in our new whistle. With the Storm selling retail for six dollars while cheap East-Asian made sports whistles were selling for a little over two, Vicki and I decided that our new target price would need to be somewhere close to four dollars each.

In order to achieve the lower price, we decided to double the size of the manufacturing tool so that the per piece price would drop by half. In addition, we learned that if we incorporated a modified design to the Windstorm whistle halves, the change would make the sonic welding process quicker and easier, which would also lower the price. All in all, the new Windstorm all-weather whistle hit the market at an in-store retail price of $4.95 filling our lower price objective while still providing the same profit margin as the original Storm.

Again, I employed Pete Buckert to make the tool and quickly trademarked the Windstorm name with the help of our new lawyer, Morland Fischer.

Morland Fisher was referred to me by my brother who had used him in the past. Morland was knowledgeable, communicated exceedingly well, produced only the most exacting of work and finished everything quickly. Best of all, Morland charged half of what I paid the other patent attorneys always telling me upfront what things cost. It was odd finding a patent attorney so easy to work with until I realized he wasn't an attorney at all. Morland Fischer was a patent agent.

Patent agents specialize in obtaining patents. They are trained specifically to prepare, file, and execute both patent and trademark applications as well as appear in front of the Patent Trial and Appeal Board. Unlike attorneys, patent agents are not legally allowed to practice law. What this means is that a patent agent cannot give legal advice such deciding if your invention is "infringing" on an existing patent or discuss the feasibility of a non-disclosure agreement. Their job is to simply write and file a patent in the most effective way possible.

For me a patent agent was exactly what I needed.

# Chapter 23:
# Brand Diversification

*"You can't wait for inspiration; you have to go after it with a club."*

Jack London - American Novelist and Journalist

One of the unfortunate aspects of living with ADHD was dealing with the side effects of my self-imposed concentration methods. Utilizing my focusing technique of "keep your head down, make a list and charge," had made me successful as a student, but was now starting to hinder the growth of our product. I still depended on lists and relied upon the "microtask" system to get things done, but I hadn't updated the original flowchart I drew up and, like those kiddie cars at Disneyland that ran the same track day after day, we were finding ourselves in a marketing rut. It was clearly time to develop a new set of goals and diversify our approach to obtain greater markets.

The well-known self-help authority Tony Robbins has been quoted as saying, "Stay committed to your decisions, but stay flexible in your approach." We were in our third year of manufacturing whistles and while sales were good, I felt vulnerable functioning in our tiny slice of the whistle market. I knew we needed to somehow branch out.

I shared this marketing challenge with one of my dental patients who was a big-time account executive and advertising guy with a nearby clothing company. He mentioned that he had just read an article in one of our local business papers about a Mr. Ashton, who was supposed to be a marketing guru, who just retired from the world famous Pet Inc. My patient and friend, between the buzz of my handpiece and the beep of my UV curing light, said that I should try to get ahold of him, but warned that according to the article, this marketing genius could be very difficult to work with.

The next day during lunch I called around and, after a couple of inquiries to Pet Corporation's headquarters, was assured that Mr. Ashton would be contacted and given my phone number. I had told the secretary at Pet that I was doing some research on marketing and wanted advice from an expert. Oddly enough, just as the secretary was about to hang up, she too warned me to be careful and that the retired 'guru' could be a bit of a curmudgeon.

A few days later I got a call from Mr. Ashton and, after comparing our schedules, we agreed on a time we could talk,

"So, what do you want to know?" he asked over the phone getting right to the point.

"I run a company that makes whistles," I responded, "and we basically have one product and I am concerned because I want to diversify but..."

"You need more than one product, he interrupted.

"Yes, well unfortunately I only have one whistle. I am working on a smaller one..."

"You're not listening, damn it!" he screamed into the phone. "You need another two or three products, at least, or you will go bankrupt and lose that one whistle you have."

I stopped and thought about what to say next. "I think that would be great, but I don't have any more ideas, I don't have any more products. I guess I am kind of a one hit wonder..."

"Why don't people listen?" he yelled. "You idiot. What is it? Are you slow in the head?"

"Maybe, but if I could come up with another invention I would, but I only have the whistle."

"You are the stupidest most idiotic fool I have ever met," he shouted, "and I have worked with some of the most pathetic slobs on earth."

"I'm trying to understand here, but I ...."

"Ok. Crap, it looks like I am going to have to grind it up into baby food and stuff it down your throat."

I waited and held my tongue as I prepared for the next onslaught.

"Do you seriously think that all the bread you see in the stores comes from different bakeries? Well? Do you?"

"Actually, I do." I answered meekly.

"Oh my God," he gasped in disgust, "you are an idiot."

" I just thought..."

"Nearly all of those different loaves of bread come from the same factory!" he shouted. "They are just packaged differently. You don't need to come up with another invention, you just need to package it differently and push it to another market."

"Oh, I see," and I did.

He hung up.

I started by making a list of every market that uses a whistle and next to each entry outlined what each of those markets demanded most from the whistles.

Sure Mr. Ashton was crass, hateful, ill-spirited and mean, but he was also right. God had blessed me with a great idea, and I had taken it and put it into a tiny box. It was time to truly step back and think outside the box and reach out to a wider market. Diversifying the Storm whistle meant adding pink whistles to our line and making them available to women's groups. It meant smoothing one side of the Storm whistle, so we could effectively pad print corporate logos on them and sell them to Fortune 500 companies as giveaways.

Within the next twelve months we were selling five times more whistles to industrial safety suppliers , women's groups, police and general sporting goods companies than all the diving distributors put together. We also made our packaging more generic in order that it would be compatible with a greater customer base.

I became particularly aware of how important the diversification of our marketing was when Vicki and I attended a Dive Equipment Manufacturer's Association (DEMA) convention in New Orleans. Trident Diving Equipment invited us to come along and we jumped at the chance. We were walking around the convention hall with our Storm whistles around our necks and our sellers' badges clipped to our shirts when suddenly we were called over by a man and woman working a booth selling dive hose clips.

"You must be the Whistle King!" the older man called out from behind a cloth-covered display table. "How are those whistles doing?"

"Great," Vicki said, "Trident is doing a wonderful job getting our whistles into dive shops."

"Cool," the clip manufacturer said with a smile, "we have been making dive clips for five years and have done pretty well also."

"Fun, isn't it?" I chimed in.

"A blast," the vendor agreed. Then leaning forward, the clip maker waved us closer, "I bet I can tell you exactly how much money you are making on those whistles."

Smiling back, skeptical, I asked, "Really? Alright, tell me how much."

Holding his index finger to his temple and closing his eyes like a carnival magician, he whispered, "I bet you sell a thousand whistles a month, and you make a dollar and a half per whistle. That's a little over twelve to fourteen thousand dollars a year. Tell me I'm wrong."

"Very good," I smiled impressed. "You are absolutely right. How did you know?"

"I've been doing this for a long time. Yep, that's just about what we do also," he grinned. "Pays for the convention and a little to put away."

"Sure does," I said as we waved goodbye and walked away.

A moment later when we were way out of earshot, I looked over to Vicki and said, "He was right about the diving revenue, but what he doesn't realize is that we make that much in each of our different markets: boating, corporate sales, industrial safety and sporting goods."

Vicki smiled, "Whistle King?" Then shaking her head laughed, "Don't let it go to your head."

Mr. Ashton, the retired Pet corporation marketing guru, may not have been the nicest guy in the world, but what he taught me about diversification and expanding a product's market was invaluable. Stephen Jay Gould, the world-renowned evolutionary biologist said, "Evolution is a process of constant branching and expansion."

What I learned was that, by giving the Storm whistle the opportunity to expand into unfamiliar areas, we were able to develop otherwise unseen areas of growth and in doing so expand our capabilities and strengthen our brand.

# Chapter 24:
# Getting Knocked Off

*"In every battle there comes a time when both si•es consi•er themselves beaten, then he who continues the attack wins."*

Ulysses S. Grant - 18th U.S. President

E very year during the holidays, Vicki and I would host our annual St. Louis Dental Christmas party. It was a small affair where we would give out the Christmas bonuses, have dinner and just relax together with our staff, talking about what we were thankful for. There would be Christmas music, decorations, the usual. That year, as 1997 ended, I got a shock that I would never forget.

My dental assistant, Carol, had gone shopping the day before and visited our local Buck Bargain Store (not their real name) looking for cheap stocking stuffers. While perusing the various items the discount outlet offered, she happened upon a rack hanging six deep and four across covered with what looked like my whistles in strange packaging.

Carol had heard a lot about the Storm whistles and knew I would never sell them for just a buck, so she decided to purchase one to show me. It was my whistle, identical in every way with the exception that along its lower edge where I had Pete Buckert write "Made in USA," someone had replaced it with "Made in China."

I felt violated, and rightfully so, because I was.

The next opportunity I had, I visited my patent attorney (my third and counting) and he suggested we send a "cease and desist" letter to Buck Bargain Stores demanding they pull the whistles off the shelves. I had heard that fighting a company that had knocked off a product was time consuming, frustrating and expensive. Within twenty-four hours I found that all three were true.

"Is your dad home?"

It was a Saturday morning and some guy was at the door talking to my daughter Jessica. She was ten years old and had just pulled herself from Tiny Toons to make the short run from a morning of cartoons to the front door, beating me by two seconds.

"I'm Doctor Wright," I replied, stepping up to the half open door. "What do you need?"

The squatty-looking older man looked like he was dressed for a casual meeting: an open shirt, sports coat and dress pants. He leaned forward and under his breath told me, "Get rid of the kid."

"Excuse me?"

"Get rid of the kid!"

Jessica first glared at the man and then at me. "What's going on, Dad?" she asked as she raised an accusing single eyebrow.

"Please go back inside, Jessica. I want to talk to this man privately."

After a moment she ran back inside whereupon the mysterious man handed me a folded letter.

"You're being served."

"What for?" I asked.

"I don't know; I just deliver them." And the man was gone.

An hour later there was another knock at the door. This guy was scruffy looking, more in a hurry.

"You Howard Wright?" the man asked, looking around as if he expected to get jumped at any moment.

"Yes," I replied.

"You're being served." He handed me an envelope.

"Great," I answered back.

It just so happens that I was being sued by some attorney firm that I had never heard of for both false advertising and the illegal transportation of hazardous materials across state lines.

Vicki looked over the papers, "You have to be kidding." But they weren't.

Buck Bargain Stores, Inc. was attacking our company by throwing me into multiple lawsuits in an attempt to drain my resources and undercut my confidence. These lawsuits were completely frivolous and designed to harass me for being bold enough to dare demand that they remove their bogus, knock off whistles from their shelves, and now I had to answer the assertions despite the absurdity of the charges.

While hiring an attorney to fight these frivolous lawsuits, I learned that the cheap knock-off of my whistle was in hundreds of Buck Bargain Stores from coast to coast with over 35,000 having already been sold and around 30,000 more in stock. I was crushed emotionally.

After delivering my cease and desist letter, my attorney demanded all correspondence relating to my whistles be presented to the court. It took months for them to answer, but when they did, we were presented with a memo from Buck Bargain that was written to a Chinese manufacturer asking that my Storm whistle be duplicated. I was shocked. Unequivocal evidence that the cheating weasels at Buck Bargain got ahold of one of my whistles, sent it to China and had it copied.

I figured I had them dead to rights. Figured that this would be a simple case and they would fold, admitting their error and pay us a miniscule amount of money for the damage they caused and that would be that. Unfortunately, that was not how things worked. They denied any wrongdoing.

Buck Bargain made the next move by offering to withdraw the two lawsuits they had initiated, if we dropped our lawsuit that accused them of patent infringement. Yes, they would stop selling the whistle, but refused to admit they copied our product and refused to compensate us for any attorney expenses or lost profits from the cheap knockoff whistles.

At this point, defending ourselves against the two lawsuits had cost us over five thousand dollars with tens of thousands more due if we actually had to go to court. Vicki was livid at the idea some company would try to steal our product and possibly destroy our company by dumping cheap fake whistles onto the market. We were furious that an American company would use our own court system to bring frivolous lawsuits to cripple our company and blackmail us. We were both outraged and troubled to the core. We decided to fight long and hard because it was not just illegal, it was immoral.

Threats and finger pointing went back and forth until the attorneys on both sides got together and decided to attempt "binding arbitration" before a judge. Binding arbitration is when everyone involved meets face-to-face and attempts to come to an agreement with a judge present to act as a mediator.

Vicki, my attorney and I, walked into the courthouse on Market Street in downtown St. Louis, went immediately to the third floor and entered a large well-lit conference room. The room smelled old and musty, the wood paneling dark. In the center of the room sat a table that was at least a dozen feet long, easily able to accommodate twenty people or more. We sat huddled on one side of the table, Vicki and I fuming at the idea of meeting the thieves who were trying to destroy our company. Waiting infuriated for the owners of a company that was ten thousand times bigger than our little whistle company yet intent on obliterating us.

Ten minutes later, in walked our opponents, the contingent from Buck Bargain Stores having just arrived from Chesapeake, Virginia, where they had their headquarters. Buck Bargain, I had learned over the last few months, did over twenty BILLION dollars in revenue, had over a hundred and fifty thousand employees and a reputation for knocking off small products. They sat on the other side of the table looking both put out and pissed off.

Soon after the Buck Bargain group got seated, in walked the judge. He was an older man, graying hair, slim build with a rather upbeat demeanor. He took the seat at the head of the table and started by having everyone introduce themselves. Attorney number one representing Buck Bargain said her name, said she was from Virginia and presented her business card to each of us. Attorney two, same thing, Attorney three, same thing. Buck Bargain's Attorney four was from St. Louis as were attorney five and attorney six. Next came the Buck Bargain Store's executive.

He was tall, slim and looked like he had just left the beaches of Italy. He sat there smug, his expensive gray suit, ironed monogramed dress shirt and silk tie looking like they were straight out of GQ magazine. His gold cufflinks and gold watch glimmered in the lighted room like they cost a mint and probably did. His hair was impeccable, his nails polished and as he sat listening to the introductions from the judge, he seemed as relaxed and tranquil as anyone I had ever seen.

I, on the other hand was as nervous as a mouse in a room full of hungry cats. My company was being attacked by an insatiable giant, and we were in way over our heads.

"My name is Robert Rogaczski," my attorney said with a smile. "Lawyer for All Weather Safety Whistles."

The executive from Buck Bargain just sat there self-righteously as he stared at me as if I didn't even exist. Looked at me as if I was a tiny worm and he was about to step on me.

"Hello," Vicki said with a nervous smile, "my name is Vicki Wright, my husband and I own All Weather Safety Whistles."

Still the executive just sat and stared like this was the biggest waste of time in the world. Was it an act? Did this lawsuit really mean so little to him? My whole world was being torn apart and it seemed like he was totally unfazed.

Then I got an idea. It was a wild idea I came up with at the very last second to mix things up a little, just to "test the waters."

It was my turn to introduce myself. My turn to state who I was and then toss my business card on the table like I was tossing a dry twig on a bonfire.

In addition to being a high school wrestler, I was also on the South High School gymnastics team. My event was the stationary rings where I would perform a series of spins, handstands, front levers and the iron cross. While clearly not the best on the team, I was agile enough and powerful enough to hold my own.

As I sat in the dank room I decided that, instead of tossing my business card on the table, I would toss myself onto the table. To jump out of my chair and land like some kind of deranged alley cat right in front of Buck Bargain's senior vice president just to see how he would react.

It was my turn to introduce myself and as everyone looked my way I kicked my chair back, sprang up and landed with one knee on the table, my face moving to within an inch from the executive's nose. Balanced like a bobcat on a rock, I then screamed as loud as I could, "My name is Dr. Howard Wright and I'm the guy you're trying to destroy with your damned company!"

Vicki shouted, my attorney grabbed me, the other attorneys and the judge yelled for me to stop. Oddly enough, however, the executive didn't move. He didn't blink, he didn't flinch or try to block my advance. He truly didn't care, and it was at that moment, as I knelt an inch from his face, that I realized I was indeed up the proverbial creek without a paddle.

Two hours later, with no consensus reached, the arbitration was ended and we each went our separate ways. I had already spent thousands of dollars defending myself from the frivolous lawsuits and spent another ten thousand defending the patent. My back was up against the wall and Vicki and I were ready to give in and just agree to everything Buck Bargain wanted. Then I remembered something.

Buck Bargain was ignoring me because I was tiny and insignificant, representing nothing of any importance. I had to find some way I could represent a threat to Buck Bargain, and jumping on a table was definitely not the answer. It was clear that "doing the right thing" meant zero to Buck Bargain, daily profits their only incentive.

Actually, that was not true. Buck Bargain was a publicly traded stock where millions of dollars were invested daily based on what would happen to the stock over time. It was the public's perception of what Buck Bargain Stores would be worth in the future that mattered because it is that future value of the company that drives the all-important stock price. If we could somehow get in the news and make investors question, even in a small way, the direction Buck Bargain stores was heading, that would bring down the stock price the same way our company was being brought down. The only way Vicki and I could get that to happen was if we went all the way to the Supreme Court.

I had to unequivocally convince Buck Bargain that I was going all the way. That this lawsuit was the hill I was willing to die on and that they would not leave the fight unbloodied.

Perhaps the crazy act of jumping on the table may have been useful after all.

As we descended the stairs leaving the courthouse, I looked at my attorney and told him, "I don't care what it costs. I will sell my house and everything I own. I will drag this to the Supreme Court if I have to because we have solid documented proof they stole my idea and I will not stop till I get justice."

My attorney, after telling Vicki and I that we were out of our minds, called Buck Bargain Stores and informed them I was going the distance.

The next day we got a call from my attorney. "Buck Bargain says that they will destroy all the counterfeit whistles and pay your attorney fees."

I said, "No. I want compensation for the thousands of counterfeit whistles they already sold."

An hour later they agreed.

# Chapter 25:
# Toothpaste, the Idea

*"A problem is a chance for you to ₂o your best."*

Duke Ellington - American Composer and Pianist

It was 1998. Vicki and I had secured the revised whistle patent, streamlined the manufacturing process and after pushing back against Buck Bargain stores, were doing well enough to start putting some money aside.

There was some push back from having worked with Walmart. Despite the fact we held the line on the retail price, some companies resented our partnering up with a discount department store. We had been included in the L. L. Bean catalog and had sold a fair number of whistles but after about a year they got word that the Storm whistle was in Walmart and quickly canceled our account. Their reason was simple. They carried an exclusive line of products and couldn't be seen having any goods sold in a discount superstore. I understood.

The businesses had been running smoothly at both the All Weather Safety Whistle Company and St. Louis Dental until one day while preparing to place a simple filling, everything was suddenly pulled in a completely new direction.

"Hold on! Hold on!" the dental patient asked as he waved his hands just as I was about to give the shot. "How did you invent that whistle I've been hearing so much about?"

Clearly the question was a delay tactic. I had treated thousands of individuals and seen most every trick in the book used by apprehensive patients to put off having a shot, but I do love telling the story and if waiting a few moments would calm him down a bit, why not?

I placed the syringe back on the bracket table and smiled, "Alright. The essence of invention is filling a need. When I was a kid, I invented the Storm whistle because I needed a noisemaker that worked underwater so we could play Marco Polo and not get yelled at by frustrated moms."

I started reaching back to the table and he again called out, "I don't understand. You mean it's the old 'necessity is the mother of invention' thing?"

I turned back to my dental patient and thought for a second, "First there is a problem, then there is a solution, an invention, that solves that problem. Take, for instance, the fact that most kids don't like brushing their teeth. If only we could invent something to fix that and make kids want to brush."

Looking at me with a suction hose in the corner of his mouth, a cotton roll between his lip and his teeth, the patient asked, "So how can you make kids want to brush?"

"Well, what if we could, somehow, get the toothpaste to do the Macarena on the child's tongue; then they'd brush. If we could get the toothpaste to dance right on their tongue, we would have a winner. Right?"

"Good idea, but how could you get a toothpaste to dance?" he mumbled.

"What if instead of dancing..." I asked, "what if we could get the toothpaste to change color?"

Over the sound of the suction the patient asked, "How could you get it to change color and it still be safe to use?"

I thought out loud, "Red and blue make purple. What if we could have the toothpaste that comes out of the tube in streams of red and blue, so as the kid brushes it turns purple?"

The patient offered a crooked smile and as he did, before he even knew what I was doing, I slowly and painlessly injected a small amount of numbing solution right above his decayed tooth.

Fifty years ago, Dr. Seymour Cray, the architect who designed what would be for decades the fastest, most powerful supercomputers in the world, was asked how he could visualize the millions of parts, wires and connections and make them all work so amazingly fast. He replied, "I never used lined paper, it restricts my thoughts."

With Cray's quote in mind, I spent the rest of the day visualizing how I would build a color-changing toothpaste. Was it feasible? Would it work? Would it sell?

That night I went home, but not before stopping at our local drug store and buying two tubes of toothpaste, one red (Closeup) and one blue (Colgate Gel).

Vicki had dinner cooking on the stove and the children, Tom, Angela and Jessica were scattered around the house doing homework and watching TV. I had put together in my mind just how I would run the experiment. Moving directly to the kitchen cabinets, I grabbed a white mixing bowl and a small metal spoon.

"Kids," I called out from the kitchen. "Come here. I have a new invention I want you to see."

Tom, Angela and Jessica always enjoyed seeing things I would put together around the house and now that there was the possibility of there being a new invention in the works, they bolted into the kitchen within seconds, crowding around the table.

"What I am hoping to create is a magical new toothpaste for kids," I explained waving my hands through the air like some kind of circus entertainer. "A toothpaste that changes color as you brush."

The kids screamed their approval while Vicki smiled.

I reached into the small shopping bag, pulled out the tubes of red and blue gel toothpaste and laid two thick ribbons across the bottom of the porcelain white bowl.

Vicki, being an artist who painted landscapes in both acrylic and oils, leaned forward and laughed, knowing just where this was going,

"You're going to make the red and blue turn purple," she said with a smile.

"Don't spoil the surprise," I whispered under my breath as I slowly took the spoon, and holding it like a magic wand, gradually mixed the two toothpastes together.

As the gels combined and the colors spun, the first tinges of purple peaked through; first as soft pastels, then in striking swirls of deep purple, the colors erupted like flames from a fire, reaching in every direction.

The kids sat shocked and amazed as they watched the colors dance until suddenly, the entire mass of multicolored toothpaste turned white as snow. It was a burst of white foam that stole the color change of its brilliance. Bubbles oozed from the toothpaste, spreading out and covering the purple gel, producing a sea of white froth where a moment ago churned a purple fountain of color.

"Well," I said, as the kids sulked back, looking toward me with an air of disappointment. "That was short lived."

My son Tom reached over and picked up the bowl, pressing his fingers into the thick smudge of foamy white toothpaste and remarked "The bubbles, they're messing with your color change, Dad."

"Yes." I said with slight nod of the head and a frown, "You are correct, son."

Then all of a sudden, I had an idea.

I looked at Vicki and my children with a wide grin, grabbed my car keys off the kitchen counter and started to head to the door, but not before turning to ask, "And what gets rid of gas?"

The room was quiet.

"Gas-X. You know, the stuff that stops you from farting. Gas-X."

Vicki thought I was crazy, but the children thought I was hilarious. I burst out the door and headed back to the drug store.

Fifteen minutes later I returned with a box of Gas-X soft gel capsules.

Everyone huddled once more around the table as I held the slippery gel cap carefully between my fingertips and snipped off the end with a pair of scissors. I squeezed gently and in no time the gooey ointment, free of its ampule, flopped into the mass of bubbly toothpaste.

The foam disappeared almost instantaneously; the purple pastel that had shone before now reappeared in its previous glory.

"Oh my gosh! That is a beautiful purple," Vicki called out, excited. "You have to figure a way to deal with that foam. Can you just leave it out?"

"I don't know," I replied. "I find it hard to believe that nearly every toothpaste in the world adds a foaming agent just for the heck of it."

"Could it be that the froth helps the toothpaste clean your teeth?" Vicki mused as she stuck the spoon into the purple goo at the bottom of the bowl.

"I'll do some reading online and in the journals." I commented, "I'll also search around to see if any kind of color-changing toothpaste has been patented. No use wasting our time on something we aren't legally allowed to make."

I spent the next month searching through the internet to see if there was any mention of a color-changing toothpaste patent and found nothing in the literature. There was still, however, the all-important question concerning the color eliminating foaming agent and whether or not it was a critical ingredient in the toothpaste.

With the whistles doing great and the dental office running smoothly, I wasn't particularly motivated to start a new project, until about a week later when I came upon something very special while reading one of my dental journals.

I was sitting at my desk at lunch when I happened upon an article that referenced a study written up in the Scandinavian Journal of Dental Medicine. The article stated that after completing a prolonged study, it was found that there was a dramatic increase in the number of canker sores found in both adults and children when a toothpaste was used that contained a foaming agent. The researchers went on to say that there was no clinical reason for the foaming agent, sodium lauryl sulfate (SLS) to be in toothpaste, especially in children's toothpaste. Furthermore, it was stated that SLS should be removed completely from toothpaste and that the only reason it was added nearly two hundred years ago was so that the paste looked like it was doing something.

I called Vicki directly and told her this entire idea of developing a "SLS-free" color-changing toothpaste might just work. I studied further and found that the reason kids complained so much about brushing their teeth was largely two-fold in nature. The primary reason kids hated brushing was because the SLS that caused the foaming, burned their mouths. In case after case, kids complained that the toothpaste tasted "hot."

This burning of the child's tongue and mouth occurred as quickly as five seconds after the children started brushing and was caused by the extremely caustic nature of the SLS foam. As I looked into the literature, I was amazed at the number of cases where the SLS chemical got into a worker's eyes, nose or mouth, causing severe burns. Why a children's toothpaste contained that same ingredient that initially aggravated the tissues and then actually caused open sores seemed beyond moronic.

The second and equally important reason why kids hated brushing was because of the way the foam from toothpaste blocked the back of their throat. Before the age of six, a child's nasopharynx is vastly underdeveloped, making breathing through the nose nearly impossible. With difficult nose breathing and a mouth half filled with burning toothpaste foam, a child spends as much time in misery as they do cleaning their teeth.

Between the burning of the SLS foaming agent and the thick mass of bubbles clogging half the child's mouth, the recommendation by the American Dental Association that kids brush their teeth for a full two minutes was foolish. If, however, I could make a SLS-free toothpaste that could save kids from the burning, the choking, and the canker sores, while at the same time entertaining them with a mesmerizing color change, they might just be able to brush the required two minutes happily rather, than with tears.

It was now time to find a qualified patent attorney to search the prior art to see if my idea was indeed novel. I had to know definitively if someone already held the patent on the idea of mixing primary colors in order to create a secondary color as a tooth brushing timer. If I was indeed the first to come up with the idea, I had to grab it first. Most importantly, I had to find an attorney that could actually see the patent process through without messing up the entire procedure.

I searched around and found a person who was considered by many to be the number one patent attorney in St. Louis. He specialized primarily in pharmaceuticals, worked at one of the largest firms in the state of Missouri and came with a slew of great recommendations. We met in his large corner office where he asked all the right questions and told me he would start the patent search straight away.

Three weeks later I received the good news. While other inventors had come up with bizarre and complicated ways of having toothpaste change color using acids and bases or time releasing capsules, I was the first person to ever think of mixing colors of toothpaste in order to get kids to brush longer. Two months after that, the patent was submitted, and I officially had a patent pending on the world's first color-changing toothpaste.

# Chapter 26:
# SmithKline Beecham

*"In preparing for battle I have always foun• that plans are useless, but planning is in• ispensable."*

Dwight D. Eisenhower - 34th U.S. President

Having a great idea is just the start. It is a fantastic start, but it's still just the start. With the knowledge that we had a really cool idea that could change the way kids all across America brushed their teeth, Vicki and I sat at the kitchen table and tried to decide what we would do next.

To bring the color-changing toothpaste to market came down to basically two options. We could either sell the idea to someone else to produce or we could manufacture it ourselves.

Selling the idea was simpler, cheaper and had less risk. Doing it ourselves gave us more control and more profit, but was also much more difficult, time consuming and we ran the risk of losing a great deal of money.

"Let me try to sell it," I told Vicki. "Let me see what the mega toothpaste manufacturers like Colgate or Crest think of the idea."

Having decided to try to peddle the color-changing toothpaste, I went straight to my basement office where I sat down and, after two hours of struggle, wrote pitch letters to three of the largest toothpaste manufacturers in America.

*Hello,*
*My name is Dr. Howar• Wright. I am a successful •entist an• inventor*

*of the Storm All-Weather Safety Whistle, the lou•est whistle in the worl•.*

*The reason for my letter is that I just obtaine• a patent pen•ing for the most amazing color-changing toothpaste ever ma•e an• woul• like to show it to you. If you want to meet, just sen• me a note. It will knock your socks off.*

*Sincerely,*

*Dr. Howar• W. Wright*

*Presi•ent St. Louis Dental*

*CEO All Weather Safety Whistle Co.*

Within two weeks I got responses from all three companies. Colgate-Palmolive said no thanks, Procter & Gamble (makers of Crest) said no thanks, SmithKline Beecham (makers of Aquafresh) said they would talk to me, but only if I flew out at my own expense.

Vicki got two plane tickets to New Jersey's Newark Liberty International Airport, made reservations at a cheap motel fifteen minutes from SmithKline's headquarters in Parsippany and rented a car to get us there.

We landed in the morning and drove straight to the one o'clock appointment. We parked our rental car in a huge parking lot, left our luggage in the trunk and walked hand in hand slowly toward the headquarters of one of the largest toothpaste manufacturers in the world. I carried my old briefcase that held the same white porcelain bowl from our kitchen, along with a mockup of the toothpaste tube and a couple of white toothbrushes that would best show the color change.

It was strange as we entered through the tall glass doors of SmithKline Beecham's twelve story building. As we registered at the front desk, I learned that they had been in business for over a hundred and fifty years, samples of their products both from the middle eighteenth century to present day proudly on display.

Within less than five minutes of arriving, we were met by an executive secretary, issued badges, signed nondisclosure agreements and were taken upstairs to the top floor.

The elevator opened directly into a boardroom and as Vicki and I stepped out, we were immediately awed by the expanse of the room. It had dark wood paneling covering the walls, oil paintings of old men that looked like they belonged in a museum and floor to ceiling windows overlooking a river far below. If it was the intent of the architect to impress anyone entering the room, it worked.

The room was uncluttered. At its center stood a huge marble table that ran for at least fourteen feet in length; against a far wall was a podium and behind that rested a huge executive desk.

"Welcome to SmithKline Beecham," the executive greeted us both with a handshake, the executive secretary standing to his right. "I'm Jeff Narzinski. So, what do you have for us?"

There was no messing around. No small talk. We got right to business.

With the slightest of smiles, Vicki stepped back, and I, like an entertainer in a Los Vegas lounge show, stepped forward.

"A toothpaste, Mr. Narzinski. A toothpaste that changes color like nothing you've ever seen. There are no chemical reactions, but instead this is so simple every mom in America will wish they had thought of it first." I opened my briefcase and placed the porcelain bowl and toothbrushes on the table.

With one slow squeeze, I then laid a single line of multicolored toothpaste on the bristles of the stark white toothbrush, the dual lines of red and blue running side by side like a twin-colored railroad track. "Now watch!" I called out.

Taking the toothbrush, I slowly spun the red and blue together on the bottom of the porcelain bowl like an artist preparing to paint. As I rotated the brush in tight circles, I watched the executive lean forward in wonder, speechless, as the beautiful purple gradually seeped from the melding pastes, first slowly and then in a torrent of color.

"Oh my gosh," I could hear the secretary whisper from behind.

"We've removed the Sodium Lauryl Sulfate, the SLS, so the color persists," I explained. "Children complain that toothpaste feels hot, that it burns them. Not anymore."

I handed Mr. Narzinski the toothpaste and a brush. He squeezed out a thin line of red and blue paste across the side of the bowl and mixed it himself.

"What does it taste like?" he asked, a tinge of anger in his voice. An irritation that surprised me and set me aback.

"It can be any flavor. We made this bubblegum grape," Vicki interjected.

Mr. Narzinski tasted it with his fingertip.

"Dr. Wright, did you bring the patent application like we asked?" Mr. Narzinski inquired, hard and impatient. It was as if there was suddenly something wrong, his tone more like a coach frustrated with a losing team.

"Yes, it's right here," I replied as I handed him a copy of the documentation. After a cursory review, he passed it on to his secretary.

"All right," Mr. Narzinski called out as he turned to me and, after composing himself, asked. "Can you give this same demonstration once more for the staff? Is that ok?"

"Sure" I said, curious as to where this was going.

"Helen," Mr. Narzinski called out to his secretary. "Get the entire staff in here. I want the chemists, the marketing people and counsel. Everybody. Right Now. And Helen, get Mary Ann in here to set up the Wrights."

Within moments people started to arrive. Helen was organizing the room while Mr. Narzinski was speaking quickly on the phone. It seemed like we had caused quite a stir and as Vicki and I stood with our backs to the large windows overlooking the wintery landscape of New Jersey, it seemed like we may have just pulled the golden ticket.

"What's going on?" Vicki mouthed to me as another group of scientists hurriedly entered the room. They all wore long white coats and expressions of the utmost seriousness. Among the group walked another woman in an exquisite business suit, middle-aged and very uppermanagemt-esque, carrying a thick sheaf of papers. After a short discussion with Mr. Narzinski, she walked straight up to Vicki and introduced herself.

Before I had a chance to find out what Vicki was up to, Mr. Narzinski called me over to the head of the conference table where I positioned my just-cleaned mixing bowl, toothbrushes and handmade tube of color-changing toothpaste.

I waited and watched as the last of the stragglers entered the conference room. There were probably fifteen people, most of them wearing the same kind of white coat and stern expression, not one of them dared to sit down. Along the dark paneled wall near Mr. Narzinski's desk stood two executive types in thousand-dollar suits. They looked like lawyers, their eyes dark and scrutinizing as they watched me lay out my wares.

"Excuse me," Mr. Narzinski raised his voice to the group. "I want to know why I pay all of you so much damn money and you give me nothing in return? Then, out of the blue, this solo dentist out of St. Louis comes up to me with this idea?"

The room was silent.

"Dr. Wright," Mr. Narzinski said turning to me, "would you please show us what you have?"

Suddenly I decided to change direction. I didn't like the idea that I was being portrayed as a wacky dentist that happened to come up with a new invention out of blind luck. That developing an idea like a color-changing toothpaste was simply the product of a silly dream that popped into my head after eating spicy meatballs before going to bed.

The act of developing a new idea is difficult and demands research and hard work. Standing before SmithKline Beecham's scientists and executives, after being introduced that way, created a single image in my mind. It was the image of Sir Isaac Newton.

The story is told that way back in 1677, a newspaper reporter approached Newton, arguably one of the greatest mathematicians and physicists ever to walk the planet, and asked him how it was that he came up with his theories on planetary motion and gravitational physics. It is said that Newton, looked at the reporter and replied sarcastically that he was sitting under an apple tree one day when suddenly an apple fell, hit him in the head and "*voilá*" all the equations and theorems describing how planets rotated around the sun just came to him in a flash. The reporter, not realizing that Newton was mocking him, wrote the "apple story" as fact.

I reached back into my briefcase, dug through my papers and folders and after a quick search found what I was looking for. I had thrown it in at the last moment. I held the bright fluorescent orange Storm whistle high over my head and cleared my throat. Facing the group, I called out loudly, "This is the Storm whistle, the loudest whistle in the world. I invented it when I was fourteen years old. Eight years ago, I started manufacturing and marketing it. This whistle is totally waterproof and even works underwater and is being sold all over the world. Most importantly, it has saved many lives."

I leaned forward and slid the whistle across the table until it stopped a little over halfway down. "What I have now is a color-changing toothpaste that makes brushing fun, entices kids to brush three times longer and, most importantly, is healthy for the children's teeth and gums."

I demonstrated the toothpaste.

They loved it.

Questions were asked, explanations were presented and demonstrations performed as I described how the new color-changing toothpaste could change the way kids brush their teeth forever. Finally, after a little over twenty minutes, I pulled myself from the group and returned to Vicki who was waving me to her side.

"They want to change everything around," she whispered wide eyed with delight. "They want to change our hotel to one in downtown Manhattan."

"New York?" I asked confused. "How are we going to get there?"

"Helicopter," Vicki said with a smile. "Helen says they will take care of the rental car and hotel we reserved for tonight."

"OK. So, then, how are we going to get back to the airport?" I asked more confused than ever. "We need to get back to the kids and your sister by tomorrow."

"Dr. Wright," Helen interrupted gently, "we hope you will let us reimburse you for your flights here and organize two first class tickets for you and Vicki to return to St. Louis tomorrow?"

"You are getting us first class flights back home for tomorrow?"

"Yes. And we have tickets to all the shows on Broadway. We would also like to pay for all your meals; just save all your receipts for cabs and drinks and whatever. We will reimburse you completely."

Shrugging our shoulders, Vicki and I agreed just as one of the executives approached.

He introduced himself as an attorney for SmithKline Beecham Pharmaceuticals. As he spoke, he handed me a short two-page contract, "I know this is happening fast, but I'd like you to look over this contract."

The second the executive secretary suggested we change our hotel, the warning bells in my mind started flashing. Now, with this attorney handing me a contract, the alarms hit DEFCON 1.

All I could think of was RUN AWAY and don't look back.

A contract is the weapon of choice for any lawyer and this moron had just pulled his blade from his scabbard and was flashing the steel right in my face.

"Please, just read the first paragraph," he said, his hands held up like a bank teller being robbed. "It says you are signing this without counsel and that the contract can be nullified, ripped up and thrown away at any time. It is being offered to you to show our level of commitment to your invention."

I read the first paragraph. "Ok, so this is not binding. What does the rest of the contract say?"

"We are offering you a minimum of $250,000 per year for five years plus three percent against the gross sales of any of the color-changing toothpaste."

I tried to hold back a grin as I read the rest of the contract. "So, just out of curiosity, what was your sales for kids toothpaste last year?"

"Around fifty million dollars."

Vicki looked at me and I looked at Vicki. "What do you need from us?"

The lawyer looked at us both. "Your signatures, and once the patent goes through, the rights to manufacture the first ever color-changing toothpaste."

We spent the helicopter flight watching the skyline of Manhattan pass beneath us as the Vice-President of Marketing rattled on about the different ways we could package the toothpaste. We took a cab from the heliport to an amazing hotel with gold faucets and thick soft carpets. We had dinner, slept through the last half of Fiddler on the Roof, had drinks, New York cheesecake and the next morning jumped on a first class flight back to St. Louis. All told, the receipts for a single night in New York added up to a little over twenty-five hundred dollars.

# Chapter 27:
# The Hammer Falls

*"The most beautiful people we have known are those who have known ◆efeat, known suffering, known struggle, known loss, an◆ have foun◆ their way out of those ◆epths."*

Elisabeth Kubler-Ross -
Swiss-American Psychiatrist

All that was necessary for us to solidify our relationship with SmithKline was to complete our color-changing toothpaste patent. My attorney had submitted the paperwork three months before and now it was simply a matter of waiting for the U.S. Patent and Trademark office to complete its work.

Up until that point, I had received two phone calls from Mr. Narzinski, the executive from SmithKline, asking about the status of the patent and how things were developing. I called the patent office to see where things stood.

"Hello, my name is Dr. Howard Wright and I am looking to speak to Larry Rosen. He is handling my patent for my color-changing toothpaste."

"I'm Examiner Rosen," the man replied. "How can I help you?"

"I was curious to know how things are going," I said. "What does the timeline on completion of the patent look like?"

"If you don't mind," Examiner Rosen asked, "what is the hurry?"

"Well," I responded feeling pretty good about myself, "I have a ten-tative contract with SmithKline Beecham, and everything is depen-dent on me getting this patent through."

"I am sorry to say," Rosen remarked, "That I don't have any mate-rial concerning a color-changing toothpaste here."

"My attorney sent it four months ago," I groaned. "It was my understanding that you are the Examiner of record."

"Well, this is the U. S. Government, you know, and things get lost here all the time," Rosen commented causally. "Just have your attorney resend it and we will take care of our end straight away."

I agreed and hung up. "Lost?" I couldn't believe it! The entire deal being held in the balance and now the patent is lost? I called my attorney the next day.

"We'll mail another copy of the patent to Examiner Rosen," my attorney remarked a little too nonchalantly. "I will get it out tomorrow."

By the middle of the next week I called the patent office again and got Larry Rosen on the phone.

"Hello, this is Howard Wright. I just wanted to know if that color-changing toothpaste patent application showed up. We sent it last week."

"Nope, nothing here yet," he replied, frustrated. "Why don't you send it again. I've worked here for twenty years and never known a patent to get lost three times in a row. I will let the mailroom know it's on its way."

I hung up and called my attorney again, "What is going on? This is crazy."

"Yes," he said, "this is very odd. Let's send the patent again. I will make sure it is sent priority and registered, one day express mail. Then let's see where we stand."

Four days later I called the Patent and Trademark office and asked to speak with examiner Larry Rosen. "Did you get it? The patent. The color-changing patent? If you haven't received it, I swear I will get on a plane and hand it to you personally if need be."

"Oh, I received the paperwork this morning," Examiner Rosen chuckled. "But it is all wrong. Your attorney doesn't know what he's doing. He is making all kinds of mistakes. You have clearly hired the wrong attorney."

"The wrong attorney?" I asked shocked. "He's one of the finest pharmaceutical patent attorneys in St. Louis."

"You may think so," Examiner Rosen replied slowly, "but I have a friend in New Jersey who could write this beautifully and in no time. He is a little expensive, though."

"Really?" I ask, my voice turning bitter at the suggestion. "How expensive?"

"Pay him fifty thousand dollars and I can guarantee that the patent will be yours, quick as spit." he said with the confidence of a professional embezzler. "If you choose, however, to keep your own attorney, this patent will never go through. Never!"

I held the phone's receiver tight in my hand as I could feel my blood pressure rise. I couldn't believe it. An agent from the United States Patent and Trademark Office was shaking me down; he was trying to kidnap my patent and hold it ransom. This thief was trying to embezzle fifty thousand dollars from me in return for a completed patent.

"No." I responded through gritted teeth. "I don't work that way. We do it straight, no money under the table, no shady deals. I came up with the idea of a color-changing toothpaste, this is my invention and I'm not giving in to your threats."

"Have it your way," he chuckled.

He hung up.

I immediately called my attorney and told him what had happened.

He didn't believe me.

"What?" I ranted on the phone. "You think I'm making this up?"

"I am just saying, Howard, that you must have misinterpreted what he said."

"Oh, well, what the patent examiner said was that you're a horrible attorney and I should use one of his choosing. That if I gave this "other attorney" fifty grand then this would go through like crap through a duck. Otherwise it will never happen."

"Well, I can't answer to that," my attorney replied, acting as if he got this kind of call every day. "I am just saying we should hold strong and wait him out."

I hung up and redialed the only other person I felt I could trust, the only other person that seemed to be on my side and wanted this to go through. I called Jeff Narzinski, the executive from SmithKline Beecham.

"Hello, this is Howard Wright with the color-changing toothpaste."

"Yes, Howard," Mr. Narzinski answered. "How are things progressing with the patent? Are we good to go?"

"Well, that is why I am calling," I told him. "We are having a problem with the patent."

"Let me guess," he replied, a sad hollow somberness to his voice. "You got Examiner Larry Rosen handling your patent."

"Yes, exactly. How did you know it was Rosen?"

"Dr. Wright, SmithKline Beecham has been in the business of making toothpaste for over a century and we've seen it all. Are you going to pay him?"

"No." I answered.

"Well, that is admirable. I'll have our attorneys write letters questioning the hold up. Maybe we can convince him to play it straight."

It made me sick to think that this goes on all the time; that this was almost commonplace in our government. Like an idiot I thought I was the only one that ever had been embezzled, defrauded by the very people we payed to protect us. Now it seemed like it was the way that our and every other government worked and that I better get on board or pay the consequences.

SmithKline wrote the letters to Larry Rosen in an attempt to get things moving ahead and so did I, but nothing came of our attempts to get things moving forward. The patent was stalled, and we never did get any cooperation from the patent office.

My own personal patent lawyer said over and over that we should sit tight and let things run their course, that if we just stood back and waited, it would all work out at some point; but nothing did "work out."

Six months passed, then a year, then two years.

It was two and a half years after our first meeting with SmithKline that I dejectedly got the letter that I knew would be coming; SmithKline Beecham rescinded the contract to buy the toothpaste. They said that because I couldn't secure a patent for the color-changing toothpaste, the deal was off.

It was many years later that I came to understand, at least partially, why my spineless attorney did nothing when I told him how I was being extorted by Examiner Rosen from the patent office. I learned the truth while watching the wonderful 2008 movie "Flash of Genius".

In the true-to-life movie, the story is told of how the auto industry attempts to steal the intermittent windshield wiper patent from the inventor Robert Kearns. Kearns' patent attorney, in an act of self-sacrifice, encourages Kearns to fire him and find another attorney to sue the auto industry. The reason Kearns' attorney asked to be fired was because he knew that to participate in a lawsuit against the car makers, the very clients he depended on for business, would be financial suicide. Robert Kearns fired his attorney and ended up winning a settlement equaling nearly 30 million dollars from the auto industry.

In my case, I had asked my attorney, who's entire career revolved around pharmaceuticals and the U.S. Patent Office, to investigate the very people he depended on for his livelihood. My attorney, unlike Robert Kearns' attorney, had no scruples and instead of asking me to release him and expose the extortion, instead refused to defend me and became part and parcel to the larceny.

If I was smarter, I would have seen through my attorney's selfishness and fired him straight out, hired another lawyer to attack the patent office and perhaps sued my attorney for his malfeasance. Like an idiot, I foolishly thought things would work out and instead of exposing the thieves, I ended up with nothing.

I was devastated. Despite the fact that I thought I couldn't feel any worse after being embezzled by the U.S. Patent Office and losing the toothpaste contract, I received more bad news. Walmart, after ten years of growing sales, discontinued the whistle and replaced it with a cheap Chinese sports whistle. The only positive aspect to the entire Walmart rejection ordeal was that they didn't copy the shape of the whistle, but instead replaced it with a "New" Chinese whistle that was both cheap and toy-like.

There is an old adage that states that bad news happens in threes, and in my case, it bore true as true can be. Three months after losing the toothpaste and one month after losing Walmart, the third piece of bad news arrived in the form of one of my dental patients who, as a part-time ambulance chasing lawyer, sued me for malpractice.

It all started when I received a call from her at around eight in the evening at my home.

"Hello. Is this Dr. Wright?" the woman on the phone asked.

"Yes, who is this?"

"I am a patient of yours, I've been going to you for about three years. I am just calling to tell you that I am going to sue you for malpractice. I just want to tell you that if you just agree to settle, that your insurance company will pay everything and there won't be any problem."

"What the hell are you talking about?" I yelled into the phone, "Malpractice? Won't be any problem? Is this some kind of sick joke?"

"I am just asking for $80,000, which your insurance will pay without a fight. But if you argue this and take this to court, I will go for punitive damages and take your license to practice dentistry."

"What?" I yelled into the phone, "Who is this?"

"I am just saying, don't take this personally. Just let your insurance company handle it and there won't be any problem."

"Don't take it personally? Screw you!" I screamed and slammed the phone down.

The next day I was served with papers outlining her malpractice suit.

She worked for one of those contemptable law firms that advertise on park benches and billboards and now she was acting as her own attorney against me, accusing me of not telling her she had gum disease. The court documents said that because I didn't notify her of the gum problem, she was now facing the possibility of losing her teeth and that I was responsible. I needed to pay for any and all dental work she may need in the future.

I remember distinctly laying sleepless in bed as I tried to figure out if I had indeed made the mistake of not diagnosing her gum disease. I was disturbed to my very core at the idea that I could have treated her for three years and that neither I nor my dental hygienists noticed any gum problems. If she truly had gum disease and I failed to either fix it or refer her to a periodontist, that was indeed malpractice.

The next day I arrived early to the dental office, checked the patient's dental chart and saw that she had indeed visited my office, clearly had gum disease and that there was nothing to indicate I informed her of the problem.

The dental chart is a legal record detailing everything that transpires during the treatment of a patent. I dictate to my dental assistant and it is the assistant's job to write down what I see and how I plan to respond to any problems I do detect.

In this patient's case, the chart did show that I found periodontal disease and that the gum problem had progressed fairly far and could indeed result in her losing her teeth. There was nothing further written down as to what I did next, if anything. According to the chart and the chart alone, I found the gum disease, wrote down the presence of the gum disease, but stopped right there and never gave the patient any further instructions.

In twenty years of dentistry I have never left a cavity or gum problem left unattended; maybe the patient was the one who made the mistake and just forgotten that I told her to get treatment and my assistant forgot to write it down?

I decided to fight the lawsuit.

True to her word she, withdrew the request for $80,000 and was now suing me for $250,000 and trying to take my dental license for seeing a problem, but not fixing it.

I underwent hours of depositions, sat through meetings with experts and months of worry as I met with attorneys, always with the blatant fact staring me right in the face: I clearly wrote down in the chart that she had gum problems, but there is nothing written down about me telling her of the periodontal disease and there was no referral to a periodontist. If I truly forgot to tell her of the problems she had and if I truly failed to refer her to a periodontist, then I was truly guilty.

Maybe I just made a mistake? I had thousands of patients and I treated each one for a myriad of problems. Maybe I didn't tell her. Maybe I just forgot. Maybe I am guilty.

The actual civil trial was about four weeks away. The hearing before the Missouri Dental Board where they would decide if I should lose my license was two weeks away. It was then, with my back against the wall, that I had an idea. Something my attorneys or I should have thought of months ago.

Lying in bed at three in the morning, Vicki asleep alongside me, I wondered to myself, "What if I did in fact advise her that there was a problem?"

I was a good dentist. I tried my best always to treat patients properly. What if she was setting me up? What if I did tell her she had gum problems and she decided to ignore my recommendation to get it fixed and my staff just didn't write it down?

It happened all the time. I would tell a patient that they have a wisdom tooth that needs extracting and then send them to an oral surgeon. It was their choice to get the procedure done. What if, rather than me being negligent in not telling her she had a problem, instead she just ignored my advice to get treated by a specialist, a periodontist?

If I did indeed tell her that she had a gum problem, I would have sent her to one of four different periodontists that I knew and referred patients to in the St. Louis area. Maybe they had a record of her visiting them or contacting them and then she backed out of the treatment?

The next morning upon arriving at the dental office, I wrote down the names of the four periodontists I worked with and their phone numbers. One by one I called the periodontal offices, giving them the rough time frame and asking if they had seen or been contacted by the patient.

It was twenty minutes later that I got a call from the office of a specialist in Crestwood, a small municipality thirty minutes from my office.

"Hello, Dr. Wright," the receptionist replied. "You asked if a patient named Jane Jones contacted our office in August."

"Yes," I answered my eyes shut in anticipation. "Did she ever see you or visit your office as a patient?"

"Well, yes," the receptionist said. "I looked back in our scheduling book and she made an appointment for a periodontal evaluation, root plaining and scaling just a few days after that date you gave me, but it says here in our ledger that she canceled it two days before the work was to be done. It says she wanted to postpone the procedure till a later date. She never called back."

It was as if the weight of six months of pain, frustration and heartache had just been wiped away in one powerful swipe. The periodontal office had done what I failed to do, they documented everything.

"Please," I asked as calm as possible. "Can you copy that page and send it to me by FAX today?"

"Of course," the receptionist replied. "You'll get it in just a minute."

I thanked her profusely.

The patient lied. I did tell her she had gum problems and I did tell her to go to a periodontist and I, as a matter of fact, gave her a referral to a periodontist to get her gums treated. She lied about everything. She didn't tell anyone that she made an appointment and then canceled her appointment with the specialist. She lied about the entire episode and was willing to destroy my reputation, revoke my dental license and ruin my office all for $250,000. She was a lying thief.

I was completely exonerated by the Missouri Dental Board and three weeks later, was found not guilty by the Circuit Court of Missouri. She, on the other hand was found guilty of misrepresenting herself, lying to the court and therefore was responsible for paying my legal fees.

After the ordeals with the toothpaste, Walmart and dental office law suit, I decided it was time to make a change.

Losing Walmart was a hit, but it wasn't unexpected. We knew that at any moment they could drop us, and with that understanding, made a point of putting all the money we earned into a special account for our retirement. We always considered every dollar we made off Walmart a gift.

My failure to acquire the toothpaste patent, however, was incredibly tough on me though. I believed in the idea and could see millions of kids all over the world using the color-changing toothpaste. What was even worse, SmithKline Beecham understood the simplicity and value to the idea and was willing to put money and resources behind it. Losing the toothpaste was a major hit for me.

It took me a great deal of time to forgive Larry Rosen from the patent office who destroyed my dream with his greed. In his attempt to embezzle $50,000 from me he ended up stealing a great toothpaste from the smiles of children all over the world. But I forgave him, or at least I think I have forgiven him. Sometimes I cannot help but remember the disappointment that squeezed my heart when I was told by Rosen that I would never get the patent.

The dental office lawsuit hit me in a way that was different and strangely more personal than how I felt with Walmart or SmithKline. I will never forget how the selfish, lying dental patient told me that first night I shouldn't "take it personally." But that's crazy! I had always seen myself as a caring and decent dentist, so when that witch of an attorney lied about me and tried to steal the money and threatened to take my dental license, I couldn't help but be hurt down to my soul.

I continued to work drilling, filling and billing, always careful to write everything down in the patient's chart, but the joy I had creating beautiful smiles had diminished. Was there another patient right around the corner willing to destroy my career and put me through that pain again in order to turn a quick buck? Dentistry is a unique combination of art, engineering, medicine and a doctor's passion for the patient. Unfortunately, the litigation knocked the passion out of the entire equation, leaving behind nothing but work. I decided to make a change.

I didn't need to put St. Louis Dental on the market to sell it. Barnes Hospital, one of the largest hospitals in the area, had been trying to establish an organization of dentists to serve the St. Louis area and needed the downtown area to complete their network. To that end, they contacted my office about every three months suggesting we hook up and work together.

What drew Barnes Hospital to want to acquire St. Louis Dental was not just because of its location or the number of patients we had or even the professionals we employed. What I think Barnes really wanted out of my practice was my close association with the labor unions.

# Chapter 28:
# Starting Anew

*"Change is the law of life. An• those who look only to the past or present are certain to miss the future."*

John F. Kennedy - 35th U.S. President

Late in my sophomore year at Washington University School of Dental Medicine, I was invited by my soon to be brother-in-law Stan's house for a get-together with a bunch of guys who were going to watch a Cardinals baseball game. Understanding proper party etiquette, I brought along a large bag of chips and a six pack of beer. What I didn't understand was that, during that time, many people considered St. Louis a one beer town and that all other breweries were strictly taboo and never to be touched.

"Hi, Howard," Stan greeted me. "I'm glad you could make it."

Yeah," I said as I shook his hand, "it should be a good game."

"Uh? What is that?" he said, pointing down to the six pack of Coors.

"Well," I answered. "I like beer."

"Yeah, sure, but what's with the Coors?"

"It's cold and refreshing and I've drank it since I was in college."

Stan just stared at me and shook his head slowly. "No. Come with me."

I followed him through the living room and back to the kitchen where he grabbed the six pack of Coors from my hand and held it up as if he was holding a dead rat by the tail.

"Howard," Stan explained, "St. Louis is a strict union town. Here we buy only union beer made by Anheuser Busch"

"You're joking, right?"

Stan tossed the Coors into the trash and opened the refrigerator. Inside, between the plastic containers of leftovers, milk and eggs were two kinds of beer, Michelob and Busch, both made by Anheuser Busch. He leaned down, grabbed two beers and handed me one.

"Nobody jokes about the unions."

And I never forgot that.

In downtown St. Louis there were a large number of very large unions. There was a union for the postal workers, the railroad, the power company, the police and another for Anheuser Busch. All in all, there are as many as fifty unions in St. Louis, each and every one employing tens of thousands of fully insured downtown workers.

What I realized early on was that by catering to a union's insurance companies, I could secure a top position with the workers, and by treating those individuals promptly, competently and with respect, I could then be seen as part of the "union shop." In the same way that Stan insisted that I honor the union label when I drank beer, employees of the downtown unions started to see my office the same way, beating a path to my door.

Barnes Hospital, appreciating the power of having a close relationship with the unions, came to me with a proposition. They offered to buy my office for a great deal of money along with a three-year contract to work four days a week making more than I was making before working sixty hours a week. I wouldn't have to run the office, pay the bills or worry about insurance. In exchange I could spend more time doing just dentistry and have more time to be with my family.

I took it.

It was a wonderful three years having three-day weekends and spending more time with Vicki and my children. I hadn't realized how much pressure I was dealing with every day taking care of the dental office, dealing with employees, insurance companies and all the equipment it took to make the office work.

Before I knew it, the contract was up, three years had come and gone. About that time, I received a letter from Barnes Hospital saying they liked what I had done over the past years and requested that I re-new the contract and stay on for another three years with a pay raise. It seemed like a good idea and I asked them to stop by with a contract, which I signed.

My twin daughters, Angela and Jessica, had just completed the sev-enth grade at a wonderful Catholic school that taught girls from kindergarten through high school. Despite having done very well and excelled, oddly enough my daughter Angela approached Vicki and I saying she wanted to make a change.

"Dad? Mom?" Angela said as we sat down for dinner. "I don't think I want to go to Visitation next year."

"I don't understand," I said. "I thought you liked it there."

Angela looked at me, and after thinking for a moment said, "I do like the school, it's been great."

"So why the change?" Vicki asked.

"Well," Angela said, looking at us both. "I've been at Visitation Academy since first grade and I'm just afraid that five years from now I will have the same friends, the same teachers, the same cafeteria, the same everything and I want something different."

Angela made the change.

I got a call two days later from the executive from Barnes Hospital.

"Dr. Wright." he stammered nervously. "I have some bad news. We can't find your contract anywhere. I know you signed it, but it's nowhere to be found. Is there any possibility you could stop by our office and sign another copy?"

"Sure," I said. "I can stop by after work and we can get this thing finished up."

That evening I drove to the corporate offices of Barnes Hospital where I found the executive waiting for me with the new contract.

"I am truly sorry for this inconvenience," he apologized. "I don't know where the contract could have disappeared to."

"No problem." I commented as I read through the new contract, making sure nothing had changed.

Then picking up a pen I prepared to sign on the dotted line, but I stopped. I couldn't sign it. All I could think of was my daughter Angela.

"I am so sorry," I said putting the pen down, the unsigned contract lying on the table. "I am not going to be able to sign this."

The executive was stunned, "I don't understand. Did you want more money? Did you want a company car?"

"No," I laughed, "it's just that, three year from now, something tells me that I will be sitting at this same desk signing this same piece of paper." Then after a half second, I stood up and shook the manager's hand and said, "Three years from now I will have the same friends, the same teachers, the same cafeteria, the same everything and I want something different."

I turned and walked away from dentistry.

# Chapter 29:
# Teaching

*"When you have solve◦ the problem of controlling the attention of the chil◦, you have solve◦ the entire problem of its e◦ucation."*

Maria Montessori - Italian Physician and Educator

Vicki helped me decide what I was going to do after dentistry. It was a couple of months before I officially retired from St. Louis Dental and we were working late at night in the basement filling orders. We had made an agreement that we would not work past midnight and we were five minutes from our self-imposed quitting time.

"This order is for Canada," I replied as I put twelve blister-packed orange Storm whistles into a small shipper box and taped it closed. "They want two hundred eighty-eight total, so we need only six more of these to complete the purchase order."

Vicki didn't respond. Typically, we chatted as we worked; we talked about the kids, whistles, what was going on with her or what was going on with me, but now it was quiet.

"And that police and security catalog we just picked up," I said from the other side of the worktable. "They have a circulation of like twenty thousand, so that could be really good."

Vicki just kept her head down and continued filling out an invoice sheet, folding it over so the address showed clearly then quickly slipped it into one of those windowed adhesive envelopes. Walking over to where I was filling the order, she unceremoniously stuck it to the top of the box, smoothed it down and turned away.

It was at that moment that I noticed she was crying.

"What's wrong?" I asked, totally unaware of anything that could cause her to be so upset.

Vicki turned and looked at me, sadly wiped away her tears and said, "You know I never wanted to work in a warehouse. I always wanted to be a teacher."

I immediately stopped what I was doing and got up, walked over to where she was standing and hugged her. In the time it took for me to walk across the basement floor, I understood why she was crying, why she seemed so sad and how I was responsible.

"I am sorry," I said taking her hands in mine. "For the last twenty years everything has been either about the children or about me. Everything."

"It's ok," she muttered trying to turn away. "Really, I'm just tired."

"No, it's not ok." I said holding her softly. "Go back to school, study to be a teacher. Really, I think it would be great."

"Are you serious?" she said with an odd smile.

"Serious?" I shuddered at the accusation, "Call tomorrow and find out when classes start. I bet some of your nursing school classes will transfer."

"I'll do that," she grinned. "I'll call tomorrow," and she kissed me.

I was lying, of course. Just the idea of Vicki becoming a teacher and running off by herself to do something new and exciting without me left me feeling empty and alone. As a teacher, she would have summers off, interact with young people and learn all kinds of new things while I was considering going to law school to be a patent attorney (ugh).

So, in order to stay part of Vicki's life I, for the first time ever, considered becoming a high school teacher. This was a completely crazy idea since I truly hated school; for me, school was both confusing and demeaning. Being in school was torture. It was like I was in some kind of twelve-year long obstacle-course wearing a hundred pound pack, lost, and without a map or compass.

When I told Vicki that I was also thinking of teaching, she thought I had lost my mind and to a large degree she was absolutely right.

It was three years prior, while Vicki and I were visiting my parents in California, that my mother unceremoniously dropped an old box of mementos from my childhood at our feet. My parents were trying desperately to get everything cleared out of their cluttered closets and it seemed that in my case, that battered cardboard box represented the last of the items I had been storing at their house.

The carton was loaded with everything from outdated video tapes to my yellowed high school yearbooks, but it was what lay bundled in the center of the box that caught Vicki's eye. Wrapped tightly with aged rubber bands and looking like a mass of old notecards were my report cards from kindergarten through high school.

"Oh, this is grand," Vicki laughed as she unbound the large stack of aged papers and with a curious smile asked, "Is this my chance to see what your grades really were like in school?"

I tried to pull them away but Vicki, having played four years of high school's basketball, hip-checked me preventing me from getting them back. Unfolding the topmost card, she held it up and read out loud my grades from my senior year in high school.

"Ok, 1974. Your senior year at South High. Howard W. Wright, C, C, D, C, D, C," Vicki looked at me, shocked.

All I could do was wince.

Taking the next report card, she flipped it open and read, "1973. C, C, B, D, F, C."

Vicki read through a few more of the dogeared and tattered documents silently till she pulled out my seventh-grade transcript, "C, C, D, D, C, C."

I could sense a deep pain in my heart as her smile turned into a frown, not one of disappointment, but more of an expression of sorrow. I had seen that expression before. It was the same look she would give our children when they hurt themselves. It was the sad face of empathy.

She filed though a couple more report cards until she stopped and started reading again, "Fifth grade, C, C, D, C, B, D. Third grade U, S, U, U, S, S. First grade S, U, S, S, S U.

Vicki's eyes were red as she recited the row of mixed unsatisfactory and satisfactory grades. "How did you survive this, year after year?"

"I don't think I did," I told her as I gently took the collection of report cards and high school transcripts from her trembling hands. I looked down at twelve years of academic failure and without a moment's hesitation, tossed them into the trash.

I stood and looked at Vicki, the prospect of finding a new career before me as I pondered the idea of becoming a teacher. I thought back to the years I spent as a struggling student. Thought back to the dozens of teachers that mislabeled me as lazy and dumb. Remembered the pain of being seen as a fool and buffoon.

"Are you sure you want to do this?" she asked, dead serious. "Do you think you'll enjoy being in a classroom again?"

"Yes," I said with a confident smile. "If I, the slowest and most scatterbrained dope in the world can learn to study, I think I may end up being a pretty good teacher."

The next day I got on the phone and started looking into what it would take to become a teacher. As I searched the internet for information on teaching classes and state requirements, I pictured myself in front of a crowded classroom. I visualized the kids in the back of the class throwing crumpled pieces of paper at one another while bored boys and girls doodled on their desks.

I quickly learned from the central office of the St. Louis Public Schools that I would need a valid teaching credential to teach in a classroom and that my only other option was to be a volunteer "helper", working as a tutor or mentor. While being a volunteer sounded great, it wasn't what I was looking for.

"You say I need a current teaching credential. What about my four years of college and four years of dental school? I was hoping to teach biology. Can't I transfer those credits?"

The woman on the other end of the phone was unimpressed, "You will need at least thirty hours of college-recommended teaching classes, complete a minimum of 60 hours of student teaching and then pass the designated assessment test."

"So," I asked a little frustrated. "There is no way of getting around me having to go back to school for two, maybe three years?"

There was a pause on the phone and then the administrator asked, "Why would you want to get around that?"

"I see your point," I agreed. "Thanks."

I hung up.

My son Tom was in his sophomore year at Chaminade College Prep, a large, highly respected Catholic all-boys school with classes that went from sixth grade all the way through high school. It was an academically challenging school located about thirty minutes from my house, had been established a little over a hundred years ago and had over 900 students.

While trying to determine if teaching was right for me, I decided to call Chaminade and offer, as a parent, my services as a lecturer to discuss how I invented the whistle, marketed it and sold it all over the world.

Amazingly, they agreed and permitted me to give a short lecture to their honors business class being offered to seniors. Pulling together some sales figures, drawings of the Storm whistle, and a few whistles to give away, I showed up ready for my first attempt at teaching.

I could feel cold sweat dampening my palms as I was directed to a third-floor classroom accompanied by an administrator who acted as part mentor, part guide and part prison guard. As I entered the room I was shocked at how big and old the kids looked. I don't know why I was surprised, seniors in high school are between seventeen and eighteen years old. Looking around the class I swear the average kid was at least six foot one, two hundred pounds.

As I walked into that classroom of sullen students, I decided from the outset that it was with the blade of curiosity that I would break them from their melancholy. That if I could prod them into asking themselves "why?" I could capture their attention and direct them to learn.

Walt Disney once said, "We keep moving forward, opening new doors, and doing new things, because we're curious and curiosity keeps leading us down new paths." I decided, right then and there, that it would be by tapping into the student's innate curiosity that would propel them forward.

I began the lesson by holding up two cans of soda: one Coke, one Pepsi. "Why do you buy one and not the other? Don't tell me it's the taste, because we all know you can't tell the difference." I waited for a decent answer and tossed the Coke to the student. Another good answer and I gave away the Pepsi.

I talked about inventing the whistle when I was fourteen; how I built it from odds and ends around the house. One kid in the back said under his breath, loud enough for all to hear, "I don't believe it."

I point at the troublemaker, smile and say, "There is nothing I like more than being 'unbelievable'." The school administrator was amused as I first asked questions, then used their answers to explain marketing, price point and profit. Always asking, never telling.

Benjamin Franklin once remarked that you should never argue; that the best way to change a person's view is by laying a trail of questions that guides them to your opinion. I made every effort to lay a wide trail of questions, and as I did, watched as more and more of the students became involved. I strung together questions, the lesson developing into more of a competition than an inquisition. The students ate it up.

After thirty minutes I ended the class with a story, "I never meant to sell a million whistles. I wanted to make enough money to go on vacation, pay for my kid's college. But now I have gotten letters from seven people who have had their lives saved."

Suddenly, from the back of the class I see a student and he is furious. His eyes are red with tears, his hands are clenched tight with rage and pain as he yells out to me, "You don't know what you're talking about!"

"Please, what don't I know?" I asked as I watched the boy stand, his body shaking as he moved towards me. He is a full five inches taller than my height of five foot ten as tears poured down his cheeks.

"You have no idea what you're talking about!" he screamed. "SEVEN?"

The entire class watched in silent horror as their classmate moved across the room towards me seconds before. The administrator had been leaning against the door jamb relaxed and amused, but now moved to intercept the student. I waved him off.

"Tell me," I implored the student as he sobbed. "I want to know. What is bothering you? How am I wrong? Use your words."

"Seven?" he repeated the question softer, almost a whisper. The entire class watched, shocked as their classmate cried no more than six inches from my face.

The student shook his head no. "It's not seven, it's eight."

He rubbed the tears from his face and stared burningly right into my eyes, "It was Christmas time. My mom was coming out of the Target store and heading to her car when three guys grabbed her and started dragging her to the back of the parking lot. She had that whistle - your whistle - and she blew it and they ran away."

Wiping his tears on his shirt sleeve, he cleared his voice and said, "It's not seven. It's eight."

From that moment on, I knew I would be a teacher. I didn't know how or when, but I knew to the very bottom of my heart that I would teach in a high school.

I started looking into the local community colleges, figuring out what classes I needed to take. I had taken one introductory teaching class while attending college and found it to be slow, pointless, and boring. I wanted to take classes that were inspiring. A class that would teach me the tricks of the trade.

It was two weeks later that I got a call from my son's tutor, Mrs. Jente. She was a wonderful instructor and when I was told she had an important news for me, I was a bit surprised.

"Hello, Dr. Wright," she said sounding rather upbeat. "I just heard that Chaminade is looking for a chemistry teacher. Are you still looking for a job?"

"Yes," I replied, feeling more than a little trepidation at the idea of teaching chemistry. "Yes, that is my hope."

"Well, they are looking for a chemistry teacher and are interviewing right now. Can you teach chemistry with all that balancing equations, electron shell stuff? And don't forget the labs."

Her question took me aback. Chemistry was a tough subject. It kicked my butt in high school and was a struggle from start to finish in college. And the labs. Knowing which chemicals to mix, the measurements and all the lab reports.

"Chemistry? Really? No problem." I exaggerated, "I love chemistry."

The next day I worked up enough courage to call and was surprised to learn that they wanted me to come in for an interview the next day.

Walking into the interview I carried my curriculum vitae, a recommendation from the administrator who watched over me when I spoke for the business class and an outline of my philosophy on teaching.

The principal was Jim Gerker, and after asking a few cursory questions, he sat back and looked me over. "I have a question... Assume for a moment you have a boy in your class that is causing problems. He won't listen, he is disruptive and, all in all, out of control. Who do you approach first with this troublemaker: the head of the science department, the Dean of Discipline or, the child's parents?"

I had anticipated a number of questions I would be asked but had not been ready for this one. Who would I contact if a student was beyond my control? Another teacher, an administrator, the parent? I thought back to my own time in school and how my parents would ground me for months at a time. How they would tell me I was stupid, lazy and dumb.

I answered, "I am not sure if I should first speak with the head of the science department or the Dean of Discipline." Then, leaning forward, I spoke with absolutely no equivocation. "But what I do know is that the parents are the very last person I want to talk to. In my experience, they are typically the core of the problem."

Jim Gerker grinned and slapped his hands together. "Perfect, we will call you within the week."

I got the job.

It was the summer of June 1999 and for the next two and a half months I focused as hard as I could on studying chemistry. I went into battle mode and opened an area in the basement just for studying. I installed a large ceiling light, got an old wooden door from the Salvation Army and used cinder blocks from Home Depot to make a desk.

I was hired to teach four classes of general chemistry and one course described as introductory chemistry. There was another teacher at Chaminade that taught the other two honors chemistry classes, but he had a busy schedule during the summer and couldn't seem to find even five minutes to acquaint me with the textbook, test schedules, lab setup or curriculum.

At the time I was upset that he ignored my calls and gave me absolutely no direction. I didn't know when exams were to be taken, what material should cover or how grades were to be entered. I didn't know how to take roll, where the library was or how the lab was set up. It wasn't until later that I realized his letting me alone was truly a gift from God. Without a mentor telling me how things were done, I basically had full reign to do whatever I wanted.

I opted after re-learning chemistry, that the typical course was setup horribly wrong. Chemistry teachers had a habit of frontloading all the hard math to the first few months of the course. This was particularly detrimental for the slower students who were often mathophobic. Placing all those calculations first, acted to simply overwhelm the underachieving kids before they had a chance to fall in love with blowing things up and creating amazing science.

I decided instead to teach the basics of chemical properties like it was a board game and then at the end drizzle the math in slowly. I chose to ignore how the textbook chapters were laid out and disregarded their interpretation of how chemistry should be learned, choosing to instead jump around a little. The students seem to love it, nobody was left behind and according to the student counselors, the parents were delighted.

I expected the first day of school to be a challenge, but I never expected it to be such a trial by fire. In the initial five minutes of my first class, a student from the second row rose to his feet and said, "This is bullshit." He was a junior, probably seventeen and looked like he had already spent hard time in prison.

Containing my fear, I screamed back at him, "Get out of my classroom! I've got a one-year contract, but you...I'll have you on the street by noon. Leave! Go down to the Dean of Discipline's office before I really get mad."

He left slamming the door.

I then turned to the class and with a smile asked, "So, how did I do?"

There were wide grins on all the students' faces, "Great, Doc. Like a pro."

My second class of the day was uncomfortably small with somewhere between twelve and fifteen students. It was the course in introductory chemistry. The textbook was pathetic cartoon written more like a Batman comic book and made less sense than a street map of downtown Los Angeles. I threw the book away.

I soon found out that these students were both the behavioral and academic rejects, the worst students in the junior class. They, according to the dean in charge of academic affairs, would be best served by a course in chemistry that was void of facts, physics or math.

Ignoring the dean's recommendations, I again relied on the student's curiosity and competitive nature to work through the curriculum. I covered the identical material in basically the same fashion and same rate as in my other four general chemistry classes.

The students in each of my classes understood quickly that if we got the work done, stayed on task and worked together, I would end the day with a story. Tales of whistles and toothpaste, scuba diving and surfing. Stories about bar fights I ran from and tragedies I ran toward. Every day during the last five minutes of class I would tell another story because the kids were consistently fantastic.

Near the end of the first semester of my first year, I was confronted by the head of the science department. She was one of those in-your-face, no-nonsense kind of administrators who had apparently gotten ahold of my grade sheets. Realizing that I had given a little over half the class A's or B's and the rest of the class was getting C's, no D's, and no F's, she was now so angry she could spit.

"Your grading," she fumed, "is way off. I want to know how you can rationalize giving all these A's and B's?"

Up until this point in the semester she had not said more than five words to me, so it shocked me that she was all of a sudden so interested.

Looking at her with a smile, I explained calmly, "There are two ways to grade a student's performance. On the bell curve where you give the top 20 percent an A, the bottom twenty percent an F and then divvy up the other 60 percent between B's, C's and D's. I don't like that way. The other approach, the method I use, is to give exams and if the student knows between ninety and a hundred percent of the material, they get an A. Eighty to ninety percent a B, seventy to eighty a C, sixty to seventy a D and anything lower than that an F.

"Well, your tests aren't hard enough." She glared. "I want to see your last exam."

"I'll get one and put it in your mail ..."

Interrupting, her face squished into a fierce scowl, she put her finger in my face and demanded, "I want to see it now!"

I walked to the rear of the supply room, unlocked the filing cabinet and pulled out the most recent exam. It included a hundred multiple choice questions along with ten essay questions that covered most of the first semester's work. It had everything from balancing equations to stoichiometry, polarity to moles, atomic modeling to questions from the labs.

She snatched the five-page exam from my hand and read through scrutinizing each question.

"You're telling me that this is the exam you gave to your general chemistry students?"

I looked at her and smiled, "That's the exam I gave to both the general and introductory classes. Most of the kids got eighty percent or above."

She handed the exam back, suspicious, a surprised and kind of disappointed expression etched across her face. "Don't change anything."

After that introduction, she rarely talked to me again.

It was during that, "in-your-face," encounter with the department head that I got an idea. These kids of mine were doing pretty well, especially those "flunkies" in the introductory chem class. Maybe I could do something special for the kids? On a whim, I asked the other chemistry teacher if I could borrow the chemistry exam he gave to his honors students. He said sure and a few days into the new semester, gave the introductory class the honors chem semester exam just for fun.

The average score of the introductory kids was an eighty five percent. The average the honors kids got on the same exam three weeks before was an eighty-two.

Armed with the facts, I went to the administrator in charge of all academics, showed her the students' scores and requested that the introductory class be renamed general chemistry. To my surprise she agreed.

The kids went wild.

# Chapter 30:
# Extracurricular Activities

*"Success is not the key to happiness. Happiness is the key to success. If you love what you are ＊oing, you will be successful."*

Albert Schweitzer – Writer and Humanitarian

In addition to teaching chemistry, I began coaching varsity wrestling. Later on, I was asked to assist with varsity cross country, tennis, middle school football and robotics. The extracurricular activities were enjoyable, but nothing compared to the experience of being in the classroom.

It was after I had taught for three years that Vicki completed her classes and earned both a teaching credential and ultimately a master's degree in teaching ESL (English as a Second Language.) She was offered positions at a number of schools, but after considering all her options, she decided to work at Chaminade, spending half her time in the middle school teaching public speaking and art and spending the other half with international students teaching ESL.

Vicki from the start was an amazing educator and the students loved her. Besides teaching her classes, Vicki coached basketball and varsity tennis. I truly adored working together with my wife at Chaminade. We would go to the school athletic events to watch football, basketball, soccer or wrestling, always surrounded by students clamoring for our attention.

One of the most enjoyable times as a teacher was mentoring students while they participated in the various school mission programs. Chaminade College Prep would send students out into the community to help with food drives, soup kitchens and outreach programs.

On occasion, we would hear of an elderly homeowner whose house was condemned due to excess trash, or poor upkeep. We would go out with a group of kids along with a knowledgeable builder and remove the debris and make the necessary repairs.

Our goal was to instill leadership skills, social awareness and compassion for the poor. Vicki and I had the opportunity to mentor the students not only in St. Louis, but as far away as South Dakota and Mexico City.

On one such student trip, we were invited to Central Mexico in hopes that the students could help build an irrigation system for a poor rural town. Normally, Vicki and I served as chaperones, helping where we could. In this case, we were asked to do more; they wanted us to do dentistry.

Hearing that I was a retired dentist and Vicki a retired nurse, the nuns in charge of the local Mexican church felt that as healthcare professionals our time would be better spent working with a medical group nearly a hundred miles north of the students. The administration at Chaminade high school liked the idea of their teachers working hand's on with the project and, realizing we had more than enough adults to watch the kids, they agreed. For three days of the seven-day mission trip, Vicki and I left the students, went north and spent our time pulling teeth in one of the most remote valleys in Mexico.

Vicki and I liked the idea, but as the saying goes, "No good deed goes unpunished."

Sitting three across on the bench seat of a small dilapidated pickup truck, the driver smiled as he handed Vicki and I bandanas to cover our faces. It was still early morning and I was already sweating, so I really didn't want to put it on, but when the driver tied his tight over his mouth and nose, I thought we should probably follow his lead. I laughed as I tied mine on, the neckerchiefs making us look more like wild west bank robbers then missionaries.

Six hours later, the temperature now well into the high nineties, I didn't know which was going to kill me first, the dust, the heat or the bone jarring drops as we slowly jerked down the washed-out Central American dirt roads.

We motored through small streams where naked children played, pushed up steep ravines and careened past cavernous gullies thick with jungle vegetation. We drove for hours bouncing back and forth as we jostled loose in the uncomfortable cab.

After hours of teeth chattering travel, the small truck broke free of the wilderness and came to a stop at the edge of a large rectangular field. At the area's furthest edge was a wooden barn which we would learn later was the church. Its archaic walls were constructed from a latticework of loosely nailed sticks while the roof was made of bent and crumpled overlapping corrugated sheets. Next to the church was an outhouse, a tool shed and at the far left edge of the open ground lay three small tent-like structures that housed the medical personnel.

Vicki and I stepped free of the dust-caked pickup and brushed off the clumps of dirt that clung to our hair and clothes. We were tired, sore and thirsty as we stood and surveyed the large jungle clearing. Out of a small crowd of people emerged a lone nun in full black regalia.

She approached quickly, a bitter smirk etched on her face. "You're late," the nun shook her head, disgusted. "Those people have been waiting for hours."

I looked first to Vicki and then back to the nun. "Hi, Sister. It's good to see you, too. Where can we wash up?"

The nun just shook her head offended, "Over by the tent where your patients are waiting for you, so hurry up."

Vicki and I hobbled toward the simple awning-type structure that was constructed from a single piece of tattered blue tarp stretched between four worn wooden poles. We stumbled, slowly stepping around sprinting chickens as we tried to work the kinks out of our bones from the long drive. We were suddenly face-to-face with a young boy no older than twelve.

"*Tu eres el ₊entista? La enfermera?*" "Are you the dentist? The nurse?"

"*Si.*" I answered, "*Soy el ₊entista, mi esposa es enfermera.*" "Yes, I am the dentist, my wife the nurse."

The boy offered us a wide grin, "*Mucho gusto en conocerte.*" "It's good to know you."

Smiling at the young man I replied, "*Igualmente.*" "Equally."

"My name is Arturo," the boy continued in simple Spanish. "I am here to help you. Follow me."

Together, Vicki and I followed Arturo to a wash basin where we cleaned up, got into oversized surgical gowns and put on masks and gloves. We saw our first patient moments later; she was a middle-aged woman with a large egg-shaped swelling just below the lower left edge of her jaw.

Arturo sat her down in our dental chair, a rickety chaise lounge that looked like it belonged poolside at a budget hotel. The seat and backrest were stretched out, the dirty white plastic piping discolored to a soft brown. She sat down carefully and laid back, following Arturo's instructions. Curiously, however, Arturo wasn't speaking to her in Spanish.

It seemed that these native Indians from the deep jungles of Central Mexico didn't speak Spanish. Instead, they used a strange kind of clicking language unlike anything I had ever heard before. I spoke a smattering of Greek, French, and Mandarin, but this language was more like some clip form of German. Thankfully, Arturo spoke the dialect and so I was able to converse with him in Spanish while he translated to the local woman with the severe dental problem.

"Arturo," I began, "*Pregunte a la mujer ₊ón₊e le ₊uele y por cuánto tiempo?*" "Ask the woman where it hurts and for how long?"

Arturo then looked at the woman and said, "*Click Click thwack click squeak.*"

The woman spoke back to Arturo in the same click squeak voice as Arturo while pantomiming the parts of her jaw and neck that hurt. Arturo then looked toward me and said, "*La parte inferior izquier⋅a por tres semanas.*" "The bottom left for three weeks."

I examined the tooth while Vicki held the flashlight and passed the instruments. We treated the woman by removing the split tooth, giving her antibiotics. After cleaning up and flash sterilizing the instruments in a special chemical bath, we immediately started on the next patient. We worked without pausing, treating patient after patient till dusk. Finally, the medical doctors who were giving vaccinations, prescribing medicine and listening to hearts and lungs, shut off their headlamps and called it quits. We did the same.

Silently, the patients who were left untreated disappeared into the jungle as Vicki, Arturo and I secured our work area for the night. There were no questions from the patients we did not get to, no complaints from people who came from so far and now were forced to leave unseen.

"*Vámonos, ya es hora ⋅e comer,*" Arturo said with a wide grin as we closed up the last box of sterilized instruments. "Let's go, it's time to eat."

In the evening's failing light, we walked unhurriedly up a dusky narrow dirt path until we arrived at a rather large circular hut located atop a low hill. The hut sat on bare dirt, was constructed from thin sticks no larger than your finger and, like the church, supported a roof made from overlapping sheets of rusted metal. Centered in the middle of the roof was a single cylindrical chimney from which a thick grayish-black smoke wafted from its opening.

Vicki, Arturo and I squatted low and entered the shadowy shelter and as our eyes adjusted to the dark, found that we stood in a kitchen.

Beans, slices of chicken and tortillas cooked hot on a flat metal plate the size of a manhole cover. Over the makeshift grill we watched as a handful of women prepared the meal. The food looked and smelled delicious as we were handed small plastic plates, utensils, and cups filled with filtered and treated water.

We took our food and moved outside where we settled with a half dozen other medics on wooden chairs and benches.

"So, you're the dentist?" a young doctor asked as he slowly chewed a mouthful of beans.

"Yes. I'm Howard and this is my wife Vicki. We are from St. Louis."

"I'm from Dallas." The doctor continued. "This is my third time coming here to treat these folks."

We talked shop and discussed patients and treatments until we completed our meals.

The night was now pitch black, a coolness blanketing the valley.

"Vicki, why don't you come with us and get cleaned up?" a female nurse suggested. "We wash behind the church."

"Ok." Vicki replied easily. "Where do we sleep?"

"The women sleep inside the church," the nurse explained, and then with a slight chuckle she added, "The men? They sleep outside."

Vicki offered me a sly smile and disappeared with the other women.

After another couple minutes, I got up with the men, grabbed some clean clothes and followed them in the dark to a nearly imperceptible trail toward the bathing hole. We walked for a short five minutes to a cool stream that I could barely see and was pointed toward a shallow pond that reflected silver in the starlight.

"Strip down and hop in there." The doctor pointed, "I'll be over here."

I removed my clothes, stacked them on a large rock and then eased myself into the cool slow flowing water. It felt amazing washing the grime and stress of the day from my skin. I finished by dunking myself completely underwater.

It was surreal as I looked up at the stars and listened to the doctors as they continued their discussions of disease and treatment options. Before too long I heard the others pull themselves from the water, dry off and get dressed.

By the time we got back to the encampment, army-type cots had been set up at the edge of the field; light blankets laid out across their length.

I slept until forced awake by the glow of the morning dawn and the hushed voices of the patients as they walked out of the jungle and queued up outside the treatment tents.

I walked to our primitive dental office and met Vicki and Arturo as they organized the instruments and prepared for the day's patients.

"So?" I asked putting on my smock and pulling on a mask. "Tell me. How was your night?"

"Wonderful," she answered with a smile. "My bath was quite nice actually. I used a plastic cup and dumped water over my head while standing in a bucket. Chic, huh?"

"Not too bad," I chuckled.

"No." Vicki grinned as she laid the forceps and syringes out on the bracket table. "The bath was easy. The tough part was trying to fall asleep on the ground while these little frogs kept hopping over my legs. That took concentration."

"Frogs?" I asked, "Really?"

"Really," she laughed.

We worked all morning taking only a half hour off for lunch and then saw patients straight through till dusk. Things went well until dinner when we were approached by the nun in charge. She had not spoken with us since our first uncomfortable encounter and now seemed excited with news that tomorrow would be different. It seemed that the medical staff, along with Vicki and I, were going to a small village about seven miles to the north. This didn't mean very much until it was explained by some of the medical staff that the area we were entering was very dangerous. It was controlled by the rebels, the Zapatista, and that there had recently been killings.

Early the next morning we were taken by truck once again along the bumpy washed out road thirty minutes further into rural Mexico. I don't remember the name of the town we entered, but it was tiny, having not more than a half dozen outbuildings and a small open town center. Even before our facilities were set up, patients were arriving to receive care. Where these wonderful people lived or worked was not clear to me. It seemed that they just appeared from the dense jungle.

"Remember,." the medical nurse whispered to me in broken English as she hurried by shuttling supplies. "We have to walk out. That we won't have the truck. We must leave at least two hours before sundown. No later than 4:30."

I checked my watch. We had been working for hours and now it was a little past two. I looked at Vicki as she passed me a two-by-two gauze. "That nurse looks like she has seen a ton of action and if she is nervous, we best keep track of the time."

Vicki looked at me with roll of the eyes, "You think so?"

The dental patients were lined up all the way to the tree line and we had a little over two hours left.

From the moment a patient sat down till I finished treatment was typically no less than twenty minutes. I had been known to be quick at my work, maybe even fast, but there was no way I could treat all these people in the time left. With this in mind, Arturo and I walked down the line of patients and selected the neediest.

It was now 4:30, the nurse having passed by with her dire warnings now insistent that we leave.

"Arturo, Vicki," I said as I placed a small gauze where an infected tooth once sat. "Let's make this the last patient and pack it up. *Vamanos.*"

The words were barely out of my mouth when up stormed the nun, her face a contorted grimace of anger.

"What do you think you're doing?" The nun screamed not two inches from my face. "You can't stop yet."

"I was told we are walking out of here, so we have to...."

"No!" the nun shouted. Then grabbing a young woman who had been waiting, threw her in the chair. "One more! You have time for one more!"

I looked from Vicki to Arturo, then back to the nun. "Ok. One more, but then we leave."

I moved as fast as I could and injected the troubled area while nonessential dental instruments were sorted and put away.

Suddenly, the nun was back again. "This boy. Look at his mouth. You must help him!"

"We need to leave!" I shouted back. "It will be dark soon and..."

"You will let this boy live with this infection?" She shook her head in disgust. "You call yourself a doctor? You are a bastard!"

Vicki deferred to me. I looked across the paddock to the medical nurse. She was vehemently shaking her head no.

"Arturo!" I spit out. "*Por favor, ame una jeringa.*" "Arturo, please, give me a syringe."

I hurried not truly knowing the danger, but I recognized the dread in the eyes of the medical nurse.

We finished. I check my watch and it was well past five. We pack up and blow by the nun. She is repulsed at our leaving.

There were five of us. Vicki, twelve-year-old Arturo, two older Honduran medical nurses and myself. We had walked for nearly an hour carrying two medical bags, a large sack of sterile gauze and a box of assorted equipment. The sun had dropped to just above the horizon as we slowly stumbled down the washed-out dirt road. Suddenly, we looked up to see that our route was blocked.

Cattle. A small herd of scrawny tan and brown cows were bunched together blocking our path.

We considered moving through the jungle to avoid our bovine friends, but the foliage was so dense, not even a dwarf mouse would be able to work its way through the bramble. I had never dealt with cows before and had only seen them on television or when driving by a farm in my car. I figured they were harmless enough barring some kind of stampede.

We advanced further down the dirt road, keeping quiet in hopes of slipping through their ranks unnoticed. The herd seemed uninterested as they lazily watched us approach, the five of us forming a single-file line as we leisurely moved around the dozen or so cows with our backs to the jungle.

We were halfway through the listless herd when, without warning, they started to move, alarmed by something behind them. It was then, from inside the shifting mass of cattle, that a single bull appeared. It was larger than the other rather scraggly cows, powerful and cocksure. It wasn't skittish or frightened as it lowered its head toward us and rocked its horns back and forth. It simply looked mad.

We stood stock still as the bull angrily moved toward us, pawed the ground and snorted loudly.

"*No corras, no corras,*" I heard whispered urgently in my ear as one of the nurses clutched my arm, fearful tears pouring down her cheeks. "Don't run, don't run," she begged.

The enraged bull took a step forward and lowered its head even further, its front hoof scraping a divot in the dusty road in anticipation of a charge.

I bent down slowly and lifted a stick from the ground. It was as long as my arm and big around as my wrist. I knew it would be totally useless against the beast, but I grabbed ahold of it nonetheless.

The bull snorted loudly as it watched me stand my ground. Glared at me through slit eyes and furrowed brow as it stood posturing for an attack not more than fifteen feet away. The rest of the group huddled close behind me with the jungle at our backs. It was then, out of the blue, that I remembered something.

It was a folktale, a myth. Something that I had heard when I was a kid. It was an old Indian legend that told of a boy's encounter with a bear and how the young warrior escaped being mauled to death by doing something very clever.

The ancient story talked about how nearly every living thing fears the deadly diamond back rattlesnake. That the mere sound of a rattler will cause even the most powerful of beasts to take pause. It is said the young Indian boy used the buzzing sound of a rattler to scare the bear away and now, face-to-face with an angry bull, I was about to try the same trick.

I wet my lips and started low making the *tshhhhhhhhhhh* sound of the rattlesnake.

Louder and louder I hissed, trying to imitate the quick rolling *whirr* of a snake while Vicki and the others stepped slowly away, further down the trail.

The bull stared at me unmoving, but deep behind its flaming eyes, I clearly saw the slightest hint of uncertainty.

I took a single step back down the uneven road, then a second step, eventually escaping down the trail where I joined up with the others.

Dusk turned to night as darkness enveloped the jungle road. We continued to walk on slowly, wordlessly and stumbled often due to the ground's uneven surface as we moved ahead. One of the nurses had brought along a head lamp she used during her examinations of the medical patients and now trained its powerful light onto our path to illuminate the rugged potholed road. The light didn't last long, the batteries finally expired forty-five minutes into our journey leaving us to walk by starlight. I preferred the darkness. In the middle of Zapatista controlled territory, invisible was good.

We marched on silently until I heard the tiniest of sounds behind us in the dark. The kick of a stone, the bump of a stick. Three women, a boy and a middle-aged dentist alone in the middle of nowhere and now we were being followed.

I stopped and confronted the darkness and whatever it held as Vicki hurriedly pressed the others to move along faster.

I made out the sound in the dark. It was a horse.

I waited.

Out of the inky black darkness, up rode two boys on a single horse. They looked like brothers, no older than eight or ten.

"*Buenas noches.*" I call out.

"*Buenas noches,*" they reply in return as they steadied the horse.

"Can you tell me," I say in Spanish, "how far to the church?"

"*Más allá ↑e la curva en el camino.*" "Farther up, past the bend in the road," the older boy told me.

I noticed as the horse took a step closer that the older of the two carried a rifle.

"*Y para que sirve el rifle?*" "And what is the rifle for?"

"*Ban↑i↑os, tratarán ↑e robar mi caballo.*" "Bandits, they will try to steal my horse."

We walk on with the boys at our rear.

We find ourselves back at the encampment a short ten minutes later.

Early the next morning we stowed our gear into the bed of the same small pickup truck and prepared to leave. Despite the rough ride we will have to endure, I look forward to our departure. The nun sees Vicki and I as we make ready to go, but she says nothing. I tell her simply, "Adios."

# Chapter 31:
# Toothpaste, The Do-Over

*"No problem is so formi•able that you can't walk away from it."*

Charles M. Schulz - American Cartoonist

It was two years later, during my fifth year of teaching honors chemistry, that my life once again took a hard turn to the right. It was the first class of the day and I had just finished covering some very difficult concepts involving isomer chemistry and, as a reward to the students, found myself telling one of my "Dr. Wright stories."

I was halfway through the account where I lost the SmithKline Beecham Color-Changing Toothpaste contract because of the thieving, no good patent examiner Rosen, when a student stood up in the back of class and demanded to know why I was so quick to give-up.

Class was nearly over when the soccer player stood up and interrupted me. Chaminade had a magnificent soccer program and this particular guy was not only one of the varsity team's premiere players and a great student but he was also spitting mad.

"You just gave up? You've been telling us all year long how you have to stand up for what you believe in, and now, after this big toothpaste manufacturer canceled the contract, you just roll over and give up?"

"Listen," I replied trying to explain. "This is the U.S. government. They blocked the patent process. What was I to do? Fight the patent office?"

"YES!" he screamed. "You fight till you can't fight anymore. You don't just give up."

I shook my head at the young man, "Taking on the government is not as easy as you make it sound."

He looked me right in the eye. "Winning is never easy."

I felt ashamed for having quit; for giving in and giving up. I reached into my pocket and pulled out my phone. In front of the entire class I called the U.S. Patents Office's main call center. I got an operator and asked for the executive offices and then for the administrator in charge of the offices and then asked for her boss.

After about three minutes on the phone, I found myself on the line with an executive secretary of some super important guy named Mr. Dollie. I gave my name and left a message with her. "There is something very wrong in the patent office and I want to report a crime."

I looked past the rows of students to the kid in the back row. "I guess you could say we just started the second half," I tell him.

It was the next day at lunch that my phone rang. "This is John Dollie of the U.S. Patent and Trademark Office. What's this about reporting a crime?"

I told him the story about the way my patent was lost twice and how I was told that unless I paid the fifty thousand, the patent would never go through.

"You're making it up. You're lying. There is no corruption in the USPTO. You're wasting my time."

"Wasting YOUR time?" I yelled into the phone. "I've lost a multi-million-dollar contract and have been waiting for years for a patent. Wasting your time?"

There was a pause on the line until the patent officer in a bored uninterested reply said, "We have no corruption here."

I went ballistic. All the angry feelings that I had kept bottled up inside me came to the surface. My memory of Vicki and I in New York, my presentation to the research scientists at SmithKline, everything bubbled up. "You're right, there is no corruption, not at the patent office or in the NYPD or the St. Louis Police Department or anywhere in the U.S. government for that matter." I then went into overdrive. "You son of a &*&^^%, you &^%&*. I don't know why I waisted MY time calling, you piece of %^&**! Crawl back under your rock, you lazy good for nothing pencil pusher!" I hung up.

An hour later, when I had calmed down, I slid over to my computer and did a search on the name John Dollie. Oh crap, he was one of the top guys at the U.S. Patent and Trademark office. He was the head honcho, the main man, the big wheel. Crap.

It was three days later that I got a phone call at school. I was in the middle of a lesson and it was John Dollie. I asked him to call back in an hour when I wasn't teaching.

"Before we start, I want to apologize," I said humbly. "My father was in the Navy and he taught me you show respect to an officer whether you agree with them or not. I had no idea who you were, and I regret for not showing you the respect you deserve."

"You know," he chuckled, "I haven't been called those kinds of names since I was in eighth grade, but sometimes it's good to get pulled off your high horse."

It was after a pause that he continued. "I checked the status of your patent and something very strange came up. Somebody on the inside canceled your paperwork not just once, but twice, just like you said. And now it is in the inactive file. Very strange. I'm going to look into it."

"Fantastic," I replied jubilant.

"We'll be getting back with you soon," he assured me. "Sorry for the mix-up."

I told the students what was going on and they were over the moon with excitement. Dr. Wright was taking on the patent office.

But nothing happened.

I waited for three months until I couldn't take it anymore and was forced to call John Dollie again.

"Hello, Dr. Wright. What can I do for you?"

"Well, Mr. Dollie. I am still waiting to hear back from your office."

"What?" he yelled into the phone. "I was assured that this had been taken care of. You'll be hearing from us. I promise." The phone went dead.

I can still remember sitting with a couple of teachers at our lunch table talking sports when my cell phone rang. It had been a week since I had talked to Mr. Dollie, so when the woman on the other end of the line said she was an examiner for the USPTO, I was shocked. She told me that she had been put in charge of my patent and that after a detailed review, a full patent for the world's first color-changing toothpaste had been awarded. My patent was accepted exactly as written.

I sat stunned. "Accepted in full, all the claims, everything?"

"You will receive the final documents express mail tomorrow or possibly Friday. Congratulations." She hung up.

Unbelievable. After eight years of embezzlement, lies and frustration, I had suddenly won the rights to the world's first color-changing toothpaste. I was overjoyed. This is what I had dreamt about for years.

I called SmithKline Beecham hoping that maybe, with the patent in hand, I could persuade them to reconsider the idea of manufacturing the color-changing toothpaste, but they said that the company's focus had changed. "No, thank you," was their reply.

I approached every other medical-dental compounding businesses in the country and in each and every case they replied with a resounding, "No."

Finally, after reaching out to nearly every dental manufacturer I could find, I got a call back from the owner of a small company on the East Coast. The gentleman had started a company that manufactured small dental appliances, dental waxes and impression pastes. He had a fairly large company in New Jersey, employed somewhere around fifty workers and had been in business for over twenty years. He loved the idea of a color-changing toothpaste and wanted to partner up with me. He would do the manufacturing and sales, while I would supply the patent and be the spokesman.

Vicki and I flew out to New Jersey to meet him face-to-face and check out his facility. He seemed like a nice, intelligent and hardworking guy, the company was legit, his employees seemed happy and, seeing there were no other offers, I signed an agreement linking us together for the next three years.

Vicki said the time period was too long and that if this guy didn't come through, we would have wasted a great deal of time. The manufacturer reminded us that it would take at least eighteen months to bring the toothpaste to market and he didn't want us pulling the plug on our relationship just as we started to become successful.

After a long deliberation, I convinced Vicki to go with the three year exclusive contract. Again, she was right, and I was wrong. You'd think I would at some point learn to listen to her.

What I hadn't counted on was that, despite his promises, assurances and emails with grandiose ideas, the manufacturer would just sit there and not do anything. I would call and ask what advances he had made in the formulation or packaging and he would say, "Still considering our options. I have some great ideas I'm working on. I'll get back to you."

Six months went by, then a year. "Still considering our options."

After three years I tore up the deal. I have tried to think of ways I could have handled that agreement differently, placing performance riders in place or some such thing, but I still don't see how I could have known he was just going to sit on the idea. I didn't lose any money, just time. I would soon learn that time was actually the most expensive commodity in the universe.

# Chapter 32:
# Handing Off Operations

*"There is something about buil•ing up a comra•eship - that I still believe is the greatest of all feats - an• sharing in the •angers with your company of peers. It's the intense effort, the giving of everything you've got. It's really a very pleasant sensation."*

Edmund Hillary - New Zealand
Mountaineer and Philanthropist

With Vicki and I moving our focus more and more toward teaching, we quickly came to understand that we needed to hire someone to act as business manager and handle the day to day responsibilities of running the whistle company. Having made this decision, we forced ourselves to become seriously organized in how we handled every step of the manufacturing, packaging and selling process. We wrote down everything and developed detailed procedures for monitoring inventory levels, guidelines for proper handling of accounts payable, accounts receivable and the calculation and payment of taxes.

Once we established concrete systems to get things done, we then documented, as closely as possible, exactly how and when each of these tasks needed to be accomplished. Between grading papers, writing up new lesson plans, working with the students and participating in extracurricular activities, Vicki and I were able to put together a concise manual that detailed the exact protocol necessary to efficiently run the All Weather Safety Whistle Company.

This was great for the company. It truly forced us to look closely at how we did what we did and why. When do you reorder supplies?

How often do you go to the bank and how do you handle delinquent payments? It took us well over a month of hard work, but after about a hundred rewrites, we had finally constructed a concise, step-by-step instruction book on how to do everything from generating a quote to filling an order, from taking a credit card payment to sending an order overseas.

The procedures that Vicki and I put together for running the company were both solid enough to set concrete guidelines while being flexible enough to allow for common sense variations. My last and most important task was hiring Dona, Vicki's younger sister, to take these responsibilities and implement them.

Dona was a godsend. She cared and still does care for the company as if it was her own. Having learned everything from computer accounting to the art of upselling over the phone, the All Weather Safety Whistle Company would not be what it is today if it wasn't for her.

Because of Dona and her success at running the whistle company, Vicki and I were able to consider new projects. Projects like developing the color-changing toothpaste ourselves.

# Chapter 33:
# Making the Toothpaste

*"Men willingly believe what they wish."*

Julius Caesar - Emperor of Rome

"Why don't we do it ourselves?" Vicki asked over dinner. "Why don't we start our own toothpaste company? We can call it Wright Pharmaceuticals."

"Are you crazy?" I asked over my meatloaf and broccoli. "Do you have any idea what you're suggesting?"

"We did it with the whistles," Vicki smiled, "I don't see why we can't make a kid's toothpaste. How hard could it be?"

I stopped and tried to wrap my mind around what she was saying, "We're talking about trademarking a name and logo, generating a formula, finding a manufacturer and then developing a special package so when the two colors mix, they change color at just the right speed."

Vicki looked at me, "I know."

"But here's the thing," I responded just a little too loud as I tried to control my voice. "With the whistle we are competing against small time whistle makers. With the toothpaste we will be up against some of the largest manufacturing companies in the world."

"The color-changing toothpaste is an incredible invention," she said, trying to encourage me. "It would be a terrible thing to waste."

I leaned back and looked at Vicki, "If the toothpaste works like I think it might, we will be knocked off in a millisecond by the most ruthless and aggressive companies in the world. If it doesn't work, then we will end up losing a ton of money, along with all the grief that goes along with financially getting the crap knocked out of you. In either case, successful or not, we get crushed."

Vicki just looked at me.

"I wouldn't even know where to start," I cringed, shaking my head at the immensity of the project.

"I've been thinking about that," she replied excitedly with a quirky smile. "I have this friend…"

Three days later we walked into Drew Pharmaceutical, a mid-sized company that manufactured nasal sprays, vitamin tablets and dietary supplements. The company had been around since 1960, employed just under eighty individuals and covered about a fourth of a city block. Vicki's friend was the owner, a wonderfully intelligent and hard-working woman named Connie Drew. Connie's father had started Drew Pharmaceuticals which was now being run by the family with Connie taking a leadership role.

We were greeted by a very prompt and professional receptionist who ushered us into a simple conference room where. After a short wait, we were met by Connie and the plant manager who was in charge of the overall manufacturing, packing and distribution of the products. Connie was warm and congenial. The production manager, with his starched white lab coat and no-nonsense demeanor, was all business.

"No way."

It was Connie. After having heard my spiel, she just shook her head sadly and repeated, "No way. The production costs alone will be a disaster. You're going to need to basically take two toothpastes and fuse them together making certain everything lines up. The manufacturing cost will destroy you. Not to mention the per item price of the product. What did you want to sell it for?"

"I was thinking six dollars per tube in the store."

"Six dollars?" Connie laughed as she felt the weight of the sample tube in her open hand. "Your cost will need to be more like twelve. Shipping alone will kill you."

"Well," I gently interrupted, "I was thinking of getting ahold of a single 'dual tube,' a toothpaste tube that had a divider, a partition down the middle. It would keep both the weight and cost down."

Connie faced me with a questioning glance, "And how are you planning on filling this imaginary dual tube?"

"I don't know," I conceded.

It was the supervisor's turn to grill me. "Is this toothpaste of yours going to have fluoride? Because if the answer is yes, you might as well stop right now."

I sighed with the same guilty feeling you get having been caught finishing off an entire box of Girl Scout cookies, "Well, yes, we need to have fluoride."

Connie and the supervisor glanced at each other and shook their head, a pained expression passing across their faces.

"What?" I asked defensively, looking from one to the other. "You don't like fluoride?"

"The problem isn't the fluoride," Connie clarified, forcing her voice to calm. "The problem is the FDA. Fluoride is a controlled substance. If you're going to be adding fluoride, you have to first get past the Food and Drug Administration. The FDA makes the other government agencies look like choirboys."

Vicki and I just rolled our eyes and shrugged. We thanked Connie and her plant manager for the information and left, both discouraged and disheartened.

On our way home, Vicki and I discussed the toothpaste.

"Alright." Vicki said, a cold and somber tone to her voice. "At least we now know what we are up against."

"Yes. It's going to be tough," I replied after a moment's thought. "Let me search around and see if we can find a dual tube, and then we can move on from there. Remember the old saying: The way you eat an elephant is..."

Vicki laughed, "I know, I know. One bite at a time."

It was four months later that I received samples of the only dual tube in existence. It was distributed through a company in New York, but was actually made in China. The dual tube was a little stiff, but despite its feel was the proper size and had the inner partition and twin openings that when squeezed laid out a perfect stripe of red and blue. It had been used by Avon cosmetics for years and despite being a little on the heavy side and made in a foreign country, looked pretty slick. The cost, which included a tamper resistant seal, full-color printing and shipping was a little over a dollar each.

Now that I had the tube, I needed to find someone who could fill it. This was difficult because not only would the contract packer, or copacker, need to fabricate two colors of toothpaste, they would also need to fill both sides of the tube, monitor fluoride levels and keep track of shelf lives all while being inexpensive enough to keep everything financially profitable.

Four months later I finally found a copacker capable of doing all the things necessary to bring the toothpaste to market. The company was family owned in Bridgeton, Michigan, and had been in business for over thirty years. They had an FDA approved lab, seemed to do a good job with the required documentation and were presently making an organic toothpaste for children. The fit seemed great.

Having decided on the exact dual-tube that would be used and the facility that would both compound and fill the toothpaste, it was time to start working on the actual toothpaste formulation. This was, in my mind, going to be the easiest of tasks. Leave out the bitter SLS foaming agent, use the gentlest of silicate abrasives and demand the colorants and fillers be as healthy as possible.

With that in mind, we instructed the laboratory technicians at the Bridgeton copacker to use the absolutely lowest levels of colorants, flavors, and abrasives possible. In addition, I demanded that absolutely no foaming agent be added and that the fluoride level be held at the very lowest levels while still being considered containing fluoride.

For the formulation process, Vicki and I flew to Michigan and met with the chemists one-on-one so we could get a firsthand feel for the flavor we wanted and the colors we required.

"This toothpaste is going to get it's pop from the color change," I told the Bridgeton chemists, "not from bubbles that irritate the tissues and choke the kids."

It seemed surreal sitting at the conference table as the laboratory experts laid samples of toothpaste on glass plates in front of Vicki and me.

"This red is .04 %" the chemist explained as he laid out a strip of toothpaste. "Same as Closeup made by Crest."

"It seems too dark," we decide as we slid the sample back and forth between us. "Can we dilute it to half and make it more of a light pastel red?"

"And the flavor," Vicki remarked as she swirled the toothpaste around her mouth. "Can we try using half as much bubble gum grape flavoring?"

The lab tech shook his head in frustration, "This is what we use in the other toothpastes, .04% colorant."

"We're trying something new here." I explained. "We want less colorants and less flavoring. This paste doesn't have any foaming agents, so we are not going to need to mask any bitter tastes. Just lower the concentrations to half normal. Please."

After another hour of mixing and tasting, we had the formulation down. The red and blue pastes had concentrations of .01 percent, less than a quarter of the colorant found in the average toothpaste, the flavoring dialed back just as far. When mixed together, the color change was amazing, a beautiful pastel purple emerging as the red and blue were mixed. The flavor was delightful and amazingly light, a subtle flavor of delicate bubble gum grape, not that icky sweet candy flavor found in other kid's toothpastes.

Deciding on the level of fluoride was tougher and became a real gamble. Typically, adult toothpastes contained between 1000 and 1500 parts per million (ppm) fluoride, with children's toothpaste having around 600 ppm. Because of my fear that children would like the new color-changing toothpaste so much that they would be tempted to eat it, we decided to lower the fluoride lever to around 300ppm.

The danger of using such a low level of fluoride was the possibility that we would fail the FDA's fluoride efficacy test. Every new toothpaste that says they have fluoride must demonstrate: 1) the fluoride level is high enough to effect cavity prevention and 2) not have so much fluoride that it is a danger to the public. Our goal was to provide the safest toothpaste while still providing strong anticavity protection. My greatest concern was that by trying to create the world's first super-low fluoride toothpaste for kids, it would fail to be strong enough to prevent cavities and we would flunk the FDA's test.

The FDA test cost was $35,000, pass or fail. If we failed the test, we would have to adjust our formula, pay the FDA another $35,000 and run the test again. We submitted our toothpaste samples and waited the prescribed eight weeks for the results.

While we waited for the FDA tests to come back, we worked on the name of the toothpaste and the associated logo. We were looking for an upbeat unisex name that both boys and girls would like, that was easy to say and called to mind a modern and dynamic product that screamed innovation. Lastly, Vicki and I wanted a name that was the same in both English and Spanish. I chose the name Vortex Color Changing Toothpaste. As our logo, Vicki sketched a brightly colored smiling octopus. It was beautiful, in one tentacle it held a toothbrush, in the other a tube of Vortex toothpaste. Octopi change color, so I thought it was a good fit.

Six weeks went by, then eight, then ten, but still no word from the FDA about our fluoride tests. I was concerned to say the least. During the down time, I built our website, put together videos of the toothpaste and organized press releases and social media outreaches. Everything hinged on the FDA approval and, after the debacle with the Patent and Trademark office, nothing was for certain.

It was after a long three months that we finally got our results from the Food and Drug Administration's lab. "Excuse me for taking so long to get back to you, but your toothpaste gave us a real challenge." It was the research scientist from the FDA, the individual who was responsible for the quantitative analysis on the toothpaste. From the tone of his voice, things clearly didn't go well.

I covered my eyes with my hand thinking crap, crap, crap as I shook my head in frustration. "I am sorry to hear you had problems. Where did we go wrong?"

"Actually, the problem wasn't on your end. Our first set of results didn't make sense, so we decided to start over and run the evaluation again."

"Didn't make sense?" I asked as I held the phone even tighter to my ear. "What do you mean, didn't make sense?"

"The way we run the test is by placing a sample of your toothpaste against a cube of simulation tooth substance, a material called Ivorine®. If your toothpaste imparts the proper range of fluoride into the Ivorine®, then cavities will be prevented, and you pass. If the Ivorine® doesn't absorb enough fluoride, then you fail."

"Ok," I said uneasy, "what went wrong?"

"According to your documentation, this toothpaste is for children and that's why you're starting levels of fluoride were so low. 300 ppm, right?"

"Yeah," I agreed, "we wanted to keep the fluoride concentration really low in case a child decided to swallow the toothpaste."

"Right," replied the researcher. "So, when we ran the tests, we expected a rock bottom fluoride level in the test Ivorine® after being exposed to your low fluoride toothpaste. We figured you'd barely pass. What we found was something entirely different."

"How's that?" I asked sitting on the edge of my chair.

"Well," the researcher continued, "the tests showed a strong level of fluoride in the Ivorine®, the test teeth. A lot more than we expected. It seems that by removing the foam from the toothpaste, the fluoride is wetting the test enamel more completely making your toothpaste more efficient in transporting fluoride."

"I don't think I understand," I replied confused.

"Look at it this way," the scientist explained, "imagine if you wanted to paint an old dingy wall white. If the wall happened to be covered with balloons, would that make the painting job easier or harder?"

"Harder," I answered, "the balloons would get in the way of the brush and the paint."

"Right," he agreed. "But what if there were no balloons on the wall, no foam. You could paint the entire wall in half the time. Your non-foaming toothpaste made it easier for the fluoride to coat the teeth. Nice job! Twice the fluoride protection with half the fluoride exposure. Congratulations."

I couldn't believe what I was hearing. This was tremendous news.

Vicki and I had successfully developed the first ever color-changing toothpaste that tasted great, didn't cause mouth sores and encouraged kids to brush longer, all while delivering twice the fluoride protection with half the fluoride exposure.

We had a winner.

I finished up the website, wrote press releases that touted the super-fluoride effect and started putting together our direct marketing campaign. All that was necessary now was to order the toothpaste tubes and get them filled.

I called the tube distributor in New York and sent him the final artwork that was going to be printed on the tubes. This artwork not only included the Vortex name and our logo, but also the UPC barcode and company information along with the mandatory "Drug Facts" required by the Food and Drug Administration.

A little more than a month after the company in China received the designs we had for the tube, they sent us back a dozen printed tubes for us to inspect. This was crucial because we had to confirm that everything was written correctly, the colors were exactly as they should be and the FDA requirements were followed to the letter. I expected the colors to be wrong and the wording blurred, but what I found was surprising.

Everything looked beautiful.

Vicki's octopus looked great, the writing was easy to read and the UPC was perfect. There was one very critical problem, however.

"Got some bad news, Howard," the New York tube salesman tossed out lackadaisically. "We can't get your batch of Vortex tubes for like six months."

"You told me the turnaround time would be four weeks," I objected, sounding a lot like one of my middle school football players after I told him he wouldn't start the game.

"Well, you got Chinese New Year, shipping problems, the yen. I'm thinking April of next year."

I felt like I was just hit in the stomach. "Fine, put the order in."

"So, what did you want? The minimum forty thousand units or go with eighty thousand?" Then with a slurred, New York kind of "I don't give a crap accent," added, "Hey, don't forget the long lag time."

"I'll get back to you," I replied and hung up.

Considering $1.20 per tube, this was an immense amount of money. Vicki and I sat down and discussed the options. What's the upside? What's the downside? Will forty thousand tubes be enough?

What if we get Walmart? What if we get Walgreens? Will they accept a delay of six to eight months if we get into the stores? Will a half a year delay getting product give our competition the time they need to knock us off and find their way into our niche market?

After a great deal of hand wringing, we decided to go with the eighty thousand tube order. We tried to always be ready for the best, but prepared for the worst. My father had an adage he loved to repeat, "The more you bet, the more you win; but never bet more than you're willing to lose." Unfortunately, people tend to leave off the second part of that saying.

Vicki and I dug deep into our savings, purchased the Vortex toothpaste tubes and waited. We had them shipped straight to Bridgeton where the tubes arrived in large refrigerator sized boxes. Now it was Bridgeton's turn to give us the bad news.

"We are going to need three months to get things started. We need time to get our machines freed up for the run."

"You assured us that you had the capacity to start immediately once you got the tubes," I replied trying to control my anger. "You told me yourself that you could fill three thousand tubes a day."

"Well," he said, sounding more like an unscrupulous auto mechanic than an experienced manufacturer. "Things have changed, so we need more time. We'll get you on the schedule in a few months."

"OK," I said, irritated, as I tried desperately to figure out how it was that every person I dealt with insisted on disregarding deadlines.

We waited the three months and then another two. We sent Edible Delights, those bouquets of food, in hopes of enticing the Bridgeton toothpaste manufacturer to notice us and get us onto the schedule, but it was about as effective as a wink to a blind horse. We were just going to have to wait.

As children, whenever we were late for anything, my father would yell at us screaming, "If you're late it's because you either are disorganized or you just don't give a damn. Pick one." I was unfortunately arriving at the realization that the toothpaste copacker was both.

After six months of delays, I flew up to Bridgeton to find out what was going on. Only after a long discussion across his dented and worn conference table was I able to pin down a final filling date.

It wasn't until the middle of February 2007 that I finally got the call from the copacker in Bridgeton. He told me they had started filling the tubes that morning and they would be in a position to send me a partial shipment by the end of the week. After fifteen years, we had our toothpaste.

It was then, as I realized that I would actually have the color-changing toothpaste in hand, that it hit me like a hard smack upside the head. I was running out of time.

Doing the math in my head and knowing full well that patents only last twenty years, I couldn't believe that I only had a little over five years left. After all this work, all the stress and all the money, I was running out of time.

Looking back, I realized where I made a crucial mistake.

It took nearly ten years to fight through the patent officer's extortion attempt. A decade of waiting until John Dollie finally got me my patent. I was a fool accepting the toothpaste patent after waiting half of its legal life. What I should have demanded was that they issue a new patent date when they reopened the case. The corruption in the patent office didn't just cost me the SmithKline Beecham contract, it lost me nearly a decade of patent protection. Looking back, I should have argued for the date to be adjusted, but I was so excited about getting the patent, the thought of changing the patent's start date never crossed my mind.

The first run of Vortex toothpaste was fifteen thousand tubes. They arrived at our home in St. Louis on a semi, the truck containing

150 shipper boxes, each container holding close to 100 tubes. For lack of space, we were forced to store the product throughout the house, their cardboard sides imprinted with the words VORTEX Color-Changing Toothpaste. The basement was now home to two companies, All Weather Safety Whistle and Wright Pharmaceuticals.

We started our guerilla marketing campaign guided by two fundamental principles. First and foremost was the fact that nearly ninety percent of children's toothpastes were purchased by the child's mother and the second was that dentists were the authority on all things dental.

With these two precepts in mind, we sent out a wave of product with the goal of informing both mothers and dentists of the features and benefits of the new color-changing toothpaste. We didn't have the money or the resources to make "sample tubes," so we opted for sending a single full tube along with product description sheets and ordering information.

We sent the first barrage of Vortex toothpaste to the most popular parenting forums and mom blogs that were frequented by modern, inquisitive mothers. These moms, hundreds of thousands of them, both experienced and new moms, discussed a myriad of topics on these blogs including everything from raising kids to organizing households. One thing these highly educated and passionate mothers loved as much as anything, was hearing about new products and how they could make their homes healthier, more organized and happier.

Vicki and I knew that these amazing women would appreciate our new healthy kids' toothpaste, so we jumped into these discussions by becoming active in their "giveaway" programs. By donating a couple of tubes of Vortex to each blog or forum, they, in exchange, would offer the tubes free to their readers in exchange for honest reviews. In a matter of weeks, we had more than fifty blogs raving about how children, who typically hated brushing, were now looking forward to brushing their teeth with Vortex Color-Changing Toothpaste.

The second volley of sample tubes were sent to pediatric dentists. There are nearly three thousand pediatric dentists in the United States so, because money was tight, we had to be selective on which dentists we sent samples. Using the internet, we separated out and contacted only those dentists that, from their websites, seemed open-minded, progressive and had the most modern and up to date offices.

Like the forums and blogs, the responses from the dental offices were fantastic. The kids liked the toothpaste, the mothers loved the fact that the daily fight to get her kid to brush his/her teeth was over and the dentists liked the idea of selling toothpaste in their offices.

At this point, six months into production, we hadn't gotten into any actual stores, so anyone who wanted to buy the toothpaste was directed toward our website where they could buy the toothpaste on-line. It was there that questions could be answered, videos shown and most importantly, toothpaste could be purchased.

The website had two separate sections, one for the public where the Vortex Toothpaste could be purchased through either Amazon, eBay or directly through our online store. The other separate section of the website was for professionals and gave dentists an avenue to purchase toothpaste in "commercial bulk packs" of six tubes.

Despite the overwhelming positive initial reaction from the public, we did find that we had two minor problems with the Vortex Toothpaste. It seems the tube was difficult for the younger kids to squeeze forcing moms to stop whatever it was she was doing and help the kids brush. While this was not a supercritical issue, it was clearly a problem that I would have to address and solve further down the line.

The other issue was more insidious and difficult to pin down.

I first noticed the problem myself a few weeks after I started using Vortex to brush my own teeth. I brushed with Vortex twice a day because I enjoyed the way it tasted and liked the way it cleaned my teeth without the foam and burning feeling. What I noticed however, was that the bristles on my white toothbrush had started to turn the slightest tinge of pink.

We patterned the red color of Vortex off the popular red gel toothpaste Closeup, using the same pigment they had used for over forty years, with the only exception being that we used a much lower concentration of the red. The Closeup brand used .04 red while we used .01. It didn't make sense that Vortex would stain a toothbrush pink while Closeup, with four times as much colorant, wouldn't.

Over the next two months our online sales increased, with more and more dentists ordering toothpaste and our reviews on nearly a hundred blogs looking great. I expanded our marketing to include an outreach to dental hygienists and exhibited at a pediatric convention. In each case the Vortex Color-Changing Toothpaste was a hit.

Despite the fact that we were getting emails daily asking us what stores carried the toothpaste, I was hesitant to approach outlets like Walgreens, Walmart and CVS. We were just getting up to speed and I didn't want to ruin our reputation by not being able to deliver.

On a whim, however, I decided to approach our local Walgreens pharmacy and present Vortex to the store manager. I told him I would give him a dozen tubes at no cost, just to try out. I didn't think much would come of having Vortex mixed in with the other popular brands of toothpaste, I simply thought it would be a fun exercise.

Following up at the store a week later I was shocked to see that he had sold over half the tubes. After a little encouragement from me, the manager called two of his colleagues, one that ran a Walgreens in Creve Coeur, Missouri, the other in Alton, Illinois. Again, I followed up at the other two Walgreens and found the Vortex toothpastes was selling fast there also.

"You should call the corporate office," the Alton manager told me. "If they OK this for regional distribution, you could end up in over two hundred stores. And if that works, you could end up in every Walgreens in the county."

"I looked at the manager, "That's a lot of stores.""

"We are talking nearly ten thousand Walgreens.""

I called the person in charge of Walgreens National sales. It took a little back and forth to get through, but I was surprised when I made the connection three hours later.

I explained my situation, the features and benefits of the toothpaste and gave the contact information for the three Walgreens that had us on their shelves. She said she would get back to me soon and, sure enough, it was the next day that I got her call.

"We are pulling you out of all our stores as of today.""

"Why?" I asked, taken aback. "What's wrong?"

"I have read two reports online that your toothpaste is turning things pink. Toothbrushes, soap dishes," she said tersely. "I don't like it, something's wrong and I am pulling them all out.""

She hung up.

I learned a long time ago that, when working a problem, it is often smart to look at the simple answer first. So, with that in mind, I got on the phone with the head chemist at the Bridgeton toothpaste man-ufacturing facility and told him about what was going on.

"We have a problem, Bill," I said, easing him into the situation. "It seems like the Vortex toothpaste is turning things pink.""

"Yeah," he said just a little too quickly, a little too brazen. "I noticed it myself when I was making up the initial batch run to fill our first order. The red gel stained my stirring rod. I thought it was odd.""

Astonished, I asked him point blank, "Bill, you realized it was do-ing something odd and you didn't think to call me?"

"No," he answered, just as shameless. "It's not my job to call you.""

"And you didn't think it was important to figure out why this was happening?"

"No," he said, sounding put out.

"Ok," I groaned, calming myself. "What concentration blue pigment did you use? Let's start there."

After a long five minute wait, he came back on the line, the sound of papers rustling in the background. ".01 percent for the blue."

"Alright. Perfect, I grabbed a pencil from my desk and wrote down the word blue, and the percentage. "Now what was the red percentage?"

There was an uncomfortable pause until Bill replied, ".1 for the red."

I wrote down the number, my hand shaking as I did.

I looked at what I read, not believing what I had heard, ".1? You used ten times more red colorant then blue. That is what you said. Correct? .1?"

There was a pause until I heard him say loudly, ".1 concentration red."

"That is like, close to two. No, that is nearly THREE TIMES more colorant than any adult toothpaste made on the planet."

The phone was silent until Bills voice came back hard and clear. "That is the amount I was told to use. 0.1 red."

"No. Check your notes. Check the emails. I told you to dial each back to a fourth of the regular toothpaste. I told you to lower the percentage for both the blue and the red to .01. We mixed them right there on your conference table."

His voice was hollow without emotion. ".1 was the amount I was told to use."

"So, what you're telling me is that all the toothpaste is wrong, that I need to recall all the tubes."

"You do what you have to do. I just did what I was told." He slammed the phone down.

I felt sick to my stomach. Literally feeling like I was going to barf. I had spent thousands of hours working on the packaging, the website, the marketing and now it was all ruined. That was bad, but the worst thing was that, as of that very moment, I didn't care if I never saw another tube of Vortex Color-Changing Toothpaste ever again.

The cold pain I felt in my heart reminded me of when I was a sophomore in high school. I overheard my "girlfriend" talking bad about me to a group of kids, joking about how I acted, how I spoke. In a flash she went from the love of my life to revolting. One moment she was all I could think of, the next she was just another bully to be ignored. I didn't want to win her back or make things different. I wanted to forget I had ever met her.

The color-changing toothpaste, in which I had so completely immersed myself, had just become my worst enemy. In a matter of a split second, the invention I had tried so hard to grow and nurture had just become totally and absolutely detestable.

Vicki pulled me aside, "Maybe we could have them redo the next batch? Start over again. We have the tubes."

"No," I said unequivocally, "I'm done with it."

"They screwed it up, we could sue them." Vicki suggested. "Have them reimburse us for the messed up tubes."

"Take Bridgeton to court? Hire attorneys?" I just shook my head. "It will take two maybe three years to get any money out of them. No. Between being extorted by the patent office, the clumsy tubes that are too difficult to squeeze and the fact that we have less than five years left on the patent and now these incompetent buffoons screwed up the formula. I'm done with it."

Vicki didn't disagree.

Over the fifteen years that we had spent working on the Vortex Color-Changing Toothpaste, Vicki and I lost a little over $350,000. To some bigtime business owners, that isn't a lot of money. To us it was a massive fortune.

All said and done, I am glad I made the attempt. It was a great experience trying to develop the toothpaste and place it in a big-box store. I learned all about marketing on the internet, how the FDA works and doesn't work and the importance of checking everything yourself. There were fun times with laugh-out-loud moments and there were horrible times when I wanted to scream, but the truth is, I don't regret making the attempt.

What I've regretted more than anything in my life are those instances where I didn't act. Where I failed to take the risk and instead, ignored a potential life changing discovery.

One such neglected opportunity occurred back in the late 1980s while I was turkey hunting about a hundred miles outside of St. Louis with my brother-in-law Stan. We were trying to spot one of the gobblers in the cuts and valleys on a friend's farm when, walking along a streambed, I wandered upon a long set of dinosaur's tracks.

I have always been fascinated by anything related to dinosaurs and on many occasions taken the children to nearby Illinois where we would search for trilobite fossils. On this one particular winter's day I had just stepped out onto a flat run of limestone when I saw what looked like turkey tracks running across the rock. The only thing was, these weren't turkey tracks.

The footprints were larger than a dinner platter with each impression separated by as much as six feet. The four toed prints looked like huge peace signs and ran straight down the middle of the streambed until they disappeared into the base of a steep bluff, each print measuring at least two fingers deep. If this was a turkey it was a at least twelve feet tall, weighting in the hundreds of pounds.

I was astonished by the footprints but for some reason just dismissed the observation, walked off and kept looking for a bird to shoot. During my life, I had spent hundreds of hours looking for fossils. Days walking around museums staring at dinosaurs' bones and now, standing in the presence of a remarkable paleontological find, simply ignored what was staring me right in the face. It would be no different than seeing Bigfoot and then saying "Cool" and just walking on.

Years later, I offhandedly mentioned the dinosaur footprints to an expert in Missouri paleontology who said I was crazy and that no such dinosaurs lived in the area. I couldn't prove him wrong because I failed to document the prints. I've regretted blowing off the discovery ever since.

# Chapter 34:
# Back in the Saddle Again

*"Patience an♦ perseverance have a magical effect before which ♦ifficulties ♦isappear an♦ obstacles vanish."*

John Quincy Adams - 6th U.S. President

The implosion of the toothpaste company was incredibly hard on me. To spend so much time, effort and money on a dream and then to have it perverted by an examiner from the U. S. Patent and Trademark office, to have it squandered for three years by an incompetent partner from New Jersey and lastly, to have the formulation tainted by a bungling lab tech from Bridgeton, left me mentally devastated.

In my mind's eye, I visualized Vortex toothpaste being used all over the country by kids smiling as they brushed their teeth. I saw my own children being part of a great company that sold a healthy product that not only would have made tens of thousands of moms' lives easier and kids healthier, but one that also gave back to the community. I saw Wright Pharmaceutics as the Ben & Jerrys of toothpaste.

But it didn't work.

Maybe it was narcissistic thinking that I could actually pull it off. Maybe I just didn't have the resources to make it work or perhaps it was just a bad idea. Then again, maybe everything worked out just as it should have.

I don't know what Christ had in store for me and it is not our place to try and second-guess God. Should I have done this, should I have done that? I don't know. What I do know is that God has a plan for me. In Jeremiah 29:11 the Bible states, "For I know the plans I have for you, declares the Lord, plans for welfare and not for evil, to give you a future and a hope."

It was difficult for me to even consider inventing something new after the toothpaste's collapse. I had always come up with novel ideas, interrupting Vicki and the children with my next great invention. Now it was as if I was lost, abandoned in some kind of mental wasteland, awake but in a creative desert.

It took a combination of family, friends and prayer for me to get beyond the toothpaste failure and stop whining. Everybody, at some time in their lives, has had their hopes and dreams demolished in one form or another. I had to stop being such a short-sighted fool and instead of focusing on the bad, turn my sights on the future.

Helen Keller, when Anne Sullivan died, fell into a deep depression. After months of feeling sorry for herself, Helen decided to stop looking at the past and wake up, accept the horrible loss and move on to the next task, the next responsibility, the next adventure. She expressed this in her quote, "When one door of happiness closes, another opens; but often we look so long at the closed door that we do not see the one which has been opened for us."

Part of the disappointment I embraced after the loss of the toothpaste revolved around the guilt I felt knowing that I had quit. Making the decision to fight on and not give up, or quit and walk away, is incredibly difficult. Faced by my flailing product, I was forced to really look at things in my life and decide what truly mattered.

The question I ultimately asked myself was, "Is this the hill I want to die on?" For me the toothpaste wasn't worth the anguish. There are only a handful of things I would be willing to sacrifice everything for, and toothpaste was not one of them.

I read a story many years ago about a professor at Harvard's prestigious business school. He stood motionless and waited before a packed class of graduate students. Once they were all settled, he placed an empty glass in front of them and asked a simple question.

"Is the glass empty or full?"

All around the class, voices called out, "Empty."

"You are correct," the professor agreed.

He then reached inside a nearby box and pulled out three large stones and placed them carefully in the glass.

He looked across the class and asked again, "How about now, full or empty?"

"Full," the class replied.

"No, not quite," the professor disagreed.

Slowly, the instructor turned back to the box and taking some gravel, poured it between the rocks while shaking the glass filling in every nook and cranny. When finished he asked, "Is the glass full?"

The Harvard students caught on and said, "No."

The instructor grinned, "You are learning." Then taking a hand full of sand, he added the fine grains to the glass. When finished he again asked, "How about now, is it full?"

"No," the students answered.

Finally, the teacher took a glass of water and poured it over the rocks, gravel and sand, filling the glass to the very brim.

"Now the glass is full," the professor declared. "So, what have you learned?"

The class was silent for quite a long time until the professor explained, "Before you place a single item into the glass, you must know what is most important, and put those items in first. Once that is set, you can then just fill the extra space with whatever you like. The same thing goes for life. Find out what matters and bring that into your life first. Everything else is just filler."

For me, the toothpaste didn't make it into the glass.

After losing Walmart, the humiliation of the malpractice lawsuit and then the failure of the toothpaste, I couldn't seem to get the bitter taste of failure out of my mouth; it hung there like the putrid taste of vomit and I just didn't want to taste it again. What I had to do was empty my life of the useless and senseless extra filler and then focus on what I needed to put in the glass first.

I guess I just lost sight of what mattered, but worse still, and even more foolish, I had become ungrateful. Ungrateful of the blessings I was given by God. Ungrateful for the love of my wife and my children. Ungrateful for having had the opportunity to develop a product and sell it worldwide. Who cares that some witch tried to destroy my dental office with a frivolous law suit, that Buck Bargain Stores tried stealing my whistle or some bonehead lab tech from Bridgeton messed up my toothpaste? None of this was going to last anyway; nothing does.

About this time, I got a call from my brother Ken who told me he was having a new surfboard shaped and encouraged me to come along and watch Phil Becker, one of the foremost board shapers in the world, create yet another work of art.

Twenty years before my brother had his first Speedshape fashioned by Becker but now, after two decades and thousands of waves, he needed a new ride.

Creating a surfboard that fits both the surfer and the wave is serious business. Surfing is the melding of a rider and a wave, the board acting as the "interface" between the two. In order to tightly fuse the surfer's ability with the dynamics of the wave, surfboards are often custom made by true artists called shapers. Phil Becker was a shaping genius and he was about to retire.

Clearly, surfboards can be purchased "off the rack," but when you're shooting down the face of an eight-foot wave, it's nice knowing your board is in harmony with you and the three hundred tons of water hurtling toward your head.

We walked into Phil Becker's nondescript warehouse, passed an old dented and rusting sliding metal door and made our way along a narrow hallway past eight, ten and twelve foot long blocks of white foam "blanks" stacked against the walls of the corridor.

These "blanks" were tantamount to Michelangelo's blocks of virgin marble. Over the next few days, they would be systematically cut, shaved and sanded down to create some of the most amazingly beautiful custom surfboards known to man.

We passed through a cluttered antechamber and entered a small room, the walls covered with cardboard patterns, wooden templates and yellowed pictures of boards, surfers and most importantly, waves. The area was well lit, the floor covered with no less than six inches of shaved foam making the ground look like some kind of winter wonderland. In the center of the room stood a pair of wooden saw-horses, the tops overlaid with natty swaths of old carpet.

Atop the saw-horses rested a half-shaped board, its rounded nose and tapered tail having had just been freed from a block of four inch thick Styrofoam. Next to the partially shaped board stood a masked craftsman. In his hand he held an electric sander that shifted and shook as it was dragged along the curved outer surface of the surfboard. With each pass the small tool howled as it ejected a shower of snowy foam onto the already covered floor.

He stopped, flipped the hand tool to silent, pulled the mask down and greeted us with a smile.

"Hey, how can I help you?"

This was Phil Becker. He looked like a fit Pablo Picasso as he stood shirtless in his worn old boots and tattered gym shorts. His eyes were keen while his hands looked old, his demeanor casual while at the same time incredibly intense.

"Hey," my brother said, stepping up and offering his hand, "I'm Ken Wright and I made an appointment to have a custom board shaped."

"Great. I'm Phil, So, what are you looking for?"

"You made me a board twenty years ago," my brother explained, "and I just love it. It's getting pretty beat up, so I was hoping you could shape me a new one. I have the original; the old one's outside in the car."

"Cool," Phil said as he placed the sander onto a workbench and moved the board he was crafting to an open piece of wall space in the corner of the room. "Bring it in."

Ken left to get his board and now, left alone with Phil Becker, I stepped up from the back of the room and asked him a single question.

"Hi, I'm Ken's brother. I am a high school teacher and I try to explain to my students what it takes to be great. I was wondering what it takes to be great at what you do?"

Phil, not understanding, gave me an odd kind of, "What are you talking about?" look, so I explained.

"Couple of years ago I met a pro football linebacker and asked him the same question. He said, 'Everybody gets knocked down. To be great you have to get up fast and get back in the play.' A professional boxer I met told me, 'Don't be surprised when you get hit. Keep fighting.' I was wondering what you thought was key to being a world class surfboard shaper?"

Phil Becker, a man who is said to have been interviewed only once in his life, refused to wear a watch and hated to be photographed, stepped forward and looked me straight in the eyes. "Tell the kids to always follow your stoke."

"Follow your stoke?" I repeated, unsure of what he said.

"Yeah. You'll always be a success when you do what you love; follow your stoke."

My brother was back with his old board and instantly the conversation turned to shapes and contours, fin design and fiberglass.

Two hours later my brother had taken the first step toward getting a new board and I had taken the first step toward a new outlook on life. A month after that my brother had a new board and I had a new invention.

It was at a New Year's Eve party at a buddy's house that I came up with the idea. Vicki and I were enjoying the evening eating appetizers and toasting this and that with a fine red wine when halfway through the night, Vicki noticed that our lips and teeth had turned a soft pink-ish red from the wine.

Vicki looked at me with a wide pink Cheshire Cat smile and said, "If only there was a way to keep the wine from turning our lips and teeth red. Now that would be a cool invention."

Opening my mind for the first time in what seemed like a million years, I asked, "What if it also worked with coffee, tea and smoking?"

Vicki grinned, realizing I was back to thinking outside the box. "Ok, 'Whistle King.' How could you do that without hurting the teeth or making what you're eating or drinking taste different?"

"I have an idea," I told her.

Realizing that people were spending tons of money on bleaching gels and whitening strips only to have their beautiful smiles made dark by coffee, tea, wine and cigarettes, I decided to work on creating a clear emulsion, a gel, that you could apply to the teeth in a matter of seconds and protect them from stains.

The gel would be like lip balm, but flavorless, invisible and not toxic; you could eat it. It wouldn't stay on your teeth permanently but remain there for about two to three hours. The ointment wouldn't change the flavor of the food or the drinks you were tasting and about three seconds after applying it you couldn't even feel it on your teeth. It would be like lotion for your hands, but totally invisible, tasteless and temporary. It would function simply to protect your teeth from stains.

I decided to call the balm *Dr. Wright's Lip an◆ Tooth Stain Protector* and it worked like a charm. It was just a fun idea, nothing too weird. A simple all-organic stain barrier for teeth and it was great fun developing it.

One aspect that made the stain shield particularly wonderful was that I wouldn't need to go through the trouble of obtaining patent protection. To keep *Dr. Wright's Lip an◆ Tooth Stain Protector* from being copied or stolen, I simply had to keep the formula a secret.

Another aspect of *Dr. Wright's Lip an◆ Tooth Stain Protector* that made the entire process glorious, was that lip gloss and tooth waxes were not controlled by the Food and Drug Administration, the FDA. I didn't need to spend over thirty thousand dollars having my new product checked out because it was made from waxes and oils that are used in everyday products.

I discovered the exact formulation for the stain protector by first running tests on the tooth substitute Ivorine® that I found at a local hobby shop. Once I began catching sight of a good working formula, I moved to experimenting on my own teeth, trying every combination I could come up with. I studied different kinds of waxes, their properties and how I could combine them in order to get just the right effects. After trying a ton of different variations and creations, I came up with an mixture that was totally flavorless, stayed on the teeth and temporarily blocked stains from both the teeth and the lips.

I now needed a manufacturing copacker, a company that could formulate, fill and label a tube that could dispense my tooth and lip stain blocker. When it came to producing the whistle or the toothpaste, finding a manufacturer was a Herculean task demanding months of work and tens of thousands of dollars. Lip balm was different.

I checked the internet and found there were a slew of manufacturers of ointments, nearly each and every one of them capable of making, packaging and shipping whatever you needed. It took me less than a day to find an amazing company out of Cincinnati, Ohio that made specialty organic salves, lip balms and ointments.

After about a month of back and forth, we finally settled on the exact formulation and the packaging. Two weeks later I received a shipment of *Dr. Wright's Lip an⦁ Tooth Stain Protector*. From start to finish, the entire project cost me less than a thousand dollars and I have been selling them ever since.

# Chapter 35:
# Writing

*"Writing in a ♦iary is a really strange experience for someone like me. Not only because I've never written anything before, but also because it seems to me that later on neither I nor anyone else will be intereste♦ in the musings of a thirteen-year-ol♦ schoolgirl."*

Anne Frank – German-born
Jewish Diarist

I have always loved to tell stories. Always enjoyed recalling good times and bad, trying desperately to convey to others the constant whirl of emotions that passed through my head. Oftentimes the stories were true to life and recounted the panic, the joy or the surprise I felt during a time or event. Other stories I made up out of pure dream-stuff just for fun.

Stories were important to me. It seemed that as much as I liked telling them, people seemed to enjoy hearing them. Often on road trips, while waiting in line at the grocery store or just before bedtime, I would tell stories to Tom, Angela and Jessica to help pass the time. They would shout out characters or events and I would build a story around their suggestions. It was always great fun.

One very special story I made up was created to pass the time while the family waited for the killer whale show to begin at Sea World in San Diego. Vicki, the children and I, had arrived twenty minutes early to get good seats for the program and in order to pass the time, I made up an adventure story about ancient Hawaii. The story told of a boy Pahula, who defied his father, got lost at sea and, after nearly losing his life, was found again.

It was a simple story with a solid beginning, middle and end. There were hungry sharks and terrible bullies, near drowning and dangerous surf. I considered working with my sister Joanne to make *Pahula* into a kid's book but decided against the idea. It was just a story and despite being somewhat entertaining, had no real purpose.

I lost interest and forgot all about the Hawaiian adventure story for over twenty years until Vicki and I traveled to the island of Oahu to visit a close friend. It was then, while we were enjoying the beautiful island beaches and wonderful people, that I totally re-examined the idea of the Hawaiian adventure book.

Vicki and I were walking down the boulevard just off Waikiki Beach on our way to breakfast, when I looked down and noticed a word deeply etched into the sidewalk. The script was beautiful, obviously molded into the concrete when the sidewalk was first laid. It was the Hawaiian word *Aloha* and underneath in a smaller font was the translation: greetings, regards, kindness, compassion, affection, love.

Later that day I read an article in a local newspaper that discussed the abundance of movies and television programs that distorted the traditions of the ancient Hawaiians. It talked about how a high percentage of native Hawaiians had forgotten their own customs and language and how a large number of educators were trying desperately to preserve the true history of the Hawaiian people.

Vicki and I had always loved Hawaii. It started when we spent our honeymoon on Maui where we had the opportunity to meet so many wonderful people and visit so many amazing places. Years later, I became close friends with a fourth generation Hawaiian who, while surfing and hiking in and around Oahu, shared stories and tales of ancient Hawaii. He told of the gods Lono and Ku, the precious traditions of the Hawaiian people and what the Aloha spirit was truly all about.

It was during the Hawaiian vacation that I decided to revisit the story *Pahula* and not just write a kid's picture book, but instead write a true historical fiction. An adventure story that would not only capture a young person's imagination, but also accurately describe what ancient Hawaiian villages, traditions and people were really like.

Just as I did in college and dental school, I began by sketching a comprehensive outline of what I hoped to accomplish and then, step-by-step, filled in the details. I established a routine where, every day, I would wake up at five in the morning, make my decaf coffee and work on setting distinct micro-goals to be achieved by eight when Vicki would typically wake up.

For hundreds of hours I researched books, articles and academic papers that described, in detail, the majesty of the Hawaiian customs, religion and language. I watched documentaries, studied manuscripts and listened to numerous accounts from native Hawaiians, all in the hope of constructing an accurate rendition of ancient Hawaiian life.

Working with Vicki, who taught English as a second language, I incorporated over forty words of Hawaiian into the story in hopes that, by the time the reader got to the last page, they would have learned dozens of words of Hawaiian without even trying.

One of the most important steps in producing the book was my work with the incredible native Hawaiian historian and Hawaiian language expert Maile Keliipio Acoba.

"First off," Maile seethed over the phone, "the name is horrible. Why don't you just call the book Bill or Bob. This whole affair makes me sick."

I couldn't believe it. Maile, the wonderful native Hawaiian woman who agreed to read my book, an educator who not only taught students to speak Hawaiian but was an expert in Hawaiian folklore, hadn't even gotten past the title page and she was already beyond angry.

"Please, I want to understand. What did I do wrong?"

Gaining her composure, Maile continued, "Hawaiian names always mean something. You don't just make up a word."

"Ok," I replied feeling like the ignoramus that I was. "By any chance do you have a suggestion?" I held my breath. This is where she had the choice of either just hanging up on me and abandoning the entire project or decide to work with me and make it better.

I waited.

"Yes," Maile replied hesitantly. "I have a name, but what are the odds you are actually going to use it?"

"I want this book to be great." I countered, "What is your suggestion?"

"*Puhala*," she said with an air of reverence.

Moving to my computer I quickly flipped to Google and typed in the word *PUHALA* and searched. It was a tree, a beautiful indigenous fruit tree that was revered in ancient Hawaii. It was used for clothes, decoration, and mats.

"Consider it changed." I replied, "Sorry for the misstep."

"Really?" Maile answered back, skeptical. "Do you really expect me to believe that you just changed the name of your book?"

"Not just the name of the book," I responded. "I am going to go through the entire manuscript and change every name in it making certain that each one has a true Hawaiian meaning."

"Ok," she said, and for the first time I sensed a smile over the phone. "Now about the word *kahuna*. They're not just priests. They were, and are, both men and women, healers, mentors, teachers, hunters and builders. Anyone who would be considered the top expert in their discipline."

I worked with Maile and two other incredible consultants, Sanoe Marfil and Sabra Kauka, reading and re-reading the manuscript of *Puhala an• the Temple of Refuge* until, to the best of my ability, it accurately depicted life in ancient Hawaii. It told of an ancient civilization that thrived five hundred years before British Captain James Cook arrived and changed everything.

I wrote *Puhala an͠ the Temple of Refuge* because I liked the story, love Hawaii and delight in the amazing traditions that lay at the foundation of who the Hawaiian people are. I focused my outreach toward Hawaiian middle school teachers hoping to make their difficult job of teaching folklore just a little bit easier. I also saw *Puhala an͠ the Temple of Refuge* appealing to educators introducing diversity to their students.

Diversity lessons for middle schoolers are intended to open the student's eyes to people with a completely different culture. They try to teach students that there is more than one way to see the world. *Puhala an͠ the Temple of Refuge* was written to do just that.

It took me a full year to finish *Puhala an͠ the Temple of Refuge*. A full year to create the story, research the history and make it all flow together. By the time I finished, I had in mind a sequel that looked at the same ancient Hawaiian society but from the perspective of a young girl. I called it *Puhala an͠ the Revenge of the Matu*.

The third Hawaiian adventure book is called *Puhala an͠ the Secret of the Menehune* and discusses ancient traditions and what they mean to the Hawaiians.

Writing the Puhala series has been a delight. Meeting the Hawaiians, visiting the amazing Bishops Museum on Oahu and studying the wonderful history of Hawaii has been more than captivating, it has been life changing.

# Chapter 36:
# A Framework for Success

*"Out of pain an♦ problems have come the sweetest songs, an♦ the most gripping stories."*

Billy Graham - American Evangelist

In the book of Ecclesiastes, it says, "Cast thy bread upon the waters: for thou shalt find it after many days." Whenever I read that I hear God saying to me, "Invest even just a fraction of yourself into the remarkable world that God has created, and you will be amazed to see what emerges." That is exactly what I have tried to do: Make a change, take a risk or try something new. When you toss the proverbial bread upon the water, it is amazing what comes to the surface.

A group of scientists did a study where they took a clean sterile fishbowl, round and smooth, and filled it with clean sterile water, opened it to the air and waited. In the course of a month they found six kinds of microbial animals and plants swimming around. With little diversity you find little variation.

They then added a single small clean stone to the bowl. In no time at all, over fifty different kinds of plants and animals were found populating the vessel, all interacting in a complex interactive ecosystem, thriving in nooks and niches that didn't exist before. That stone offered diversity, opportunity, options. A single stone that generated fifty different chances for a multitude of species to hide, grow and flourish. Like finding one more door to be opened, one more gear to be turned, one more opportunity to pursue.

In my case, I tossed my dream of being an inventor into the fishbowl of life and, stirring the water, stood back and watched how, in a very tiny way, I was able to change the world.

It is humbling to think of how much God loves us. How he has given us a front row seat to witness just what the world had to offer in all its beauty and, yes, all its deceit. I watched as my silly dream of building an underwater whistle develop into the loudest whistle in the world sold in over eighty countries and saving dozens upon dozens of lives. I saw the simple act of introducing myself at a prayer group result in my meeting an amazingly smart and confident strawberry blond nursing student, a blessed meeting that blossomed into an unbelievable family.

I saw the whistle inducted into the Museum of Modern Art in New York. I witnessed my color-changing toothpaste go from a funny chairside story to an amazingly unique product and then ultimately a complete and absolute failure. I watched as I went from a student who hated school to a successful teacher, mentor and coach. I also saw my knack for telling stories transform slowly into a successful writing career.

I realized early on that God's plan for me wasn't so much that I should become a dentist, whistle manufacturer, toothpaste creator, writer or teacher. His plan wasn't that I should be a husband or father, inventor or missionary. All these professions, goals and dreams are fine. But I believe what God has always wanted for me was simply to have a sincere, holy and strong relationship with Him.

I believe God thought it was a good idea to create us. He thought it would be wonderful. He thought it would be fun.

But it wasn't always fun; for either one of us.

Once sin came into this world it destroyed that amazing God - man relationship. Tore apart the special bond God intended between us and him. I came to understand that it is Christ's role to repair the rift. Restore our relationship with God by paying the price for our sins.

As I learned from the beginning, confusion is the enemy.

In this modern world where there are twenty-four hour in your face newscasts, where the mass murder of a dozen people is considered old news after a day. Where social media, even for the most disciplined individual, is nearly impossible to ignore, it is difficult to know what constitutes senseless prattle and what really matters.

For me, the key element to my life, the stone I learned to put in the glass first, was realizing that I was not alone. That God does exist, truly does love me and has a plan for me.

I was reminded of the importance of keeping focused on what truly matters a number of years ago when night diving off the breakwall near Redondo Beach, California.

It was well past nine at night in late January when I dropped down from the deck of a buddy's boat to hunt lobster. Wearing my thick winter wetsuit, SCUBA gear, lights and game bag, I descended to sixty feet, hit the bottom and headed due east toward the base of the breakwall just outside King Harbor.

To catch lobsters, it was critical to dive at night. It was then, well past sundown, that the bugs, (that's what we call lobsters) came out of their burrows and scavenged for food. During the day the lobsters remained out of reach, hidden deep within the rocky seawall, well away from the sharp teeth of the local harbor seals. At night, however, the largest of the bugs scurried from their hiding places between the rocks and moved out into the open to forage.

When I dove, I typically brought two lights with me. A large underwater light I carried in one hand and a smaller mask light I attached to the strap of my facemask. I almost always dove alone, always kept an eye on my down time and always was aware of my depth.

The dive was going well, the water feeling warmer than usual, the sea both clear and calm. I had already caught five "keeper" lobsters and felt great as I searched for the sixth and seventh in order to secure my limit. Lobsters can be difficult to spot underwater, their dark reddish-brown color melding with the copper-colored seaweed that rose thick from the bottom. California lobsters don't have claws, but do have a pair of long stiff antenna, a jagged spiny tail and are about as big as a football.

To find the lobsters on the breakwall, I first glided to the bottom and searched the base where it was easy to see the bugs scurrying over the ocean floor. Once I had searched the lower aspect of the wall, I then rose upwards and hunted around the huge seaweed-covered rocks that make up the body of the steep jetty.

On the sand, the lobsters looked like large loaves of dark brown bread on a tan bedsheet and were easy to see and to catch. When they were in the rocks however, it can be difficult to find them; often the only telltale sign hinting to their whereabouts was their long boney antenna sticking up like stiff rusty wires.

The problem on that particular evening started when I looked up from the bottom where the boulders met the sand and, flashing my light up the nearly vertical rock seawall, noticed a giant lobster resting on a craggy outcrop ten feet above me. These big bugs were easily spooked, so turning off my main light and shifting it behind me, I advanced, slowly illuminating the giant with only my weaker mask light.

The behemoth was the largest bug I had ever seen. Its body as long as my shin was from my knee to my foot. It showed antenna that looked more like fishing poles, its legs as long as new pencils.

As I rose in the water column to approach the lobster it shifted, first facing me and then backing up halfway into a deep crevice between two huge boulders. Hoping to keep from spooking it further I stopped, placed my hand over the mask light and floated unmoving, my body nearly invisible in the black water.

One full minute went by and then a second. Slowly I opened my hand and let the dimmest of light seep through my gloved fingers and as the hazy glow illuminated the rocks, the lobster once again came into view. I crept inch by inch toward the brute.

The lobster withdrew again retreating back further into the breach in the seawall until only its head and large antenna shown from the cleft.

A creature of this size would typically be grabbed with two hands like lifting a baby from a crib, but there was no way I could snatch him properly at the angle I was facing. Realizing that I was a short arm's length away and seeing that the bug had almost completely disappeared within the rocks, I knew I would have to be bold and make a grab for its twin horns on the front of its head.

Waiting till I was ready, the oceans soft in-and-out swell moving me closer, I reached out as fast as lightning and grabbed the lobster with my left hand and held on tight as it forced its way backward, deep into the hole.

The demon fought my grip and writhed out of control as it wiggled its way deeper and deeper into the space between the rocks by spreading its legs wide, holding fast to the small stone cave it had wedged itself into.

Keeping a tentative grasp on the monster with my left hand, I reached deep into the underwater cave with my right and tried desperately to clutch the lobster's underbelly, but it was no use. I just couldn't stretch far enough into the hole to wrap my fingers around it and extract him. The cavern was too narrow, the bug too wiry, my equipment too bulky, my regulator hose was getting in my way.

I needed just six more inches. If only I could squirm just another hand's distance deeper into the cavern, then I would have my trophy. Then I would be able to prove to everyone what a great diver and hunter I was.

As if being presented with a special gift, an idea came to me in a flash of brilliance. If I could get rid of my SCUBA regulator, my only source of air, I might just be able to wiggle deep enough into the underwater cave and snatch the monster.

I reached up with my right hand, and taking two quick breaths, removed my regulator from my mouth, placing it behind me, out of the way. With both hands now in front of me, my head and torso wedged tight between stacked boulders at night in forty feet of water, I suddenly realized what I had done.

In pursuit of a foolish trophy, I was now going to drown, killed by my own selfish greed.

I could feel the terror envelop me. It felt like a million fleas were crawling up my legs, the way the horror of being trapped inside the underwater cave exploded inside of me. First came self-doubt and then the maddening sensation of pure panic making me want to thrash and scream. I struggled to calm myself; to relax my frantic mind and quiet every muscle in my body.

I held my breath as the fear that boiled inside me battled against my forced calm.

I remember that I closed my eyes against the panic and prayed for strength. Prayed that I would not leave my wife and children alone. Prayed to God that he would forgive my selfishness and stupidity.

Slowly the terror was held at bay leaving me calm, but still trapped.

Like some kind of moronically stupid worm, I wiggled back and forth using my elbows to wedge myself inch by inch out of the hole. Finally, clear of my self-imposed trap, I again felt a renewed surge of panic as I groped blindly for my regulator that was caught behind my tank. Sweeping again and again with my arm in the inky dark water, with seconds to spare, I hooked my regulator and quickly placed it in my mouth.

It is odd what you think about as you wrestle with panic; seeing your life on the verge of being snuffed out. Odd how your priorities change when faced with death as all of your hopes and dreams come to an unexpected and abrupt end.

I realize now that it was arrogance that lead me into the small cave in the rocks. A kind of senseless pride borne from the idea that I would prove to everybody that I was king of the world.

In the Gospels from the Bible, Jesus tells the story of a son who squanders his inheritance, reneges on his responsibilities and turns against his loving father. Realizing his foolishness, the prodigal son returns to his father rehearsing his apology as he makes his way home. The father we learn, has been watching the road, longing for his son's return. Upon seeing his boy from afar, the father runs to him and interrupts the apology of the repentant son mid-sentence to welcome him.

All the father wants is his son back. Not a perfect son. Not "cured." Just back with the knowledge that his father loved him enough to pay the toll, pay the price.

God redeemed us totally with unconditional love through Christ.

The whole idea of unconditional love was difficult for me as a young man. I had rarely experienced love without some kind of threat linked to it. Love for me was like a loan that had to be paid back with some kind of bookie's interest attached. "If you loved your father, you would get better grades." "If you loved me, you would clean your room."

My inability to understand unconditional love affected the way I saw myself, the way I saw the people around me and even affected my marriage. It was Vicki who taught me what true, unconditional love was. Somehow, she saw my skewed perception of love right from the beginning and knew she had to deal with it quickly.

It was right after we got married that she confronted me about my understanding of true, unconditional love. I was in my third year of dental school and Vicki had just started as a nurse on the Ears, Nose and Throat floor of Barnes Hospital. I would go off to Washington

University's dental clinic at around eight in the morning departing just minutes after Vicki got home from her eleven to seven shift at the hospital. We both shared chores around the small house we rented: cutting the grass, putting out the trash, doing laundry, cooking meals and washing the dishes.

But she saw an underlying problem at the heart of it all. A problem I had never considered. "Hey," she said looking around our small rental. "You did the dishes and finished the laundry. You didn't need to do that."

"I know," I smiled, "I just thought I'd help out."

"Well, don't worry about trying so hard," she replied, curious as to my incentive for doing "her" job.

Things went along fine, nothing further mentioned, until two days later she asked me to do the unthinkable. She asked me to do something my parents would have never even hinted at.

"Howard," Vicki said with an air of seriousness as she took two dishes from the cabinet and put them onto the kitchen table for dinner. "I need you to do something for me. After dinner, when I leave to work at the hospital, I DON'T want you to clean up. Leave everything just as it is. And leave the laundry on the couch. Don't fold it."

"What do you mean?" I asked confused, "I don't mind...."

She softly interrupted. "Just leave everything alone," Vicki insisted, "just the way you see it."

It was soon time for Vicki to go to work, the house suddenly quiet with her departure. As I settled myself at the kitchen table writing out the dental treatment plans for the next day in the clinic, I thought of how Vicki would feel returning home to dirty dishes and unfolded clothes. Would she still love me knowing I left the house a mess? Would she still care for me if I didn't care for her? I had to win her love all over again. I had to prove that I was worth the commitment she swore to at our wedding. I had to show her how I deserved her love.

I again straightened the house, and once finished, relaxed, knowing I had again justified myself. Proved again that she made the right decision choosing me.

The next morning, standing in her nurses' uniform after a long night's work, she stood and seethed, her tired expression a mixture of frustration and regret. I thought she would be pleased that I had cleaned the house, happy that she could now relax and put her feet up, but she would have none of it.

She walked over to the clothes I had so diligently folded and tossed them to the floor. Vicki then walked to the kitchen where she took clean cups, bowls and plates and spread them messily over the counter. She snatched forks, knives and spoons from their little slots in cabinet drawers and tossed them onto the small kitchen table her mom had given us.

"Now!" she raised her voice, her finger in my face. "When I come home tomorrow morning, I better see every cup and plate right where they are. And the clothes, you better not touch one sock!"

I left for school confused, a cold pallor hung heavy over our relationship. It killed me to see her so angry after I tried so hard to simply show her my love.

That evening we ate dinner between a mass of scattered plates and cups. Our conversation was short and curt as Vicki left for her rotation on the graveyard shift at eleven.

The next morning, I heard her force the house key into the front door lock and slowly move through the front hallway toward the kitchen. I met her halfway to welcome her home; at my feet lay crumpled t-shirts, pants and shirts. Behind me on the table lay plates from last night's dinner, dirty pots on the stove and all manner of cookware strewn across the counters.

Vicki walked up to me, took my hands into hers, and looking deep into my eyes, said, "You see, the house is a mess and I still love you."

I broke down and cried.

The idea of love without conditions was totally foreign to me. Vicki, by forcing me to stop working tried to show me that. Teach me how those little acts of sacrifice I was doing are fine, but often distort what true love is really all about. I was missing out on the power of her unconditional love by me constantly trying to justify myself through gifts of work and in so doing failed to see the depth of her deep caring. I think the same goes for God

The Bible has taught me that my good works are nothing but filthy rags compared to His Saving Grace, His love. I have done nothing to warrant Christ's sacrifice on the cross: nothing to gain his love. My reading of the Bible doesn't earn his love, but I am drawn to its Truth. My attending church doesn't earn his love, but it strengthens me and brings me closer to Christ.

I had no idea what God had in store for me or what plans He had for my future. Why He would inspire me to make the loudest whistle in the world? Why He would drag me fifteen hundred miles straight south to go to school in Central America and force me to learn Spanish? Why He would hook me up with a crooked patent examiner? Why would He introduce me to Dr. Allen, only to snatch him away with cancer?

All I truly do know is that I am not alone and that I trust God completely.

# Chapter 37:
# Moving Forward

*"If we fail to a·apt, we fail to move forwar·."*

John Wooden - NCAA basketball coach

B etween playing tennis, diving and surfing, I now devote most of my days writing and spending time with my children and grandchildren. When I was young, I looked forward to and delighted in owning my first car. With time, my hopes and dreams turned to marrying Vicki, raising children and, one day, building a prosperous career. Interesting enough, considering all the amazing events I had looked forward to and anticipated, I never considered the incredible gift of having grandchildren.

Perhaps the mere thought of knowing my children's children was too difficult for me to get my head around. In any case, my grandchildren have been one of the true highlights of my life and, to a large degree, the motivation to write this book. Their cries of "Hap," (they call me Hap, short for Grandpa Howard), tell us the story about the lobster," after having told them of the encounter a half dozen times, compelled me to put the stories on paper; the lessons I learned and the experiences I have had preserved in print. The grandkids are a blessing I had never dreamt of when I was young, but enthusiastically embrace as I grow old.

There are a number of things I hope to share with my grandkids. Stories recalling places I have been and the experiences I have had. I look forward to speaking with them about God and love, success and failure. And, just as important, I look forward to listening and learning as much as I can from them. Being part of their dreams, thoughts and hopes.

Of the great number of life experiences I hope to share with my grandkids, there are four central principles that have been key to my achievements. Four crucial lessons that were instrumental in solidifying my success. Techniques that, when woven together, have allowed me to visualize my dreams, create solutions and ultimately fulfill my aspirations.

The first lesson I hoped to convey to my grandchildren dealt with confronting adversity. In today's world, it's easy to fall into an attitude of hopelessness. As I watched my product copied and then sold for a fraction of its cost, I was left devastated. Forced to deal with corrupt government officials, inept attorneys and a toothpaste manufacturer whose carelessness destroyed my product, I was again left mentally crushed. As I watched my friend and partner Dr. Allen, finally succumb to cancer, the man who lifted my dental practice from near bankruptcy and taught me how to truly practice dentistry, I was completely overwhelmed with grief.

So, how do you keep from giving up when you see yourself as a grain of wheat, the world a merciless millstone?

It took me a lifetime to learn to deal with tragedy, crooks and the cynics. A lifetime to develop the fundamental skills necessary to fight back against a seemingly relentless barrage of challenges that slammed me from every side. But I did learn, and with time I ultimately changed from the slow, timid and stuttering introvert that I was, to become the responsible husband, father, teacher and business owner that I became.

One of the most valuable techniques I utilized that enabled me to keep moving forward once confronted by major disappointment was not to say "Why me?" but instead to ask myself, "What can I learn from this?" By seeing challenges as a chance to grow made each problem into an opportunity to advance, each hurdle a learning exercise.

More importantly though, what seeing a lesson in the midst of a trial also did, was to force me to take ownership and responsibility for what went wrong. If I faced a challenge with the notion that, "it wasn't my fault," and denied any blame or culpability for the outcome, I became simply a helpless victim to the assault.

Instead, if I was able to embrace the problem and accepted responsibility, I moved myself into a position to own the solution, make a change, repair the damage and hopefully, make it so it could never happen again. Most of my difficulties in school occurred because I blamed my teachers and refused to take responsibility and change my bad habits. Many of my problems with partners or associates came about because I would condemn them for what they did without truly understanding my responsibility in the relationship. Once I saw adversity as a challenge that I could learn from, I immediately became part of the solution and a step closer to success.

The second crucial skill I depended on involved the importance of surrounding myself with positive, upbeat and wonderful people. It is said that our thoughts are our own, but I disagree. It is amazing how fast my goals became muddled by a pessimist, skewed by a skeptic or upended by the slightest of negative innuendos. In college I learned to surround myself with support groups in the form of tutors and study classes whose members aspired for greatness. In business I learned to associate with the most experienced and knowledgeable people available. Individuals that were committed to doing their best and achieving the highest level of excellence.

At home my greatest partner and colleague, the person who kept me upbeat and strong through it all, was my wife, Vicki. She stood by me through the ups and downs, constantly encouraging me forward through gentle nudging and frequent affirmation.

It isn't just negative people who pushed back on my creativity and hampered my success. Watching mindless television and reading social media with its constant barrage of super-negative news and hyped-up success stories also worked to obliterate my focus and crush my ability to think. I recall my Grandmother Wright telling me, "Be careful what you put into your mind, because, once inside, it is nearly impossible to get it out." As a boy I didn't appreciate her words of wisdom, but as an adult I understood.

By making every effort to ignore the disingenuous expectations of the mass media and, instead, surrounded myself with positive input that both raised my spirt and lifted my hopes, it was amazing how quickly my mind cleared and I found myself on the fast-track toward success. Even to this day I wake up early every morning and, before I look at a single email or read a single news report, try to visualize my larger goals completed in the clearest and most specific detail possible. Before I look at one tweet or one text, I think about those things for which I am grateful and thank God for his grace. Then, once my mind is clear and open, I plan the day.

The third factor that helped move me towards success involved techniques I developed while struggling in school. My attention deficit disorder required that I break every task into a series of detailed attainable steps. Forced me to construct itemized daily lists and then follow those incremental steps until I worked my way through achievable goals and then ultimately to a completed objective. If I became stumped by a task, I broke it into smaller and smaller microtasks until it could ultimately be accomplished.

My fourth and equally important key to success, was the practice of establishing deadlines. Maintaining a timeframe in which a task must be completed was critical to my success because, first and foremost, it established a sense of urgency. By setting a timeframe in which to get a microtask completed, I not only got more things done but I was also able to celebrate the completed chore. Being able to promptly check off successfully finished tasks gave me an opportunity to be grateful for a job finished, even if it was the completion of a single microtask in a list of a hundred.

Is there more to being successful then these four key lessons? Without a doubt. The importance of perseverance, detailed goal visualization, preparing for the unexpected and intelligent risk taking must be given the most serious of attention. Most importantly, however, it should never be forgotten that that life, with all its twists and turns, is really about the journey and not the destination.

Am I finished inventing, teaching, writing or volunteering? I don't think so. Even now I am working on a number of inventions, one of my favorites being a solar cell device I designed twenty years ago that, according to my data, generates nearly twice the power of the best solar cells made anywhere in the world.

I actually borrowed the idea from the common dragonfly and its ability to catch tiny insects at night, midair, in near total darkness. Incredibly, the dragonfly has adapted an amazing pair of behavioral and anatomical features that enable it to utilize the lowest levels of light while still being able to see with astonishing acuity. What I did was build a machine that basically achieves the same effect as the dragonfly's eye using lenses, shifting platforms and micro-solar cells all networked together. My device was crude, but it worked.

Once I started getting results, I reached out to an expert in photovoltaics, a Dr. C. Wu, the professor of Electrical & Computer Engineering from the Missouri University of Science and Technology's.

"In all my work studying photovoltaics, I have never seen anything like this," Dr. Wu exclaimed emphatically. "You must go to NREL"

I looked at him confused, "NREL? What is NREL."

Dr. Wu shook his head in frustration, NREL, The National Renewable Energy Laboratory in Golden Colorado. You must go there and show them what you have developed and confirm your data."

The next day I did just that. I made an appointment with one of their top scientists at the federal government's laboratory dedicated to research and development of renewable energy. I made the appointment for later the next month to have my solar cell device evaluated and as a highlight, invited five of my best students along with their parents to accompany me.

The Dragonfly Device, as I called it, was housed in a wooden box that was as large as a typical microwave oven and weighed a little over ten pounds. I constructed it myself, and to say the device was crude was being generous. The outside walls were made from plywood, the light aperture constructed from a number 12 steel washer and the motor that shifted the solar cells constricted from an old drill motor.

I knew it wasn't much to look at, but neither were the first models of the Storm whistle or the Vortex toothpaste. It was the concept that was key, and with the prospect of going to NREL and working with some of the most knowledgeable minds in the country, I was beyond excited.

We flew to Colorado on a Friday morning and went directly by rented van to the government compound.

From the outside, the NREL facility looked amazing. Banks of solar cells could be seen laid out in every direction while lines of five story buildings that held some of the most advanced laboratories in the world crisscrossed the campus. We arrived at the central building as directed and was met promptly by a scientist decked out in the typical lab tech's long white coat and pocket protector.

"My name is Dr. Howard Wright," I introduced myself, "these are my students, and this is the Dragonfly Device I have brought to be tested against my own data."

"Welcome to NREL. My name is Dr. Mike Hannan," the tall middle-aged scientist replied, "let's get started."

We went upstairs, me carrying the Dragonfly Device, the students and parents following close behind.

After passing a number of empty hallways and vacant workrooms, we entered Dr. Hannan's laboratory. It was fairly small with one entire wall covered with digital measuring devices, oscilloscopes and computers. At the back of the room was a large work area; at its center sat a cluttered desk and well used swivel chair.

Taking a seat, Dr. Hannan twisted around in his chair and, staring at me over his glasses, told me the very last thing I wanted to hear. "First of all, it's not going to work."

I looked at the him not quite understanding what I had just heard, the students and parents that surrounded us confused, puzzled expressions drawn tight across their faces.

"What are you talking about?" I asked shocked, "I haven't explained how it works yet! You haven't even hooked it up."

"The wood. The wood on the outside. It's going to warp in the rain."

I looked at the scientist confused. "Warp? This is a prototype. This is a test model."

"And the screws, are they rustproof? It's never going to last."

Excuse me," I said as I tried to explain, "I have brought a preliminary model for you to evaluate. We are here to see if my own test data coincides with an independent lab. NREL's lab."

"I'm just saying it won't work." Dr. Hannan mumbled.

The students looked at me in disbelief. I had explained to them what I had been building and told them what to expect when we visited the lab, but this attitude was something I never anticipated. I had prepared them for the possibility that the device would fail miserably, I warned them that, more than likely, the results I obtained at home were in error. But having the research analyst condemn the device before it was even tested was ridiculous.

I tried to calm down, "Can we just run the device and see if you get the same results I recorded in Missouri?"

"No." He waved me away, "Not with that wooden box around it. I not about to hook that up to my equipment with all that stuff attached."

"You want me to take it apart? It will only work if all the parts work together as a unit."

"No way," he replied adamant. "Remove all this 'stuff' and then I will check it out."

"You don't understand. This is an integrated system, the lens, the shifting of the solar cells, the movement. This entire concept is about dynamics."

The scientist just stared at me. "No. It's you that doesn't understand! This is my lab and we do it my way."

I ran through my options. Walk away, argue longer, take it apart.

I took it apart.

After twenty minutes of pulling it to pieces, all that was left of the Dragonfly Device was my modified solar cells hooked up in series and a poorly aligned magnifying lens.

We ran the experiment.

"We just registered a two percent increase in voltage over baseline." The scientist called out excited.

"That's nothing!" I shot back angry. "If you would've tested the device the way I brought it in at the start, it would have raised the output by twenty percent!"

The NREL scientist, Dr. Hannan, raised himself from his chair, stood and glared at me. "Don't tell me it's 'NOTHING!' I've spent the last four years trying to eke a half percent out of a solar cell and you raise the percentage by two percent."

He looked totally out of sorts as he reviewed his notes, the students suddenly seeing hope in an otherwise failure of a day.

"I need to call my superior," the scientist mumbled as he snatched the receiver into his hand and dialed, "I can't believe it, a two percent increase."

"Hello, Director, Yeah. This is Mike, Mike Hannan in test. I have a..," then looking at a piece of paper on his desk continued, 'I have a Dr. Howard Wright here from St. Louis, he brought in an interesting solar cell configuration and we just jumped two percent on output."

There was a pause until the scientist looked at me and asked. "The Director wants to know; what kind of doctor are you?"

The students and parents all looked at me as I answered, "I am a dentist, retired."

Mike chuckled as he relayed the information over the phone. "He says he's a dentist. Yeah, retired. Ok, I'll tell him."

Mike hung up the phone. "I am sorry, we only deal with double Es here at NREL"

"Double Es?" I asked irritated, "What's a double E."

With a sad grimace Dr. Hannan looked at me like I was some kind of pathetic creature. "A double E is an Electrical Engineer. Double E. We only work with double Es. I suggest you submit your gizmo to a university to study. We won't consider it here."

The students and parents couldn't believe what they had just heard. I just stood there feeling both insulted and disgusted. Disillusioned, the students and I left NREL and returned to Missouri the next day.

What have I learned from this? Don't trust the government. It is only God who will show you the way, the truth and the life.

Despite my exasperation, I actually took the advice offered by Dr. Hannan at NREL and sent descriptions of the Dragonfly Device to over a hundred universities and government offices across the nation hoping to spark some interest; but despite all my efforts, I never heard back from anyone. Not a single comment.

I haven't given up on the Dragonfly Device. Often time I find myself thinking about how I could improve it, develop it beyond the rudimentary prototype phase and create a true working model and then get the word out.

But that is another story.

THE END

Made in the USA
Monee, IL
16 July 2020